THE CATHOLIC REDISCOVERY
OF PROTESTANTISM

The Catholic Rediscovery of Protestantism

A History of Roman Catholic Ecumenical Pioneering

by

Paul M. Minus, Jr.

PAULIST PRESS
New York/Paramus/Toronto

Library of Congress
Catalog Card Number: 75-44804

ISBN: 0-0891-1944-7

Published by Paulist Press
Editorial Office: 1865 Broadway, N.Y., N.Y. 10023
Business Office: 400 Sette Drive, Paramus, N.J. 07652

Printed and bound in the
United States of America

Contents

FOREWORD 1

PREFACE 5

I. JOURNEY THROUGH A WILDERNESS 17
  Prophets Dimly Heard 13
  Voices of Promise 20

II. A VISION NOURISHED BY HOPE 29
  Pope Leo XIII (1810-1903) 30
  Fernand-Etienne Portal (1855-1926) 36
  Fr. Paul of Graymoor (1863-1940) 38
  Antagonisms Revived 42

III. REDISCOVERING THE OUTSIDER 48
  Crisis for Christendom 49
  Intellectual Revival 51
  The Malines Conversations 55
  Encounter with Eastern Orthodoxy 58

IV. MEETING A "NEW" PROTESTANTISM 74
  The Ecumenical Organizations 75
  Neo-Orthodox Theology 80
  The Liturgical Movement 81
  Facing Common Threats Together 84
  New Categories and Attitudes 87

V. FOUR MODERN PIONEERS OF ECUMENISM 98
  Yves Marie-Joseph Congar (b. 1904) 98
  Paul Couturier (1881-1953) 107
  Max Josef Metzger (1887-1944) 112
  Josef Lortz (b. 1887) 115

VI. A TIME FOR SOWING 125
  World War II 126

   Return to the Sources 131
   Encounter with the Postwar World 136
   Postwar Protestantism 142

VII. Toward a Promised Land 159
   Peacetime Acceleration 159
   Pius XII and Catholic Ecumenism 166
   The Pace Quickens 174
   Pope John XXIII (1881-1963) 183

VIII. Conceptual Reformulation 197
   The Protestant and His Church 197
   Reassessing Luther 204
   The Emerging Catholic Vision of Unity 210
   Doctrinal Restatement 110

IX. The Council's Ecumenical Achievement 224
   A Schooling in Ecumenism 225
   A Pervasive Theme 230
   The Decree on Ecumenism 235

Index 255

Foreword

Almost no one is unaware of the great ecumenical breakthrough accomplished in Roman Catholicism during the pontificate of John XXIII. This gentle pastor, as the present volume tells us, doggedly "refused to be a prisoner of his church's sectarian history." Vatican II, guided by the spirit of Pope John, issued a magnificent *Decree on Ecumenism* and built a strong ecumenical dimension into all its major documents.

Great shifts of this character are never the result of chance nor are they ever the work of a single man, even though he be a pope. Behind the ecumenical achievements of Vatican II lies the dedicated toil of several generations of ecumenical pioneers, who labored amid suspicions and misunderstandings, with full consciousness that they would never live to see the harvest of what they were seeking to plant. To appreciate the meaning of Vatican II it is necessary to study the earlier apostles of ecumenism: leaders such as the Abbé Portal, Dom Beauduin, Max Metzger, and Yves Congar, many of whom accepted humiliations and contradictions for a cause which, in their estimation, was far greater than themselves. Congar, perhaps the greatest theologian among Catholic ecumenists, was fortunate enough to see many of his ideas written into the documents of Vatican II. Since the Council he has continued, with energy, discretion, and optimism, to press for further advances in the apostolate of Christian unity.

This long and patient labor of preparation is splendidly set forth in the pages that follow. Dr. Minus makes it clear that ecumenism is not a blind flight into some kind of supraconfessional stratosphere; it is not a renunciation of one's own confessional heritage. At its best, it has been an effort to combine sincere loyalty to one's own tradition with a cordial openness to all that is valid in the insights of other Christian groups. Ecumenism has something of an adventure about it; the practitioner is always walking a

1

kind of tightrope. He allows himself to be torn between conflicting values, to feel the tension and to try to absorb it in his own person. Before any kind of union can be effected between confessional bodies, that union must take place in the minds and hearts of ecumenists themselves. They are the advance scouts of a unity yet to be achieved.

The author of this book, a Methodist scholar highly esteemed by his professional colleagues, is beginning to become known to a wider public. Contenting himself with the role of a historian, he strives in these pages to tell the story of men and movements he admires. He writes in simple and straightforward prose, adapted not only to specialists but to a wide range of readers. His book, however, is no mere popularization. The author has travelled widely and consulted leading experts in various countries. As the footnotes certify, he has perused nearly all the pertinent literature, both Protestant and Catholic, in several languages. His judgments are moderate and carefully weighed.

This book keeps faithfully to its theme: the Catholic rediscovery of Protestantism. The fact that this story can be so ably told from the Protestant side is evidence enough that a companion volume could well be written, perhaps by a Catholic, on the Protestant rediscovery of Catholicism. After several centuries in which Catholic theology was scarcely read ("Catholica non leguntur," as the maxim had it), Protestants have begun to see Catholicism with fresh eyes. Some of their scholars can speak of inner-Catholic theological questions with the assurance of experts. To this select company Dr. Paul Minus and his theological mentor at Yale, Dr. George A. Lindbeck, unquestionably belong.

Running through this book as a kind of *leitmotiv* is the tension between what the author identifies as the preservationist and the transformationist patterns of ecumenism. The preservationist is concerned with full loyalty to his own confessional tradition, even at the price of some friction with other communities. The transformationist, not satisfied with retaining what has been handed down, seeks to advance beyond the limited positions of the past and to achieve a broader, richer synthesis. Dr. Minus, whose sympathies seem to lie with the second style of ecumenism, recognizes the legitimacy of both concerns. "Faithfulness to the preservationist task," he points out, "requires dedication to the companion task of self-transformation." The two styles of ecumenism must, in the last analysis, support each other. A purely static loyalty to the past would not effectively preserve the living reality that it hands down to us. And a pure transformationism, uninhibited by the tradition, would lose touch with the vital sources by which Christianity must forever be inspired. The desire for reconciliation, therefore, must never lead us to discard what is valid in our own tradition. Conscious of this principle, Dr. Minus refrains from denigrating the more cautious ecumenists of the present and the recent past. The objectivity and respect with which the author treats the various schools of thought within the Catholic ecumenical spectrum is one of the commendable features of this book.

Initiated into the ways of ecumenism by Gustave Weigel, my Jesuit professor and later my colleague at Woodstock College, I personally experienced the excitement of the decade between the Evanston Assembly of the World Council of Churches (1954) and the Vatican II *Decree on Ecumenism* (1964). During these years I attended innumerable lectures, theological discussions, and common services of prayer and worship both here in the United States and abroad in France, Holland, Germany, Switzerland, and Italy. Everywhere I sensed a realization that something great and historic was afoot, that the Holy Spirit was at work within the Body of Christ. To this day I believe that the Holy Spirit was indeed behind that mighty impetus toward unity.

Today it is not easy to achieve the same confidence. As the final chapter of this book points out, even the gains of Vatican II appear to be insecure at present. In the religious as well as in the secular sphere, we have entered into a period of widespread resentment and distrust, not untinged with cynicism, anger, and bitterness. In the words of Dr. Minus: "So many ideals have been compromised that people do not readily commit themselves to the ideal of Christian unity"—an ideal that calls for long-term strategies "rather than the instant remedies in vogue today." Under the circumstances, critical questioning tends to become the prerogative of iconoclasts; devoted believers flee all too easily to the comforts of the familiar but divisive patterns of previous centuries.

The question must therefore be earnestly asked, has the brief summer of ecumenical pioneering come to an end? Are Christians moving into the dark winter of mutual isolation once again? Will there still be pioneers of keen idealism and wide vision, unafraid to risk themselves for a future unity that still lies hidden in the designs of God? These questions are not merely rhetorical; they are real and hence difficult to answer.

This book, together with others, will help to determine the answers that history will give to the questions just raised. It may inspire in its readers a more vivid sense of ecumenical urgency. It will, God willing, enable some few to make their own the words that Paul Minus quotes from Fernand Portal: "We did not begin this work because we believed it to be easy of accomplishment . . . He who has inspired us to begin this work will, in his own good time and in his way, enable, if not us, those who come after us, to bring it to its perfect and successful end."

The Catholic University of America
Washington, D.C.
December 1, 1975   Avery Dulles, S.J.

Preface

The Second Vatican Council unleashed forces within the Roman Catholic Church that have propelled her from long-accustomed isolation into major arenas of the ecumenical movement. Since the Council's adjournment in 1965, Catholics' involvement in the quest for Christian unity has been conspicuous and productive: they have injected fresh perspectives and energies into interchurch councils around the world; Catholic and Protestant scholars engaged in bilateral conversations have broken through traditional theological impasses; and in countless communities Catholics have joined with their brothers and sisters from other churches to claim the kinship that had been denied for centuries. In no other decade has such striking progress been made toward overcoming divisions between Catholics and Protestants.

The forces unleashed by the Council also have made the past decade one of intense conflict within the Roman Catholic Church. During this period the Roman Church's commitment to ecumenism has been caught in crossfires between partisans of contrasting convictions about the Catholic future. Some have thought their church's ecumenical advance too bold, and they have favored retreat toward familiar intra-Christian battle lines. Others, thinking Catholic ecumenical advance too timid, have called for additional steps such as membership in the World Council of Churches and a relaxing of disciplinary restraints against common eucharistic worship. Still others have believed that interest in ecumenism is a diversion from more pressing tasks.

At points the Roman Church's uncertainty and disagreement about ecumenism resemble the ecumenical ambivalence now present in other churches. Catholic ambivalence has been given unusual intensity, however, by the suddenness with which most Catholics were turned from established Counter-Reformation patterns to the dream of a renewed Catholicism and a reunited Christian family.

Before Vatican II the older, polemical views were widely accepted, and the emerging new ecumenism gripped only a small minority. At the Council their vision was affirmed—but equivocally, for its components were placed in conciliar pronouncements alongside older positions with which most Catholics had been imbued. In the years since the Roman Church's descent from the mountaintop of the Council, Catholics have demonstrated how diversely the new ecumenism has been perceived and evaluated.

I have undertaken this study in the hope of helping Catholics and non-Catholics alike to understand the vision of Christian unity that was nurtured quietly for decades and then surprisingly affirmed by the Second Vatican Council. The emergence of this vision is, I believe, one of the pregnant developments of modern Christian history, and the vision itself is a resource rich in potential for all the churches. If the Roman Church's commitment to ecumenism grows and deepens, her increasing involvement in the ecumenical movement can measurably strengthen all phases of the quest for Christian unity. And if she and other churches around the world learn better to implement the solidarity arising from their "one Lord, one faith, one baptism," I believe that together they may well make a substantial contribution to the search for a peaceable future for the human family.

The most dramatic expression of the Roman Church's hesitant conversion to ecumenism has been her adoption of a fresh stance toward Protestantism. Vatican II's acceptance of Protestant churches as instruments of salvation was made possible by the little noticed preparatory work of Catholic pioneers. Father Yves Congar has aptly depicted the setting of Pope John's historic initiative in the early 1960s: "At the moment when the Holy See emerged from semi-absenteeism in ecumenical matters, it found the ground tilled and sown and covered with thickset and high-grown grain."[1] This book attempts to explain that lush growth by studying the persons, events, and ideas that fashioned an irenic Catholic approach to Protestantism in the years between the Reformation and the Second Vatican Council.

As I have viewed the succession of Catholic ecumenical apostles from the time of Erasmus to the time of Cardinal Bea, I have become impressed by their courage, wisdom, and hope. My growing acquaintance with these men has led me to discover three fundamental facts about the Catholic initiation to ecumenism which I believe are significant for the future of ecumenism and which merit continued reflection by all persons concerned about the future course of Christianity.

The first of these facts is the remarkable degree to which changes within the churches and the world during the twentieth century have made our time propitious to the Catholic rediscovery of Protestantism (and to the Protestant rediscovery of Catholicism). This is not to say that ecumenical progress has occurred without interruption or recession; indeed the first decade after Vatican II illustrates the characteristic ebbing and flowing of the ecumenical tide, as well as the difficulty of determining the prevailing direction of movement at a given moment. But in this decade as in the previous decades of the twentieth century, Catholicism and Protestantism have remained on a course that has been predominantly convergent. When one considers a larger historical frame and recognizes that "the churches have achieved more in unity in the last half century than in at least the last nine centuries of division before that,"[2] it becomes important to reflect about the significance of this shift. Do the churches stand at the beginning of an age in which they will be characterized more by concord than estrangement, and in which their impact upon human affairs will be more unitive than divisive? Or will the new tensions and conflicts erupting now within churches prove fully as divisive as those that have existed between churches?

The second fact of overriding significance emerging from this study is the conviction of modern Catholic ecumenical pioneers that the time was ripe to demonstrate the gospel's power to create life-nourishing community within the divided and distraught human family. Their affirmation of ties with Protestant kinsmen was part of a more encompassing effort to discover bonds that unite even the most dissimilar groups in such a way that the richness of their distinctive identities is not compromised. God's purpose was perceived to be the reconciliation of the whole of humankind, and unity-in-diversity among Christians was seen as an instrument to serve that larger purpose. The Catholic ecumenical dream was a bold dream, and those who became its spokesmen believed that no lesser dream accurately reflected the divine will.

The third fact to be noted is the internal struggles that accompanied Catholics' rediscovery of Protestantism. Those struggles reflected a tension present in every church's effort to be faithful to God. Such faithfulness entails both preservation of what God has already entrusted to the community and change brought by receiving what he freshly gives. Christians often have not agreed on how far the one task may be pursued without infringement upon the other. Catholics who developed a theological perspective to guide their church's ecumenical activity sought to do justice to both. They shared the ancient conviction that the Roman Church had been divinely established as the fountain of salvation for everyone. Her endowment from Christ, they believed, must be carefully preserved, for through it alone would the fullness of God's grace reach mankind, and through it alone would men realize the unity divinely intended for them. Hence all persons—including Protestants—must drink from this uniquely vivifying and unifying source.

But Catholic ecumenical pioneers recognized that the *preservationist* motif alone, however essential to their labors, neither adequately expressed Catholic responsiveness to the divine initiative nor fruitfully guided their pursuit of unity. They believed that in order to reach the compelling goal of the unity of all Christians their church must abandon certain familiar ways hindering its realization. The pioneers argued that such change dare not be eschewed, for the Lord who established the church upon lasting foundations also calls her to repent of past transgressions and inadequacies in order to receive his ever-new gifts. Therefore, with growing conviction and against constant resistance they elaborated a second, complementary theme of the Catholic ecumenical perspective: the Roman Church must take the self-transforming steps necessary both for her own renewal and for wider unity. This *transformationist* motif received varying implementations and was related in shifting ways to the preservationist motif. The Catholic understanding and practice of ecumenism have been built upon an uneasy alliance of the two, and the question of how to hold them in proper conjunction has been (and remains) a critical issue—for Roman Catholics and for all Christians.

The research that undergirds this volume began in 1960.

While a doctoral candidate at Yale University, I embarked upon a study of the Catholic reconsideration of Protestantism then underway in the French-speaking areas of Europe. The French development was part of a larger ecumenical revolution in the Roman Church, and following the completion of my dissertation I decided to attempt to view the entire movement more comprehensively, including its culmination in the Second Vatican Council.

My study of this realm of modern history has been greatly aided by institutions and scholars in several countries. Invaluable assistance has been provided by the libraries of the Yale University Divinity School, the Methodist Theological School (Delaware, Ohio), the Pontifical College Josephinum (Worthington, Ohio), the Lutheran Theological Seminary (Columbus, Ohio), the Boston University School of Theology, the Maison St. Jean (Héverlée, Belgium), the Université catholique de Louvain, the Centre St. Irénée (Lyons, France), and the Centro Pro Unione (Rome). To their staffs I happily express appreciation. My indebtedness is especially great to nine persons who have made helpful suggestions during preparation of the manuscript. Professor George A. Lindbeck, my chief guide through my doctoral program, has remained an unfailing source of stimulation. Canon Roger Aubert, Monsignor Gustave Thils, Fr. René Beaupère, Fr. George Tavard, Dr. Ruth Slade Reardon, Professor John Giltner, and the late Kenneth Scott Latourette generously shared their knowledge and experience. My wife, Nancy DeWitt Minus, has saved me from innumerable offenses against the English language, and she has been a constant source of encouragement in each of the stages through which this project has passed.

With profound gratitude I dedicate this book to my parents. They have taught me a great deal about Christian unity.

NOTES

1. Yves Congar, *Dialogue Between Christians: Catholic Contributions to Ecumenism* trans. Phillip Loretz (London: Geoffrey Chapman, 1966), p. 41.

2. Barry Till, *The Churches Search for Unity* (Harmondsworth, England: Penguin Books, 1972), p. 523.

I
Journey
Through a Wilderness

The New Testament presents an awesome and demanding vision of human unity (as in Jesus' prayer that his followers "may be one as we are one"), but never has the world witnessed more bitter and protracted conflict among co-religionists than that generated among Christians. The bleakest chapters of Christian fratricidal history recount the struggles between Catholics and Protestants. For four centuries they wandered in a wilderness of mutual hatred and contempt, forgetful of the better land to which their faith pointed.

Patterns of wilderness life had been fashioned in the most virulent years of the sixteenth century. Though outlooks varied in each camp, most Protestants and Catholics learned to view one another through strikingly similar lenses. Each side, sure that it alone preserved the faith unsullied and whole, believed the other was distancing itself perilously from the source of salvation. Each prescribed essentially the same cure for Christendom's division: the other side must abjure error and surrender to the claims of its foe. Such peace terms satisfied each antagonist's impassioned evaluation of the demands of Christian truth, but they proved a sterile basis of reunion.

Sixteenth-century polemics colored a broad range of ecclesiastical life. Theological positions were deliberately elaborated in sharp contrast to opposing positions. Characteristically, where Protestants stressed the importance of Scripture for understanding revelation, Catholics stressed the importance of tradition; where Catholics emphasized man's role in the process of justification, Protestants emphasized God's role. Forms of piety and polity similarly received contrasting emphases that accentuated the distance between the two factions.

Over much of Europe a mindset emerged that regarded Protestantism and Catholicism as mutually exclusive; one must be the true Christianity, the other a heretical Christianity. The vehemence with which fanatics on both sides viewed their religious enemies is suggested by a comment of Pope Paul IV: "Even if my own father were a heretic, I would gather the wood to burn him."[1]

So intense a religious conflict could not be restricted to the edges of sixteenth-century society. Men on both sides had inherited the medieval conviction that a primary responsibility of the Christian ruler is to support orthodoxy and suppress heresy. Religion now lent crusading fervor to Protestant and Catholic rulers already driven toward war by economic and political pressures. Soon the two groups were locked in bloody battles that recurred for a century and a half. When finally their wars ended, Protestants and Catholics settled into a long period of religious cold war. Each generation passed on to the next the contempt inherited from forebears. And because the two sides lived in hostile isolation, their encounters grew more rare and their knowledge of each other more distorted. Separation seemed normal, reconciliation impossible. In 1749 the reforming Anglican clergyman, John Wesley, soberly lamented the estrangement that gripped western Christendom: "We are on both sides less willing to help one another and more ready to hurt each other. Hence brotherly love is utterly destroyed and each side, looking on the other as monsters, gives way to anger, hatred, malice, to every unkind affection—which have frequently broke out in such inhuman barbarities as are scarce named even among the heathens."[2]

But a handful on both sides refused to acquiesce in the presence of division. Haunted by the vision of unity, they sought passages through the wilderness toward a land where Protestants and Catholics would live together as brothers. Until our own century the Catholics engaged in that venture rarely persuaded others to journey with them; indeed, most fell under ecclesiastical censure. Lonely prophets, they reached toward ecumenical horizons not perceived by most Catholics until well into the twentieth century. Their great hopefulness and meager achievement witness to a continuing Catholic determination irenically to overcome Christian disunity. They deserve to be remembered.

Prophets Dimly Heard

Soon after the onset of Luther's reforming campaign, a few prophetic Catholic leaders recognized the seriousness of western Christendom's plight and sought to forestall the calamitous rupture they feared imminent.

Appeals for reform "in head and members" had been heard long before Luther's time, but never had they won vigorous papal endorsement or implementation. Following the German friar's excommunication in 1521, however, a pope was chosen who acknowledged both the presence of grievous abuses in the Roman Church and the need for their correction. Pope Adrian VI (1459-1523), a Dutchman and former Louvain theological professor, admitted to German princes in 1522 that the clergy, especially those in the Roman Curia, bore major responsibility for the present crisis and its abatement. "It cannot be denied that up till now many inordinate, exorbitant and scandalous things have been perpetrated in the Roman Curia, and that God . . . being raised thereby to anger, has in his right judgment permitted scandals of this sort and the most pernicious errors to arise among his people." Adrian vowed so to "reform ourselves and others and to return ourselves to the path of truth" that the faithful would no longer be provoked to overthrow Roman authority. His assessment of the changes required, however, did not coincide with Luther's. The pope desired a reform of morality and discipline throughout his church, but he had no sympathy for Luther's insistence upon a recasting of Catholic doctrine. Roman transformation would not go that far. Indeed, Adrian denounced the German reformer as "a serpent whose venomous tongue, with a poison worse than that of hell, has contaminated the church and the universe."[3] Pope Adrian's hopes for reform were shared by few in the Roman Curia, and at his death in 1523, after a regrettably brief pontificate, Catholic reform under papal auspices was still an unrealized dream.

The next pope, Clement VII, evinced little interest in his predecessor's cause, but during the pontificate of Paul III (1534-

1549), such cardinals as Contarini and Pole pushed determinedly for papal-instituted reforms that would regain the allegiance of Rome's disenchanted sons and daughters. By then, however, debate had become too heated and positions too polarized for a moderating approach to overtake the centrifugal flow of events, ideas, and emotions. The Council of Trent, rather than becoming an occasion for Protestant-Catholic reconciliation as some had hoped, hardened Catholic positions and moved the Church of Rome toward the polemical Counter-Reformation stance that was to endure for nearly four centuries.[4]

Another Hollander, Desiderius Erasmus (1466-1536), was the chief architect of a companion approach to unity also developed in the early decades of the sixteenth century. The learned humanist's program for religious peace rested upon two assumptions: the revival of Christ-like love in the hearts of embittered Christians is a necessary prelude to the restoration of ecclesiastical union; such union, moreover, is not prevented by theological disagreement between Catholics and Lutherans, for their differences lie within that realm of *adiaphora* where Christians may legitimately differ and are overbalanced by their common adherence to essential doctrinal affirmations found in Scripture and the early church.[5]

The Erasmian appeal for a transformation of hearts and theological outlook was a major ingredient in union attempts launched by Catholics as well as Protestants. In the middle decades of the sixteenth century, it, together with the desire of some political rulers for peace among their subjects, led to "colloquies" where desperate attempts were made to close the rapidly widening religious and civil gap.[6] In the 1560s a Catholic disciple of Erasmus, George Cassander (1513-1566), urged Protestants and Catholics to unite on the basis of their common acceptance of the "Fundamental Articles" of Christian belief—those tenets lodged in Scripture, summarized in the Apostles' Creed, and echoed by the Fathers. On all secondary matters diversity should be tolerated. The Flemish scholar sought to facilitate Lutheran reunion with Rome by an analysis of the Augsburg Confession stressing its high degree of conformity with Catholic teaching.[7]

A like effort was made in the following century by an English convert to the Roman Church, Christopher Davenport (1595-1680), who, when he became a Franciscan, took the religious name Franciscus a Sancta Clara. Sancta Clara and other Catholics close to English royalty believed that King Charles I, already sympathetically disposed toward the faith of his Catholic wife, might be persuaded to pursue a religious pact between Canterbury and Rome. In 1634 Sancta Clara published *Deus, Natura, Gratia*, a study of key theological issues dividing Anglicans and Catholics. Those divisions, he wrote, will be healed "not by amputation but by gentle bathing."[8] The author sought to administer that bathing through an appended analysis of the Church of England's Thirty-nine Articles. His intention was to demonstrate that the Articles can be interpreted compatibly with parallel affirmations in Catholic teaching. Some of the Anglican statements posed no problem, but others reflected a keen anti-Roman animus. To discover an acceptable Catholic interpretation of these Articles, Sancta Clara had to employ exegesis that was, as a recent Catholic interpreter has observed, "laborious, and in certain cases forced."[9]

The Franciscan had been led to his imaginative comparison of the Thirty-nine Articles and Roman Catholic teaching by the conviction that even though the "bare words" of some of the Articles merit severe Catholic censure, their "hidden sense" does not, for essentially the same faith exists beneath conflicting verbal formulations of faith.[10] Anglicans' reconciliation with Rome, he believed, does not require so complete a repudiation of their positions as had been supposed. Both sides must revise their estimate of one another and of what is required for reunion. But Sancta Clara's argument convinced few, and soon the death of Charles I and the rise of Cromwell's Puritan Commonwealth brought to England a bitterly anti-Catholic atmosphere that was inimical to any Romeward movement.

Sancta Clara's method of "gentle bathing" was revived and modified in later years by other Catholics. A French Jesuit, Jean Dez (1643-1712), was commissioned by King Louis XIV to regain Lutheran Strasburg for the Roman Catholic Church. His tack was akin to that of Cassander and Sancta Clara: to show the essential harmony of supposedly irreconcilable doctrinal positions. A treatise he published in 1687 argued the compatibility of the Lutheran

Augsburg Confession with the Council of Trent's dogmatic decrees. The reunion of Protestants with Rome, Dez claimed, is "necessary for their salvation and easy according to their principles," but his position had no noticeable impact upon them. Another volume by Dez on the same subject was placed on the Roman Index.[11]

A more renowned Frenchman, Bishop Jacques-Benigne Bossuet (1627-1704), devoted considerable energy to the pursuit of Protestant reunion with the Roman Church. The age's rising confidence in the power of reason colored his method. Bossuet judged that Protestants' disaffection resulted largely from their misunderstanding of Catholic belief, a misunderstanding occasioned too frequently by the clumsy argumentation of Catholic apologists. If Protestants were to encounter authentic Catholic teaching, freed of a forbidding scholastic encasement, they more likely would embrace it. That conviction led Bossuet to publish his *Exposition de la doctrine de l'Eglise catholique* (1671), where he presented official Roman Catholic teaching (especially as formulated by Trent) on controverted theological issues. In a more polemical work, *Histoire des variations des églises protestantes* (1688), Bossuet appropriated an ancient argument of the orthodox against the heterodox by claiming that the unchangeableness of Roman Catholic dogma is a sign of its divine authorship, while the "variations" among Protestant teachings attest their human origin. He admitted that the Protestant churches retain some orthodox beliefs, but he also judged that the forces of dissolution present among them make their demise inevitable. The bishop's solicitude for those he called "separated brethren" was evident in his wish that "he who holds in his hand the hearts of men" will cause "all his stray children" to return to the Roman Church.[12]

Bossuet's irenic temper and willingness to negotiate non-dogmatic matters led him to make exceptional accommodative gestures toward Protestants. In correspondence with Gerhard Walter Molanus, the German Lutheran Abbott of Lokkum, Bossuet acknowledged that should Lutherans return to Rome, they likely would be allowed to retain a married clergy, communion in both kinds, and Luther's German Bible. Bossuet, however, would not admit the validity of Lutheran ordinations.[13]

A more radical effort for reunion was undertaken by another French Catholic. In 1717 an ambitious correspondence was initiated by Dr. Louis Ellies Du Pin (1657-1719) with William Wake, the Anglican archbishop of Canterbury. Du Pin and his chief collaborator, Dr. Patrick Piers de Girardin, were professors at the Sorbonne. Deeply influenced by Gallicanism's hope for increased independence of Rome, they believed that an alliance of the French Catholic and Anglican Churches would help curb papal intervention in the affairs of French Catholicism. Their overture also reflected a conviction about the importance of Christian unity: Du Pin wrote of his wish that "all Christians might be one fold under one supreme shepherd, even the Lord Jesus Christ our Savior. This has a chief place in my prayers, and for so good a work I would gladly lay down my life."[14]

Both parties shared their time's growing desire for tolerance of religious differences and the belief that agreement could be reached on "fundamentals." The current attraction of French and English scholars to the early church gave a common patristic coloring to both sides' understanding of the essentials of Christianity.[15] Through an exchange of letters and documents the three men sought to establish theological and ecclesiastical accord great enough for their churches to enter into communion with one another. The major Catholic contribution was Du Pin's *Commonitorium*, completed in August 1717 and devoted principally to an examination of the Thirty-nine Articles. The French scholar went further than any predecessor in altering Catholic positions for the sake of unity. He conceded that traditional Anglican practices such as clerical marriage, an English liturgy, and communion in both kinds could continue should Anglo-French union be achieved. But he insisted too that Anglicans not object to the continuation of certain distinctive Catholic traditions. Du Pin contended that the particular Articles rejecting Catholic positions on purgatory and indulgences actually pose no serious obstacle, for they had been directed against common sixteenth-century abuses rather than against authoritative teaching; surely Anglicans would not find the latter reprehensible. Regarding the eucharist the two churches must have a common mind. Du Pin conceded that the English understanding of Christ's real presence need not be expressed by the controversial word *transubstantiation;* it is enough, he wrote, for the two churches to agree that "the bread and wine are truly and really transmuted into the body and blood of Christ."[16]

The Frenchman urged that as Anglicans and Catholics neared union they eschew any attempt to assess responsibility for the six-teenth-century sundering of unity: "for conscience' sake and the good of peace" they should not ask "how the schism arose and by whose fault it came to pass." Du Pin believed that French Catho-lics could acknowledge the validity of Anglican orders. Hence they would expect Anglican bishops, priests, and deacons to continue their ministries following union. Du Pin's minimalist conception of papal authority was reflected in his proposal that the uniting churches merely inform the pope of their action and request his consent. Should he withhold it, their union would be valid anyway; "and if he resorts to threats, then an appeal will be made to a Gen-eral Council."[17]

None of the correspondents in this exchange enjoyed either of-ficial or popular support (Du Pin earlier had been temporarily ex-iled from France because of his extreme views). They hoped to reach private agreements which eventually would be communi-cated to the proper ecclesiastical and civil authorities for official approbation. A remarkable distance was travelled toward the ini-tial objective, even though Wake believed that Du Pin neither ade-quately appreciated Anglican convictions and practices nor was willing adequately to alter traditional Roman ways. But few Cath-olics were prepared to countenance what they judged to be Du Pin's too radical attenuation of the preservationist motif and too radical exaggeration of the transformationist motif. Their daring and chimerical quest for union was interrupted by mounting Cath-olic resistance to the correspondence and finally by Du Pin's death in 1719.

Only one feature of the attempted Sorbonne-Canterbury *en-tente* was pursued subsequently. In 1723 Pierre François le Courayer (1681-1776), a French priest and librarian, published a study defending the validity of Anglican ordinations.[18] The volume prompted a sharp response from a French Dominican, Michel le Quien, who maintained the more normal Catholic positions that Anglican orders were invalid and that the only way to reunion was

Anglican abjuration of error and return to Rome. Le Courayer countered with a second study that, like the earlier one, owed much to the research and reflection of Archbishop Wake. In his defense of Anglican orders, however, Le Courayer espoused theological positions that brought him ecclesiastical censure. The harried priest fled to England where he was received warmly by Anglican sympathizers.

Catholic resistance to the expansion of papal power was present elsewhere in eighteenth-century Europe. In Germany its most persuasive spokesman was Johann Niklaus von Hontheim (1701-1790). Using the pseudonym Justinius Febronius, he published a study in 1763 calling for a constriction of the pope's power so that it more nearly approximated the pattern that had existed in the early church. If the bishop of Rome did not voluntarily resume a servant role among his fellow bishops, they could justifiably request remedial intervention by the secular arm of Christendom. A major aim of Febronius's effort was to meet a critical objection of German Protestants against the Roman Catholic Church and thus to facilitate their reunion with her. The year after its publication, however, the book was placed on the Index, and in subsequent years "Febronianism" was repeatedly assailed.[19]

Febronius and earlier solitary prophets of reconciliation had sown seeds which eventually would germinate. In more propitious times other Catholics would revive the claims that an underlying unity of faith (especially with Anglicans and Lutherans) persists in spite of division, that mutual love must precede reunion, that simplistic assessments of the historical causes of division must be abandoned, and that reunion demands a reformulation of Catholic belief and a repatterning of the papacy. But in their lifetimes the prophets' lot was defeat and disappointment. Many factors account for their failure. Two are basic. The religious cleavage of the sixteenth century had placed so deep a stamp upon the emotions and institutions of western Christendom that they allowed neither widespread popular interest in reunion nor the fraternal love for which Erasmus had pled. The blood of martyrs on both sides had begotten impassioned memories, and patterns of social, political, and economic competition both nourished and were nourished by those memories. Until new forces were present that could erode the formidable psychological and sociological barriers, reunion schemes were foredoomed.

Also, most Catholics and Protestants could not accept the contention made by a few in both camps that they agreed upon "fundamentals." Theological debate in the sixteenth century had shown, they believed, that their churches were irreparably split on basic doctrinal issues such as justification and papal authority. Insistence upon the presence of underlying agreement seemed to most Catholics to bespeak a treasonable abandonment of the truths for which their church had fought in opposition to Reformation heresy. And to most Protestants that insistence seemed to signal an unconscionable dilution of the great verities that had inspired the Reformation. Reconciliation would not be purchased at the price of apparent or real doctrinal compromise. Unity must be in the truth—as perceived and preserved on both sides.

Voices of Promise

The charged atmosphere of the nineteenth century proved favorable to the search for passages out of the wilderness of mutual contempt among Christians. The political, social, and intellectual upheavals triggered by the French Revolution left few realms of western life untouched: "The world is changing its foundations," a Frenchman aptly announced.[20] Governments now were inclined to intrude less into religious affairs. Some of the century's most aggressive intellectual movements were directed against fundamental beliefs held by all Christians. Demanded of them was what the Catholic historian Daniel-Rops has called "a fight for God."[21] Although Protestants and Catholics often differed in the way they waged that battle, their unwelcome adversary unintentionally drew them nearer by attacking them on ground they shared. Moreover, some of the intellectual currents of the day (especially romanticism) colored constructive scholarly thought in both camps and gradually turned it in the same direction. In these years, too, rapid scientific and technological advances encouraged a pervasive mood of optimism; men believed they now could do what men earlier could not do. More than ever before, ecclesiastical leaders initiated projects that brought together Christians from previously isolated and competing denominations for collaborative pursuit of difficult but agreed-upon objectives. A nascent ecumenical consciousness spread to certain Roman Catholic circles, and in several lands it was given prominent expression by Catholics.

Early in the nineteenth century fresh interest in Protestantism appeared among German Catholics. Johann Michael Sailer (1751-1832), who contributed markedly to the intellectual and spiritual revival of German Catholicism, encouraged Catholics and Protestants to battle together against the continuing influence of Enlightenment infidelity and impiety. Among both groups wide use was made of a book of meditations and prayers written by Sailer.[22] Some German Catholics participated in the German Christian Fellowship, and for a short period a Catholic priest served as one of its secretaries. The Fellowship, formed in 1780 and dominated by Protestants of Pietist leanings, brought together Christians from different nations and confessions for mutual edification and service. As the first international, interchurch society, it revealed the fruitful possibilities of such association. In later years it was frequently imitated, though far more by Protestants than by Catholics.[23]

A seminal German theologian, Johann Adam Möhler (1796-1838), gave depth and maturity to the emerging irenic Catholic approach to Protestantism. A distinguished member of Tübingen University's Catholic theological faculty (which existed alongside a flourishing Protestant theological faculty), Möhler elaborated an ecclesiology stressing the dynamic, unitive quality of the church's inner life. This ecclesiological orientation, colored by Möhler's patristic study and the romanticism of his day, moved from the typical Counter-Reformation stress upon the church's juridical structure toward kinship with ecclesiological themes then developing in certain Orthodox and Protestant circles.[24]

The Tübingen scholar's chief literary contribution to Catholic-Protestant rapprochement was his *Symbolik*, published in 1832. This volume was the first major Catholic expression of an interest that had arisen among German Protestant scholars in the objective, comparative study of official doctrinal statements (or "symbols"). Möhler's irenic spirit was evident in his remarkable acknowledgment that the Reformation controversy had sprung from the most earnest endeavor of both parties to uphold the truth—

the pure and genuine Christianity in all its integrity." Like non-Roman contemporaries who were making comparable doctrinal studies, Möhler attempted to penetrate dispassionately to the core of each Protestant system of belief he examined. The crucial disagreement between Protestants and Catholics he identified as their understandings of "the mode whereby fallen man can regain fellowship with Christ, and become a partaker of the fruits of redemption."[25] Möhler did not hesitate to indicate where he judged Protestant positions to be unacceptable, but by example he also made it plain to Catholics that those positions deserve to be considered respectfully and evaluated serenely.

A new spirit was also evident among groups of British Catholics in the nineteenth century. Symptomatic was a volume published by Charles Butler in 1816. In *Confessions of Faith* the English Catholic layman objectively examined Catholic, Orthodox, and Protestant beliefs and concluded with the Pietist-like plea, "If we cannot reconcile all opinions, let us reconcile all hearts."[26] Eight years later Dr. James Doyle, an Irish Catholic bishop, addressed a public letter to the chancellor of the exchequer in which he urged consideration of Anglican-Roman Catholic union: "This union . . . is not difficult; for in the discussions which were held, and the correspondence which occurred on this subject early in the last century . . . it appeared that the points of agreement between the Churches were numerous, those on which the parties hesitated few, and apparently not the most important."[27]

Butler's and Doyle's initiatives were less consequential than unitive steps prompted by the Oxford Movement. The Anglicans engaged in this attempt to recover neglected features of the Church of England's catholic heritage gave fresh consideration to the Roman Catholic Church. Their evaluations of her and of her role in the achievement of reunion varied. Most believed that Christ's church exists in three branches—Anglican, Orthodox, and Roman —and that members of each of the branches should remain within it, working there to recover the catholicity that had been the splendor of the undivided early church. Reunion will come when what despoils catholicity in each body has been purged.[28] A smaller group of Anglicans, the most prominent of whom was John Henry Newman (1801-1890), despaired of the recovery of catholicity within their church and concluded that to become fully catholic, they must enter the Roman Church.

The positions elaborated in Newman's voluminous writings had a growing impact upon Catholic thought, especially in the decades between the two world wars. Of direct ecumenical significance was his guarded respect for the Established Church. Unlike many other Anglican converts to Roman Catholicism (and contrary to most of his earlier writings), Newman contended in his classic *Apologia Pro Vita Sua* (1864) that the Church of England performs a positive function in teaching men the partial body of Christian truth it has preserved: "The Church of England has been the instrument of Providence in conferring great benefits on me. . . . And as I have received so much good from the Anglican Establishment itself, can I have the heart, or rather the want of charity, considering that it does for so many others what it has done for me, to wish to see it overthrown?"[29]

A direct fruit of the Oxford Movement was the establishment in 1857 of the Association for the Promotion of the Unity of Christendom, the first society ever formed to foster prayer for Christian unity. The principal Catholic leader of the Association was Ambrose Phillipps de Lisle (1809-1878), an English lay convert to Roman Catholicism. By 1864 the Association enrolled approximately 5500 Anglicans, 1000 Roman Catholics, and 300 Eastern Orthodox. They pledged to pray daily that God would grant Christendom "that Peace and Unity which is agreeable to Thy will." Members were not expected to compromise their respective doctrinal convictions regarding the exact nature of the unity for which they prayed. However, the Holy Office in Rome, prodded by Henry Manning (soon to become the cardinal archbishop of Westminster), categorically repudiated the Association in 1864. It was judged to breed religious indifference by teaching that the members' churches are all "forms of one true Christian religion" and to impede non-Catholics' conversion to Roman Catholicism by fostering a groundless expectation of an eventual union of churches. Catholics therefore must not "join or in any way favor the Society in question, or any similar one."[30] Despite APUC leaders' protests that Rome had misunderstood their organization, the sweeping condemnation stood, and Catholic participation in the pioneering organization promptly ended. Not even the most visionary could have imagined the ecumenical course to be taken by the Roman Church exactly one hundred years later through the Second Vatican Council's *Decree on Ecumenism.*

* * *

The Holy Office (established in the sixteenth century to protect Catholics from heresy) had demonstrated the vigilance with which it guarded the Roman Church's endowment from Christ. It had judged that seeming Catholic acquiescence in specious claims regarding reunion obscured the singular presence of unity within the Roman Church. In future years similar bolts from Rome would rebuke others who wandered from the narrow path along which Catholics customarily had pursued reunion. Such persons risked censure because they believed the time had arrived for a more daring search for passages through the wilderness to the uncharted regions where reconciliation lay. Only occasionally were they able to commend their vision to the sympathetic interest of popes, for the Roman pontiffs normally chose to exercise their apostolic leadership on behalf of Christian unity more by preserving familiar landmarks of the past than by exploring unknown realms of the future. But late in the nineteenth century the pioneers' vision won the cautious support of the aged Pope Leo XIII. After a lapse of nearly four hundred years, creative papal interest in Christian unity resumed. Its impact proved indelible.

NOTES

1. Owen Chadwick, *The Reformation,* The Pelican History of the Church (Baltimore: Penguin Books, 1964), p. 271.

2. Albert C. Outler, ed., *John Wesley,* Library of Protestant Thought (New York: Oxford University Press, 1964), p. 493.

3. The first statement is from Adrian's instructions to the papal nuncio, Chieregati. Karel Blockx, " 'Si Quae Culpa . . . ' ," *Eastern Churches Quarterly* 16 (1964): 282. The denunciation of Luther is from a papal brief to Frederick, Duke of Saxony. J. Coppens, "Adrien VI: pape de l'union," in J. Coppens et al., *Union et désunion des chrétiens* (Bruges: Desclée de Brouwer, 1963), p. 72. Cf. L.E. Halkin, "Adrien VI et la réforme de l'église," *Ephemerides Theologicae Lovanienses* 35 (1959): 522-44.

4. Hubert Jedin, "The Council of Trent and Reunion: Historical Notes," *Heythrop Journal* 3 (1962): 3-14. Many documents reflecting Catholic hope for reform in the pre-Trent years are gathered in John C. Olin, ed., *The Catholic Reformation: Savanarola to Ignatius Loyola* (New York: Harper and Row, 1969).

5. Joseph Lecler, *Toleration and the Reformation*, 2 vols., trans. T. W. Weston (New York: Association Press, 1960), 1: 114-33; Roland H. Bainton, *Erasmus of Christendom* (New York: Charles Scribner's Sons, 1969), esp. pp. 184-96; Margaret Mann Phillips, "Some Last Words of Erasmus," in John C. Olin, James D. Smart, Robert E. McNally, eds., *Luther, Erasmus and the Reformation* (New York: Fordham University Press, 1969), pp. 87-113.

6. Hubert Jedin, *A History of the Council of Trent*, 2 vols., trans. Dom Ernest Graf (St. Louis: B. Herder Book Co., 1957), 1: 355-91; *Dictionnaire de théologie catholique*, s.v. "Controverse"; John P. Dolan, *History of the Reformation* (New York: Desclee Co., 1965), pp. 327-51; Yves Congar, *Dialogue Between Christians*, pp. 139-40.

7. Cassander's major reunionist works were *De officio pii ac publicae tranquillitatis* (1561) and *Consultation de articulis fidei inter Catholicos et Protestantes* (1565). See John T. McNeill, "The Ecumenical Idea and Efforts to Realize It, 1517-1618," in Ruth Rouse and Stephen Neill, eds., *A History of the Ecumenical Movement 1517-1948*, 2nd ed. (Philadelphia: Westminster Press, 1967), p. 38, and Owen Chadwick, *The Reformation*, p. 371.

8. John Berchmans Dockery, *Christopher Davenport, Friar and Diplomat* (London: Burns and Oates, 1960), p. 63.

9. Maurice Nédoncelle, *Trois aspects de problème Anglo-Romain au XVIIIe siècle* (Paris: Bloud et Gay, 1951), pp. 94-5. Cf. Norman Sykes, "Ecumenical Movements in Great Britain in the Seventeenth and Eighteenth Centuries," Rouse and Neill, *Ecumenical Movement*, pp. 139-40; Georges Tavard, *La tradition au XVIIe siècle* (Paris: Les Editions du Cerf, 1969), pp. 371-96; and Dockery, *Davenport*, pp. 146-9. Tavard's study also takes appreciative account of Sancta Clara's later, more substantial theological scholarship.

10. Sancta Clara, *Paraphrastica Expositio Articulorum Confessionis Anglicanae*, ed. Frederick G. Lee (London: John T. Hayes, 1865), p. 116. It should be noted that there is some question as to whether the *Paraphrastica* originally appeared as an appendix to *Deus, Natura, Gratia*; Lee thinks not, Dockery otherwise.

11. The full title of Dez' volume is *La réunion des protestants de Strasbourg à l'église romain également nécessaire pour leur salut, et facile selon leurs principes.* Dockery, *Davenport*, p. 66, n. 3; Max Lackmann, *The Augsburg Confession and Catholic Unity* (New York: Herder and Herder, 1963), p. 32.

12. Bossuet, *The History of the Variations of the Protestant*

Churches (New York: D. and J. Sadlier & Co., 1887), p. 335. See also Congar, *Dialogue*, pp. 140-1; W. J. Sparrow Simpson, *A Study of Bossuet* (London: SPCK, 1937); and A. Rebelliau, *Bossuet, historien du Protestantisme* (Paris: Hachette, 1908). According to Daniel-Rops, the first application of the "separated brethren" terminology to Protestants was made by the sixteenth-century Jesuit, Peter Canisius. Daniel-Rops, *The Catholic Reformation*, trans. John Warrington, vol. 5 of his *History of the Church of Christ* (London: J.M. Dent & Sons, 1962), pp. 58, 334.

13. Dolan, *Reformation*, p. 17. Cf. Simpson, *Bossuet*, pp. 171-5. The latter volume also discusses Bossuet's correspondence with the German Lutheran layman, Leibnitz, pp. 165-85. It should be noted that Molanus considered a similar possibility as presented to him by Spinola, a Franciscan Erasmian active in pursuit of reunion; see S. J. Miller, "Spinola and the Lutherans," in Erwin Iserloh and Peter Manns, eds., *Festgabe J. Lortz*, 2 vols., (Baden-Baden: Bruno Grimm, 1958), 1:419-46.

14. Norman Sykes, *William Wake, Archbishop of Canterbury, 1657-1737*, 2 vols., (Cambridge: University Press, 1957), 1: 258. See also T. M. Parker, "The Church of England and the Church of Rome from the Sixteenth Century to the Eighteenth Century," in E. G. W. Bill, ed., *Anglican Initiatives in Christian Unity* (London: SPCK, 1967), pp. 67-71.

15. Sykes, *From Sheldon to Secker: Aspects of English Church History, 1660-1768* (Cambridge: University Press, 1959), pp. 105-125.

16. Sykes, *Wake*, 1: 308.

17. Ibid., p. 310. Du Pin had earlier published a study of Luther, which though not favorable to the reformer, treated him more fairly than most Catholic studies of the time. See Hubert Jedin, "Changes Undergone by the Image of Luther in Catholic Works on Ecclesiastical History," in *Martin Luther: 450th Anniversary of the Reformation* (Bad Godesberg: Inter Nationes, 1967), p. 84.

18. *Dissertation sur la validité des ordinations des Anglais et la succession des évêques de l'Eglise Anglicane.* See Sykes, *Wake*, 1: 315-66; and E. Preclin, *Union des Eglises Gallicane et Anglicane; une tentative au temps de Louis XIV, P. F. le Courayer (de 1681 à 1732) et Guillaume Wake* (Paris: J. Gambier, 1928).

19. *Dictionnarie de théologie catholique*, s.v. "Febronius;" Yves Congar, *L'église de saint Augustin à l'époque moderne*, Histoire des dogmes (Paris: Les Editions du Cerf, 1970), pp. 406-8. The lengthy title of Febronius's study (in which its ecumenical intention was announced) was *De statu praesenti Ecclesiae et legitima potestate Romani pontificis liber singularis, ad reuniendos dissidentes in religione christiana compositus.*

20. Eugene Pottier, in the revolutionary hymn *L'Internationale*.

21. Daniel-Rops, *A Fight for God*, trans. John Warrington, vol. 9 of his History of the Church of Christ (London: J. M. Dent & Sons, 1966).

22. *New Catholic Encyclopedia* and *Dictionnaire de théologie catholique*, s.v. "Sailer;" Mark Schoof, *A Survey of Catholic Theology 1800-1970*, trans. N.D. Smith (Paramus, New Jersey: Paulist / Newman Press, 1970), pp. 23-4.

23. Martin Schmidt, "Ecumenical Activity on the Continent of Europe in the Seventeenth and Eighteenth Centuries," in Rouse and Neill, eds., *Ecumenical Movement*, pp. 117-9; Ruth Rouse, "Voluntary Movements and the Changing Ecumenical Climate," Ibid., p. 313.

24. M. Nédoncelle, et al., *L'ecclésiologie au XIXe siècle*, Unam Sanctam, vol. 34 (Paris: Editions du Cerf, 1960), especially pp. 27-8, 141-231, 360-73; Congar, *L'église*, pp. 416-23.

25. *Symbolism, or Exposition of the Doctrinal Differences Between Catholics and Protestants, as Evidenced by Their Symbolical Writings*, trans. J. B. Robertson, 5th ed. (London: Gibbings & Co., 1906), pp. xvi, 23. See Eduard Stakemeier, *Konfessionskunde Heute im Anschluss an die Symbolik Johann Adam Möhlers* (Paderborn: Verlag Bonifacius Druckerei, 1957); M. J. Le Guillou, *Mission et Unité*, Unam Sanctam, vol.33 (Paris: Editions du Cerf, 1960), part 2:81-2; Congar, *Dialogue*, pp. 142-4. Other sympathetic ninteenth-century Catholic approaches to the Reformation are discussed by Jedin, "Changes," *Martin Luther*, p. 85

26. Rouse, "Voluntary Movements," p. 313.

27. The letter appeared in the Dublin *Evening Post*, 22 May 1824, and is cited in Henry R. T. Brandreth, *Oecumenical Ideals of the Oxford Movement* (London: SPCK, 1947), p. 11.

28. Belief in an underlying unity (which, it should be noted, was not considered to extend to the dissenting Protestant churches) bred confidence in the outcome of theological dialogue between representatives of the catholic churches. Said E. B. Pusey, a leader of the Oxford Movement: "I am, however, more and more convinced that there is less difference between right-minded persons on both sides than these often suppose—that differences which seemed considerable are really so only *in the way of stating them*; that people who would express themselves differently, and think each other's mode of expressing themselves very faulty, mean the same *truths* under different modes of expression." Owen Chadwick, ed., *The Mind of the Oxford Movement* (Stanford: Stanford University Press, 1960), pp. 51-2. Expressions of essentially the same position go back to Sancta Clara and forward (as we shall see) to Malines and beyond. See also George Tavard, *The Quest for Catholicity* (London: Burns and Oates, 1963), pp. 148-78.

29. *Apologia* (Garden City, New York: Doubleday Image Books, 1956), p. 371. The setting and consequences of Newman's *Apologia* are discussed in Meriol Trevor, *Newman: Light in Winter* (Garden City, New York: Doubleday, 1963), pp. 331-45, and Christopher Hollis, *Newman and the Modern World* (Garden City: Doubleday, 1967), pp. 134-47. Newman's words contrast sharply with those of Henry Edward Manning, another prominent convert, written the same year: "I am afraid, then, that the Church of England, so far from a barrier against infidelity, must be recognized as the mother of all the intellectual and spiritual aberrations which now cover the face of England." *The Workings of the Holy Spirit in the Church of England*, 1864, p. 30. In their day (and long afterward)

Manning's statement was more representative of the mind of English Catholics than Newman's.

30. Edward F. Hanahoe and Titus E. Cranny, eds., *One Fold* (Garrison, New York: Chair of Unity Apostolate, 1959), p. 132. See also Brandreth, *Oecumenical Ideals*, pp. 31-9; Owen Chadwick, "The Church of England and the Church of Rome from the Beginning of the Nineteenth Century to the Present Day," in Bill, ed., *Anglican Initiatives*, pp. 73-82.

II
A Vision
Nourished by Hope

Leo's unusually lengthy pontificate was preceded by the even longer one of Pius IX. From 1846 to 1878 Pius gave determined leadership to the Roman response to assaults mounted by revolutionary forces of the age. He would brook no compromise with men whom he believed to have demonstrated outrageous contempt for the church, God, Christ, and the social order ordained by God. Eighty of the enemy's most objectionable positions were collected in the *Syllabus of Errors* (1864). That the last of them should be branded error suggests the spirit of Pius' pontificate: "The Roman pontiff can and ought to reconcile and harmonize himself with progress, with liberalism, and modern civilization."[1] But Pius was not content to condemn error; he sought also to close Catholic ranks and to fortify his flock for battle, especially by intensifying traditional religious devotions, by defining the dogma of Mary's immaculate conception (1854), and by prompting the First Vatican Council's definition of papal primacy and infallibility (1870).

The Marian and papal definitions accentuated the two doctrines particularly repugnant to the majority of nineteenth-century Protestants and thus, in their eyes, widened the Reformation chasm. Protestant objections surprised few Catholics, for Protestantism was regarded as a foe closely allied with the anti-Catholic forces of modernity.[2] With accommodation to Protestantism as unthinkable as accommodation to its secular cousins, Catholics readily agreed that the proper stance toward Protestants was demonstrated by Pius' pre-Vatican Council invitation to return to the true church.[3]

The reactionary mood of the Roman Church during Pius IX's

pontificate can be overstated. His aggressive counteroffensive—despite a proclivity for theological overkill—did help to defend the religious genius of the Roman Church against forces bent upon its subversion. The harshness of the *Syllabus* is softened somewhat when the condemned propositions are considered in their original contexts. Some of the pope's policies toward other churches were uncharacteristically positive.[4] Countervailing trends continued to evolve quietly beyond Rome. Nevertheless, it cannot be gainsaid that the enormous religious power concentrated in the papacy by the mid-nineteenth century enabled Pius to set a tone for the entire Roman Church, and that he chose to lead his flock into massive battle against the complex new forces of his time. The pope went to his grave implacably opposed to feared enemies who seemed to threaten all that he believed to be good and holy. Fatefully, his successor brought to the papacy a more discriminating and hopeful evaluation of the non-Catholic world. Because he did, the Roman Church was pointed toward another Vatican Council and another era.

Pope Leo XIII (1810-1903)

On 20 February 1878 the sixty-one cardinals who had gathered in Rome to select a successor to Pius IX chose Cardinal Vincent Joachim Pecci. For the past thirty-two years he had served as archbishop of Perugia, in central Italy. There Pecci had avidly read books and journals that kept him abreast of current social and intellectual movements. As Pope Leo XIII he sought to define a constructive role for the Catholic Church in the momentous struggles by which men were being agitated and the future shaped. Although Leo's understanding of his church's mission reflected traditional principles that had guided Pius IX and numerous predecessors, it reflected also a unique sensitivity to the beneficent possibilities of modern civilization and an awareness that ancient truths must be enunciated in accents congruent with the mind and needs of the new age. For a small group of progressive Catholics, Leo's program of adaptation was welcome confirmation of hope and action they had maintained in the lean years of Pius IX's pontificate. But most Catholics did not share the pope's commitment to adaptation. Some who were initially resistant became sympathetic. Many, however, were so wed to patterns developed in earlier years that even the greatly expanded power of the pope proved incapable of reorienting them.

Leo's policy of deliberate adaptation touched many realms. Adroit papal diplomacy produced more cordial relationships with such diverse nations as Russia, France, Spain, Germany and the United States. Leo also sought to establish new links with the urban proletariat whose disaffection toward Catholicism had become pronounced. The Roman Church, he affirmed, cares deeply for persons used as "mere instruments for money-making" and subjected to labor so severe "as to stupefy their minds and wear out their bodies."[5] In his epochal encyclical *Rerum Novarum* (1891), Leo both analyzed the causes of the malady and proposed innovative steps toward a more just social and economic order.

In time the social consciousness aroused by Leo among Catholics brought them into common secular pursuits with other Christians. A greater pressure moving Catholics toward their kinsmen in other churches eventuated from the pope's response to the intellectual ferment of his day. The major lines of that response were established in the encyclical *Aeterni Patris* (1879). Leo's immediate purpose in issuing the document was to substitute Thomism for the varied philosophies employed in the education of young priests; his long-range purpose was to equip Catholics intellectually for their mission in the modern world. Some within and many outside the Roman Church regarded Leo's deliberate acceleration of the Thomist revival (begun earlier in the century) as a retreat from effective engagement with modern life, but Leo believed otherwise. The major problems of the day, he affirmed, were the consequence of false philosophies. Intellectual error had begotten social disorder. Application of the "wisdom" of St. Thomas to the many fields of human endeavor—science, the arts, the family, the state—would restore the tranquility of society and promote its true prosperity.

Publication of the encyclical was followed by vigorous papal implementation. Soon scholars throughout the Catholic Church were giving fresh attention to Thomas' thought and time. Among them two distinct tendencies arose. One group, following the lead of theologians in Rome such as the Jesuit Giovanni Cornoldi, conceived its task narrowly as the repristination of Thomas' thought, even of his exact formulae. Revealed truth increasingly came to be regarded as capable of expression in precise propositional form. The neo-Thomists in this camp typically disdained modern thought and castigated Catholics who departed from their formulations of orthodox belief. For them the Thomist revival served to constrict intellectual horizons and intensify theological intransigence. Another group, following the lead of Abbé Désiré Mercier at the Catholic University of Louvain in Belgium, viewed its task more broadly as the rethinking of Thomas' perceptions in relation to the modern scientific worldview. These scholars hoped thereby to achieve a new synthesis of faith and knowledge as viable for the modern world as the Thomistic synthesis had been for medieval times. Among them Thomas was hailed as "a beacon and not a limit"—his role was to illumine the path of thinkers in a new age, not to stifle them by demanding slavish imitation. Even though members of the latter group eventually moved in diverse directions, for many of them the Thomist revival provided a fruitful base for theological reflection and for dialogue with modern thought.[6]

A related development among Catholic scholars, also encouraged by Leo, was an enlivened interest in the past and in scientific-critical methods of historical and literary research.[7] Protestant and secular scholars' investigations of the Bible and the church's early history often had led them to challenge positions regarded by most Catholics as unshakeable foundations of faith. A major source of Catholic interest in the disciplines of "positive theology" was the desire to refute the aggressive critics of tradition by using their own scientific methods on the very ground they had chosen.

In the last two decades of the nineteenth century Catholic historical and biblical scholarship was markedly rejuvenated. Its major centers were the theological faculties of universities and institutes in Germany, France, and Belgium. Numerous monographs, journals, and dictionaries exhibited the achievements of exegetes and historians such as the Frenchmen Lagrange, Loisy, and Duchesne; the Germans Funk, Pastor, and Denifle; and the Belgians Cauchie and Van Hoonacker.

Pope Leo's initiative was less directly responsible for the flowering of positive theology than it had been for the upsurge of Thomism. Nevertheless, he did give support and direction to the new wave of biblical and historical study. In 1881 Leo opened large portions of the Vatican archives to all scholars. His reversal of a centuries-old policy symbolized both the pope's recognition of the importance of historical study and his confidence that the historical claims of the Roman Church would be verified by dispassionate investigation of the facts; "the church," he often said, "has nothing to fear from truth."[8] In 1887 he approved the formation of the International Congress of Catholic Scholars and sent messages of encouragement to its subsequent meetings. In 1893 Leo issued the encyclical *Providentissimus Deus* in which Catholics were permitted to make cautious use of the critical study of Scripture. In 1902 he established the Biblical Commission in Rome with the intention that it propose liberal guidance to Catholic scholars treating delicate questions of biblical interpretation.

Leo could not have foreseen the far-reaching effects of the social and intellectual ferment he encouraged. Some of the changes eventually wrought doubtless would have pleased him; others not. Powerful ideas rarely remain under the control of their parents and godparents. Within sixty years of his death Catholic social and intellectual currents had converged productively with the action and thought of other Christians. In Leo's social and intellectual program lie the hidden origins of the ecumenical revolution that was quietly prepared in the first half of the twentieth century and finally ignited by the Second Vatican Council.

More overt origins of that revolution can be traced to steps taken by Leo to improve relationships among the churches. For Catholics as for Protestants, interchurch initiatives during those sanguine years were stimulated by a bracing conviction of Christendom's responsibility for bringing spiritual health to the entire world. The global expansion of European civilization prompted Catholics and Protestants as never before to envision their mission as extending to all the peoples of the earth and to all realms of life. Protestants more than Catholics began to acknowledge that that mission was seriously handicapped by divisions among Christians. Significantly, Pope Leo XIII was among the handful of Catholics who perceived that successful implementation of the Christian mission in the modern world hinged upon a more complete realization of Christian unity. Although the exact definitions of the missionary and ecumenical tasks—and of their inter-relationship—have shifted since Leo's day, most Catholic ecumenical thought has continued to affirm a close tie between the two.

In Leo's mind it was imperative that the European nations end their religious differences and establish a concord of faith like that of medieval Christendom. Should free rein be allowed for the gentle tutelage of Catholic wisdom, Europe's social and political ills would soon be healed. Moreover, such concord was necessary if the European nations were to seize the unusually propitious moment for executing their God-given mission of carrying "Christian civilization to every corner of the earth."[9] The whole world might yet become the community of Christ. To realize so bold a hope required that Leo deal constructively with ecclesiastical divisions, for many of the western nations were dominated by Christians who had rejected Roman Catholicism.

By word and deed Leo, more than any previous pontiff, brought the importance of Christian unity into Catholic consciousness.[10] His unitive efforts were directed especially toward the Eastern Orthodox and Anglican Churches. At three junctures Leo introduced transformationist features into the nascent Catholic ecumenical vision. An irenic tone replaced the characteristic harshness of most earlier papal references to non-Catholic Christians. Typically, in 1895 Leo referred to non-Catholics in England as "separated brothers," the first papal use of that terminology.[11] He placed unprecedented stress, secondly, upon the positive quality of brother Christians' faith and practice. In the same letter to English Christians, Leo noted "the frequent and manifest works of divine grace" among them.[12] In 1898 he praised Protestants in Scotland for being "assiduous in their study of and love for sacred Scripture" and acknowledged that they "love the name of Christ with their whole soul and try to follow his doctrine and imitate his holy example."[13] Leo's public pronouncements revealed a considerably keener appreciation for the traditions of the Eastern churches. The pope insisted that the distinctive liturgical and canonical practices of dissident Eastern groups would not be sup-

pressed were they to establish communion with Rome. Those practices would continue, and their co-existence with the traditions of
Latin-rite Catholics would manifest better the rich diversity embraced within the Roman Church's unity.[14] A third papal expression of the transformationist motif was Leo's affirmation of the
necessity for irenic Catholic initiative on behalf of Christian unity.
The Catholic Church, he believed, did not fulfill her unitive obligation either by passively awaiting the return of other Christians or
by polemically demanding it. Among the most aggressive measures
Leo took were the organization in 1895 of a commission of cardinals to pursue union with the Eastern Orthodox, and the establishment the same year of an annual nine-day period of prayer for
"the reconciliation to the faith of all those who are separated from
the church on questions of faith or jurisdiction."[15]

Although Leo was unusually eager for fresh moves promoting
reunion, he also proved inflexible on matters he believed beyond
amendment. In September 1896 the pope reaffirmed a well-en-
trenched position by declaring that "ordinations carried out according to the Anglican rite have been and are absolutely null and
utterly void."[16] Three months earlier, in one of the key encyclicals
of his pontificate, *Satis cognitum*, Leo had carefully explicated the
understanding of unity dominant in Catholic thought for over a
millennium. The encyclical's appearance during the dispute over
Anglican orders suggests that it had been prompted by mounting
interest in Christian unity. In both statements—and increasingly in
the future—although the Roman Church rejected the ecumenical
options that attracted other churches, she demonstrated that she
was not indifferent to their quest for unity or to the questions
raised by it. In the long years that Rome remained outside the ecumenical movement, she did not escape its impact.

In *Satis cognitum* Leo expounded the preservationist theme
calmly and thoroughly. He explained that God intends the one
church he has established to offer salvation to all men throughout
history. For this mission the church has been given the authentic
teaching of Christ, the authoritative government instituted by him,
and the "fitting and devout worship of God."[17] Unity is among the
most precious gifts to be guarded by the pope and bishops in communion with him. It is manifested principally in Catholics' assent

to the whole of revealed truth and in their obedience to the divine-ly-established government of the church. Those who leave the church and its unity "depart from the will and command of Christ the Lord—leaving the path of salvation, they enter on that of perdition."[18]

The two statements of 1896 underlined Leo's continuity with predecessors. Most Catholics expected and welcomed signs of this continuity, for they long had been taught that the church that truly preserves what Christ has given does not change. A group committed to that principle understandably will prize its links with the past, and a leader who perceives his role (as Leo and other popes did) to be the chief custodian of the group's inheritance will not normally become an agent of change. In this light the innovative features of Leo's pontificate are especially striking. Such considerations, too, help account for Leo's strategy of innovation: to penetrate behind the recent past to a more distant past, there to discover wisdom for the present and future.

Leo's policies generated a mood more hospitable to innovation and adaptation within the Roman Church, and his encouragement of historical-critical study gave a foothold to one of the most pregnant intellectual currents of the age. But an acute issue was thereby raised for Catholics. What can be legitimately changed in the church and what cannot? How are the timeless, unchanging gifts of Christ to be distinguished from their historically-conditioned, variable expressions? As Catholics were to learn, that issue bore directly upon their ecumenical task, for Catholic-Protestant rapprochement would not occur without transformation on both sides. Ecumenism would fare best in a climate which made theological concepts and ecclesiastical structures maximally responsive to fresh perceptions of the divine will, and worst in a climate which froze them into conformity with the polemical past.

Fernand-Etienne Portal (1855-1926)

Leo's interest in the Church of England had been intensified in 1894 by Fernand Portal, a French priest of the Society of St. Vincent de Paul. Portal's fascination with the Church of England dated from his chance meeting five years earlier of Charles Lindley Wood, the second Viscount Halifax (1839-1934), who was a leader of Anglicans committed to the aims of the Oxford Movement. Their friendship quickly blossomed, and over the next four decades it remained a fountain of ecumenical vision and personal strength for both men.

Portal was convinced that the Catholic pursuit of reunion required more daring departures from traditional policies than had yet been recognized. He especially hoped that Leo's approach to the Eastern churches would be applied to the Church of England. Under Halifax's influence the French priest rejected the notion of most English Catholics that the only way to Anglican-Roman reunion was the winning of individual Anglican converts to Rome. He insisted that Anglicans' reconciliation with Rome did not require their renunciation of the Church of England. That church was not the "dying heresy" some Catholics alleged; rich in tradition and devotion, it should be restored to communion with Rome as a corporate body. Reunion would benefit both churches. It must be prepared gradually by thorough study of the differences and similarities existing between the two bodies. To maximize the fruitfulness of that study Anglican and Roman Catholic scholars should meet one another and work collaboratively. Like Catholic and Anglican pioneers who preceded him, Portal was confident that examination of the doctrinal divergencies between Rome and Canterbury would reveal that a far larger area of underlying theological agreement existed than had been supposed.

Portal and Halifax attempted to open Catholic-Anglican dialogue by urging that both sides initially reconsider the traditional Catholic position regarding the invalidity of Anglican orders. In the mid-1890s, a vigorous debate on Anglican orders ensued on both sides of the Channel. A key part was taken by two journals Portal edited in 1895 and 1896: the *Bulletin* of the Catholic Association for the Reunion of the Anglican Church (the Association had been established by Portal) and the more scholarly *Revue anglo-romaine*. But the past pressed too heavily to allow the fruition for which Portal had hoped. In July 1896 he was ordered not to occupy himself further with Anglican-Roman affairs, and several months later, after an unfortunately partisan investigation of Anglican orders by Roman scholars and prelates, Leo made his pronouncement of invalidity. Portal was deeply disappointed, but he continued to study the problems of reunion and to interest other French Catholics in them. In 1904 he founded and edited a third journal, the *Revue catholique des églises*, which dealt irenically with developments among many Christian churches. After five years it too was ended, a victim of the militant Catholic conservatism aroused during the Modernist controversy. A succession of defeats did not deter Portal from his unionist interests, for in the early 1920s, through the Malines Conversations, he made his final and most germinal contribution.[19]

Fernand Portal was captured by a vision that won his complete dedication and emboldened him to move resolutely toward an objective that most of his contemporaries thought permanently beyond reach. Such persons shape history. In 1896 Portal revealed the deep roots of the mission to which he believed himself called:

Those who oppose us, who declare that the idea of corporate reunion is an idle dream, imagine that we shall be discouraged by their opposition. They are much mistaken. We know indeed that there are obstacles, obstacles many and great, but we did not begin the work because we believed it to be easy of accomplishment, but because we believed it to be God's will; and we shall continue to strive on its behalf for the same, and for no other reason. . . . Who would not be ready to sacrifice himself, to give his life, if need be, to promote the great work of reunion? But God does not ask our life. He is content with less. He asks only our self-devotion. Let us give Him our heart, our wills, all the powers of our being to further this great work of reunion in the full confidence that He who has inspired us to begin the work, will, in His own good time and His own way, enable, if not us, those who come after us, to bring it to its perfect and successful end.[20]

Fr. Paul of Graymoor (1863-1940)

Lewis Thomas Wattson, an American, was a contemporary of Portal and gave himself with equal zeal to the cause of Christian unity. Before becoming a Roman Catholic, he was a priest of the Protestant Episcopal Church whose views were strongly influenced by the Oxford Movement. In 1898 he decided to found a religious society devoted to the ideals of St. Francis. In 1900, together with a like-minded Episcopal woman, Lurana Mary White, he established the Society of the Atonement at Graymoor, near Garrison, New York, and Wattson became a monk—Fr. Paul James Francis. The conviction grew upon him that the Roman See was divinely intended as the center of a reunited Christendom, and though still an Episcopalian, Fr. Paul ardently espoused that position. In February 1903 he established a magazine, the *Lamp*, which became the principal vehicle for disseminating his views.

In 1905 Fr. Paul attempted to launch an American branch of the Union for Religious and Moral Activity. The Union had been established earlier that year in Lyons, France, under joint Protestant and Catholic sponsorship. Wattson hoped that the new organization would bind "all Christians in spite of creedal differences and ecclesiastical division into a federation of love." Members were expected to pray regularly for union (especially on Saturday nights) and to "excel in love."[21] In 1907 the American priest embarked upon a more lasting and ambitious crusade for union. He wrote an Anglican collaborator, the Reverend Spencer Jones: "What do you think of inaugurating a Church Unity Week beginning with St. Peter's Chair at Rome, January 18, and ending with St. Paul's Day? During that week a series of addresses on reunion might be made every night. . . . We have to make this a popular movement and we will not do it until we preach these things repeatedly and constantly to our people."[22] The following January Fr. Paul inaugurated the "Octave of Prayer for Church Unity." He defined the unity for which prayer was to be offered as the "return of all Christians to the Apostolic See." In Wattson's mind the first day of the Octave, the Feast of St. Peter, emphasized the Roman center of the unity intended by God, and the final day, the Feast of the Conversion of St. Paul, pointed to the need for Christendom to be united in order to win the world to Christ.

Fr. Paul's conviction about the papacy led finally to a predictable decision. On 30 October 1909 he and sixteen other persons associated with the Society of the Atonement (including four women) were received into the Roman Catholic Church. The following June he was ordained a Roman priest. Fr. Paul now redoubled his effort on behalf of the Church Unity Octave. It spread widely among Catholics in America and Europe, and in 1916 Pope Benedict XV approved the Octave and granted indulgences to Catholics who participated in it. Fr. Paul and his associates in the Society of the Atonement were disappointed that the Octave was not made obligatory for Catholics, but both Pope Pius XI and Pope Pius XII reaffirmed the official approval given by Benedict XV.

Prayer intentions were formulated for each day of the Octave. The intentions established for the 1913 Octave remained without alteration until 1959. They strikingly attested Fr. Paul's conviction that Roman unity is intended not only for all Christians but for all mankind.

January 18   Feast of St. Peter's Chair at Rome. The return of all the "other sheep" to the one Fold of Peter, the One Shepherd.

January 19   The return of all Oriental Separatists to Communion with the Apostolic See.

January 20   The submission of Anglicans to the authority of the Vicar of Christ.

January 21   That the Lutherans and all other Protestants of Continental Europe may find their way "back to the Holy Church."

January 22   That Christians in America may become one in communion with the Chair of St. Peter.

January 23   The return to the Sacraments of all lapsed Catholics.

January 24   The conversion of Jews.

January 25   Feast of the Conversion of St. Paul. The Missionary conquest of the world for Christ.[23]

Fr. Paul's deep commitment to the worldwide mission of the Roman Church led him to establish the Union That Nothing Be Lost, an organization that imaginatively and effectively solicited support for Catholic missions. Warm devotion to the Virgin Mary ("Our Lady of the Atonement") was another prominent feature of Wattson's faith. He especially emphasized the Virgin's continued love and intercession for "her wandering sheep, the heretics and schismatics," whom she wishes to restore to Catholic unity.[24]

The unitive perspective of Fr. Paul closely resembled that of Leo XIII. His remarks to and about non-Catholic Christians usually were free of harsh words. He constantly stressed the papal center of a reunited Christendom. Both men encouraged Catholics to pray for reunion. Their vision of unity embraced the entire human race. And like Leo, Fr. Paul hoped that non-Catholics would return in groups to the Roman Church; to rely solely upon individual conversions would needlessly delay the reunion of Christendom and the conversion of the world. In most respects, Fr. Paul's thought also resembled that of Portal. But the American's strong preservationist orientation caused him to stop short of the Frenchman's further transformation of the prevailing Catholic outlook. Although he was reared in a non-Roman church, Wattson never viewed those bodies as appreciatively as did Portal. The splendor of "St. Peter's Chair at Rome" shone so brightly in his eyes that he discerned other sources of light but dimly. Utterly convinced that the fullness of God's truth was preserved in that source alone, he sought humbly, charitably, and persistently to lead others to it. Their refusal to accept it, he believed, is a sign of their distance from God; indeed, he could speak disparagingly (in language unthinkable from Portal) of Protestants and Orthodox who are "fighting against God by opposing the Papacy."[25] But Wattson could also speak guardedly of the presence of God's Spirit ("a sort of movement of the Holy Ghost") among Protestants in search of the unity that, unbeknown to them, awaits them in the Roman Church.[26]

Wattson's approach to Christian unity won the support of many Catholics in the early decades of the twentieth century, for it was built upon the unquestionably orthodox foundations of firm attachment to the papacy, missionary zeal, and ardent Marian devotion. The American not only aroused Catholic interest in Christian unity but gave it an outlet in the most accessible of all religious activities—prayer. Many (including members of the Society of the Atonement) later viewed Wattson's conception of the Octave as unduly narrow, but for its time it served a useful function by awakening Catholics to their ecumenical responsibility.

Antagonisms Revived

In the early years of the twentieth century ecumenical interest spread rapidly among non-Roman churches. The conveners of several major interchurch conferences held between 1918 and 1920 invited representatives of the Roman Church to attend. The invitations were declined, and Rome deliberately remained outside the resulting ecumenical organizations during their formative years.[27]

The Roman Church's spurning of the fledgling ecumenical movement is accounted for only partly by residual Catholic scorn of Protestantism. Two other developments reinforced Catholic abstention from the ecumenical movement. A few European Catholic intellectuals had precipitated a major crisis early in the century by their attempt to assimilate prominent features of contemporary thought, especially the acknowledgment that all ideas and institutions are historically conditioned, into their presentation of Catholic doctrine. In 1907 Pope Pius X, who showed himself more akin intellectually to Pius IX than to Leo XIII, vigorously repudiated the positions of the "Modernists." Three years later all priests were required to pledge that they would not perpetuate the condemned errors. In the next decade zealous conservatives regularly reported persons suspected of Modernist leanings.

The fervent "integralist" reaction against modernism pushed Catholic thought toward the narrow channels dug by Counter-Reformation polemicists and reinforced during Pius IX's pontificate.[28] Concerted Catholic grappling with the modern mind was postponed as was the day of shared Catholic-Protestant intellectual labor. The anti-Modernist crusade, moreover, directly heightened Catholic suspicion of Protestantism, for some features of modernism closely resembled the liberal theology spread throughout early twentieth-century Protestantism and represented in the first major ecumenical conferences. The Modernists' foes noticed that kinship. Catholics sensitized to error in their own church were quick to denounce what seemed to be its twin elsewhere.[29]

Catholic rejection of the Protestant-dominated ecumenical movement was also fanned by renewed criticism of Martin Luther. In 1904 a lengthy, erudite, and passionate study of Luther was published by a Tyrolean Dominican and sub-archivist at the Vatican Library, Heinrich Denifle. Not since the sixteenth century had a Catholic scholar poured such venom on Luther. According to Denifle the German friar first had sought the church's renewal, but his pride soon led to spiritual negligence and thence to complete powerlessness before his onrushing passions. Denifle's diatribe was climaxed with the embittered cry, "Luther, there is nothing of God in you!"[30] Although Denifle's scholarship did prove eventually to have the unintended constructive effect of arousing fresh Catholic and Protestant interest in Luther's relationship to late medieval thought, the more immediate consequence was a heightening of confessional hostilities. The Dominican scholar's influence was apparent six years later in Pius X's excoriation of the early Protestants as "proud and rebellious men, enemies of the cross of Christ, . . . whose God is their belly, . . . intent not upon the correction of morals, but upon denying the fundamentals of the faith."[31]

Other Catholics writing in these years about Luther and his cohorts usually were more restrained (indeed some deliberately disputed certain of Denifle's unsubstantiated charges), but the prevailing attitude toward the German reformer and the movement he inspired remained contemptuous. The learned rector of the Catholic Institute of Paris voiced the nearly-unanimous mind of Catholicism on the eve of World War I: Protestantism, Monsignor Alfred Baudrillart warned, is "an instrument of dissolution." To Protestants he appealed earnestly, "Be quit of Luther. Return to the church."[32]

* * *

The promising shift of perspective ventured by Leo had not been pressed by his successor. At the time that other churches were receiving charter membership in the ecumenical movement, the Roman Church was being led by internal developments to turn sharply away. The great wilderness created in the sixteenth century appeared as barren and dreary as ever. Nevertheless a decisive turn had been taken. The ferment stimulated during Leo's pontificate was neither entirely stilled nor forgotten. Soon its power would be exerted over a wide range of Catholic life and thought. Ideas and attitudes that supported the Catholic rejection of Protestantism were enjoying their last years of supremacy. Furthermore, the hearts and minds of two resourceful priests had been won to a vision of Christian divisions overcome by the reconciling power of God. Despite their differences, Portal and Wattson shared the confident expectation that their unitive labors eventually would bear fruit. Without such hope men do not attempt what others have considered impossible. Doubtless the two priests' optimism was nourished by the mood of the time, but its fundamental source was the certainty that God wills unity and is able to effect what he wills. In that faith and hope they gave themselves unreservedly— "all the powers of our being" in Portal's words—to the task of preparing the way for unity. They thereby aligned themselves with formidable forces that soon would perceptibly erode the mountains of division.

In the developments considered in this chapter, one sees a pattern that was to recur repeatedly in the decades ahead. Events, people, and ideas that seemingly had no possibility of furthering the Catholic rediscovery of Protestantism nevertheless did so. Ecumenical offspring were begotten by unlikely and often unwitting parents. Thus, the neo-Thomist revival and Denifle's study of Luther appeared at the time only to widen the chasms opened in the sixteenth century. Yet each of these developments—and many others later—proved eventually to have an impact neither intended nor expected upon the Catholic initiation to ecumenism. Reflection upon that fact carries one toward philosophical and theological questions about the movement of history. It must be enough for now, however, to leave the matter with an adage that was dear to the French ecumenist Paul Couturier: "God writes straight with crooked lines."

NOTES

1. Colman J. Barry, ed., *Readings in Church History*, 3 vols. (Westminster, Maryland: Newman Press, 1965), 3:74.

2. Pius' view of the alliance is suggested by his inclusion in the *Syllabus* of several "errors" pertaining directly or indirectly to Protestantism. See nos. 15, 18, and 77. Ibid., pp. 71, 74.

3. Roger Aubert, *Le Saint-Siège et l'union des églises: textes choisies et introduits* (Brussels: Editions Universitaires, 1947), pp. 25-9; Otto Karrer, "The Council in the Roman Catholic Church" in H. J. Margull, ed., *The Councils of the Church*, trans. Walter F. Bense (Philadelphia: Fortress Press, 1966), pp. 287-9.

4. For instance, Pius ordered that Catholic prayers for the conversion of England use the word *acatholics* rather than *heretics* in referring to non-Catholics in that land. Aubert, *Le pontificat de Pie IX (1846-1878)*, Histoire de l'Eglise depuis les origines jusqu'à nos jours, 21 vols. (Paris: Bloud et Gay, 1952), pp. 478-86.

5. Etienne Gilson, ed., *The Church Speaks to the Modern World: The Social Teachings of Leo XIII* (Garden City, New York: Image Books, 1954), p. 228.

6. *Aeterni Patris* appears in English translation in Ibid., pp. 29-54. The Thomist revival has been studied by James Collins, "Leo XIII and the Philosophical Approach to Modernity," in E. T. Gargan, ed., *Leo XIII and the Modern World* (New York: Sheed and Ward, 1961), pp. 179-209; and Roger Aubert, "Aspects divers du néo-thomisme sous le pontificat de Léon XIII," in Giuseppe Rossini, ed., *Aspetti della cultura cattolica nell' eta di Leone XIII* (Rome: Edizioni 5 Lune, 1961), pp. 133-227. See also F. C. Copleston, *Aquinas* (Baltimore: Penguin Books, 1955), pp. 248-64.

7. Edgar Hocedez, *Histoire de la théologie au XIXe siècle*, 3 vols. (Brussels: L'Edition Universelle, 1947) 3:53-161; Jean Levie, *The Bible: Word of God in Words of Men* (New York: P. J. Kenedy and Sons, 1961), pp. 3-76; Henri I. Marrou, "Philologie et histoire dans la période du pontificat de Léon XIII," in Rossini, *Leone XIII*, pp. 77-115.

8. Daniel-Rops, *Fight for God*, p. 48.

9. *Praeclara Gratulationis Publicae* ("The Reunion of Christendom"), 20 June 1894; Engl. trans. in *The Great Encyclicals of Pope Leo XIII* (New York: Benziger, 1903), p. 318. Leo's vision of the entire world won to Christ led him in 1899 to consecrate all mankind to the Sacred Heart of Jesus. He considered this act the greatest of his pontificate. It manifested a spirit akin to one which in the same period led numerous Protestant youth to dedicate themselves to the "evangelization of the world in this generation."

10. Four of the thirty papal statements published in the above collection deal directly with the subject of Christian unity. The longest of the encyclicals (*Satis cognitum*) is on the Catholic understanding of the church's unity.

11. *Amantissima voluntatis* ("To the English People"), 27 April 1895. *Great Encyclicals*, p. 349. The Latin words were "fratribus dissidentibus"; see Ernest Graf, "Our Separated Brethren," *Homiletic and Pastoral Review* 43 (1943): 517-23.

12. *Great Encyclicals*, p. 344.

13. *Caritatis studium*. Cited in George Tavard, *Two Centuries of Ecumenism: The Search for Unity*, trans. Royce W. Hughes (New York: Mentor-Omega Books, 1962), p. 70. See also Gregory Baum, *That They May Be One: A Study of Papal Doctrine (Leo XIII—Pius XII)* (London: Aquin Press, 1958), p. 46.

14. Leo's policies and acts regarding the Eastern churches are

thoroughly studied in Rosario F. Esposito, *Leone XIII e l'Oriente cristiano* (Rome: Edizioni Paoline, 1961). See also Aubert, *Saint-Siège*, pp. 31-81.

15. Cited in Tavard, *Two Centuries*, p. 70. The positive role of Cardinal Rampolla, Leo's Secretary of State, in influencing the pope's ecumenical initiatives has not yet (to my knowledge) been thoroughly investigated. In 1894 Rampolla wrote Fernand Portal a remarkable letter outlining his hope for a Roman-Anglican consideration of barriers to reunion: "A friendly exchange of ideas and a more careful and profound study of former beliefs and practices of worship would be the most useful means possible to prepare the way for this desired union. All this ought to be accomplished without any touch of bitterness and recrimination, or preoccupation with worldly interest, in an atmosphere wherein one would breathe the spirit of humility and charity alone, with a sincere desire for peace, and ardent devotion to the immortal work of love accomplished by a God who prayed that all his own should be one in him, and did not hesitate to cement this union with his blood." John Jay Hughes, *Absolutely Null and Utterly Void* (Washington: Corpus Books, 1968), p. 60. One wonders if Rampolla were echoing a statement Portal had made to him.

16. *Apostolicae Curae*, in *Great Encyclicals*, p. 405. The process leading up to the condemnation is thoroughly examined in Hughes, *Absolutely Null and Utterly Void*.

17. *Great Encyclicals*, p. 369. Very little is said in the encyclical about the third endowment of the true church.

18. Ibid., p. 358. The early sources of this view of unity are studied in Walter Ullmann, *The Growth of Papal Government in the Middle Ages*, 2nd ed. (London: Methuen and Co., 1962). The place of Leo's teaching in the development of Catholic ecclesiology is discussed in Hocedez, *Histoire* 3:387-91, and Congar, *L'église*, pp. 450-5.

19. H. Hemmer, *Fernand Portal: Apostle of Unity*, trans. and ed. by Arthur T. Macmillan (London: Macmillan and Co., 1961); Albert Gratieux, *Amitié au service de l'union: Lord Halifax et l'Abbé Portal* (Paris: Bonne Presse, 1950). The Malines Conversations will be discussed in the following chapter.

20. Hemmer, *Portal*, pp. 73-4.

21. S. Butler, "Fr. Paul Wattson in the Light of Modern Ecumenism," *Unitas* 15 (1963): 93.

22. Titus Cranny, "The Chair of Unity Octave: 1908-1958," in Hanahoe and Cranny, eds., *One Fold*, p. 65.

23. Ibid., p. 69.

24. Ibid., p. 105.

25. Ibid., p. 79.

26. Cranny, ed., *Father Paul and Christian Unity* (Graymoor: Chair of Unity Apostolate, 1963), p. 137. See also Charles Angell and Charles LaFontaine, *Prophet of Reunion: The Life of Paul of Graymoor* (New York: Seabury Press, 1975), p. 128.

27. Oliver S. Tomkins, "The Roman Catholic Church and the Ecumenical Movement, 1910-1948," in Rouse and Neill, eds., *Ecumenical Movement*, pp. 680-82. The later escalation of Catholic interest in ecumenical conferences and organizations is discussed in subsequent chapters.

28. The issues raised by the Modernist controversy are carefully treated by T.M. Schoof, *A Survey of Catholic Theology 1800-1970*, trans. by N.D. Smith (New York: Paulist/Newman Press, 1970).

29. One of the first Catholic works pointing out the connection was J. Fontaine, *Les infiltrations protestantes et l'exégèse du Nouveau Testament* (Paris: Victor Retaux Libraire, 1905). Some of the Modernists' Protestant friends also recognized the kinship that existed and welcomed it; see Newman Smyth, *Passing Protestantism and Coming Catholicism* (New York: Charles Scribner's Sons, 1908). As late as 1957 an American Catholic priest wrote that present-day Protestant theology was characterized by essentially the same errors found among the Modernists. Kenneth Dougherty, "Seminary Study of American Protestantism," *American Ecclesiastical Review* 135:521-2.

30. *Luther und Luthertum in der ersten Entwicklung* (Mainz, 1904); cited in Gordon Rupp, *The Righteousness of God: Luther Studies* (London: Hodder and Stoughton, 1953), p. 23. Denifle's precursors in the second half of the nineteenth century (especially Ignaz Dollinger and Johannes Janssen) are discussed by Jedin, "Changes," *Martin Luther*, pp. 86-7. Seven years later an extremely critical but more nuanced study was published by Hartmann Grisar, *Luther*, 3 vols. (Freiburg, 1911-12).

31. *Editae Saepe*, 25 May 1910. Cited in Walther von Loewenich, *Modern Catholicism*, trans. Reginald H. Fuller (New York: St. Martin's Press, 1959), p. 266.

32. Baudrillart, *The Catholic Church, The Renaissance, and Protestantism*, trans. Mrs. Philip Gibbs (London: Kegan Paul, Trench, Tribner and Co., 1907), pp. 325-6.

III
Rediscovering the Outsider

The Roman Church's repudiation of Protestantism manifested a sectarian spirit that has reigned recurrently in Christian history. Sixty-five years before the Reformation began it had been voiced in the Council of Florence's somber pronouncement: "All who are outside the Catholic Church, not only pagans, but also Jews, heretics and schismatics, cannot partake of eternal life, but are doomed to the eternal fire of hell, if they do not enter the Church before the end of their lives."[1] Protestants soon were regarded as outsiders and remained so classified throughout the Counter-Reformation period. Most Catholics believed that these forlorn souls could possibly be rescued from the clutches of hell, and charity counseled the attempt. But admission to the ark of salvation was contingent upon converts' rejection of past ways, and few Protestants relished that alleged improvement of their lot. Most either ignored or (in league with other outsiders) assaulted the Roman ark. Non-Catholic militance intensified Catholic militance, and Catholic leaders felt obliged to maintain their ark as a battleship and to train its crew as warriors able both to repulse the enemy and to lure defectors from his ranks.

If tribalistic conflict between children of light and children of darkness is a recurrent note of Christian history (indeed of all history), so too is an affirmation of the bonds linking even the most disparate members of the human family.[2] The vision of a more inclusive, pluralistic community was not entirely absent from Counter-Reformation Catholicism, but never did it prosper. By the third and fourth decades of the twentieth century, however, forces both within and beyond the Roman Church were creating fresh Catholic appreciation of the outsider. Through that reorientation

Catholic minds were prepared for the discovery that the Protestant heretic is a Christian brother.

Crisis for Christendom

Attitudinal shifts of such magnitude are intimately related to the major events and currents of an age. Since the sixteenth century the dominant impact of those events and currents upon Christians had been divisive. In the twentieth century a grim, nearly constant atmosphere of crisis became a fertile ecumenical seedbed. For the western world its presence was jarringly announced by the trauma of the First World War. Combatant nations mobilized sixty-five million persons for battle, and by the war's end thirteen million were dead. Following the carnage, most rulers and peoples alike knew that the nations must act collectively if such wars were to be averted. Their determination created the League of Nations, which by 1926 enrolled the governments of five-sixths of the world's population.

The war and its aftermath signaled the appearance of a watershed in human history: an American historian observed perceptively in 1930 that "the greatest event of the twentieth century is the birth of a world."[3] Decades of accelerating technological achievement had laid the foundations of a global society. Communication and travel had been facilitated; new patterns of economic and social interdependence had been woven; man's knowledge of the peoples of the earth had been enlarged and disseminated; an expansive scientific-industrial culture had been forged. But as the demise of the League demonstrated, the foundations of the emerging world community were fragile. Powerful currents of national and ethnic pride stirred among peoples in every continent. Allegiance to the nation and its traditions did not preclude allegiance to the world community, for proud nations could live together in mutual respect and mutual dedication to the tasks of peace. But some nations were so seized by dreams of expanded power that they embarked upon policies of conquest and dominion. Available for their use was an expanding arsenal of potent weapons created by the new technology.

Never before had the whole of mankind faced such possibilities for maximizing both its misery and its well-being.

The opportunities and perils of the 1920s and '30s made growing numbers of Protestants recognize the appropriateness of efforts to link the churches; only through their united labors would Christianity be able to minister effectively to a precariously balanced world community. The ecumenical movement's roots were religious convictions, but plainly the atmosphere of the time prompted the articulation and implementation of those convictions.

The widespread quest for peace and solidarity encouraged some Catholics to advocate their church's involvement in the movement toward Christian unity. Dom Lambert Beauduin, a pivotal figure in Catholic unionist activity, observed that in the postwar years "the preoccupations of men are oriented more clearly than ever toward unity in all realms." Those "preoccupations," he believed, provide an immense opportunity: "The hour is propitious for the Roman Church to take advantage of these latent tendencies and to lead separated Christian groups to unity."[4]

An additional spur toward Christian unity was given Catholics by the growth and expansionist ambition of dreaded adversaries. The rise of nazism in Germany and, even more, of communism in Russia made Roman Catholics consider an alliance with other Christians and "men of good will." Catholics alone could not successfully cope with those threats to Christianity and to the social order it had helped mold. The non-Catholic Christian could be a valuable ally even if he refused to embrace the Catholic Church. Pope Pius XI (1857-1939), who reigned for most of the interwar period, gave unprecedented papal encouragement to such collaboration. There must now be, he urged in 1932, a "union of minds and forces" of all "who are proud of the Christian name . . . in order to ward off from mankind the great danger that threatens all alike."[5]

Thoughtful European Catholics, like their counterparts among Protestants and Orthodox, recognized that Christendom urgently needed both social and spiritual reconstruction. The last war and the threat of another were symptomatic of a profound disorder infecting the western world. Causes, not just symptoms, must be treated. A handful of lay Catholic intellectuals proposed theoretical foundations for a "new Christendom." A key feature of that society, they insisted, must be compassionate recognition of the dignity and rights of every person, whatever his political and religious convictions. The influential French neo-Thomist philosopher Jacques Maritain (1882-1973) urged that diverse groups collaborate fraternally in pursuit of a "true humanism." For its realization Catholics should labor unhesitatingly with non-Catholics who share their ideals.[6]

Not until another international conflagration had passed were these currents to become widespread. In the period between the two world wars they made a persuasive minority concede the folly of continued religious polarization of society: for Christians to battle one another was not only to default on their responsibility for mending the fractures of society but to aggravate them as well. The day of virtually unchallenged acceptance of the older battle lines was past. Wherever this reorientation occurred, it created an atmosphere favorable to the quest for Christian unity.

Intellectual Revival

The Catholic intellectual ferment that had been abated by the anti-Modernist furor re-emerged during the 1920s. In 1931 the British historian Christopher Dawson hailed "the return of Catholicism from exile."[7] Even though a still widespread integralist mentality required the exercise of restraint, venturesome Catholic scholars nevertheless could move more freely and creatively upon terrain from which they earlier had been restricted. Their labors in four convergent realms produced conceptual tools that were used for crafting a more positive stance toward groups traditionally considered outsiders.

Cautious use of the disciplines of critical historiography was a major feature of the revival. Previous Catholic historical scholarship often had been directed to apologetic ends, the past being searched for evidence to buttress Catholic claims and to confute those of opponents. Under the influence of the scientific historiography championed among Protestant and secular scholars, Catholic historians (especially in Germany, Belgium, and France) turned more objectively to Christian history.

One fruit of the new historical science was the discovery and appropriation of appealing theological positions formed in the early church. Some of them, notably recognition of the decisive role of God's grace in man's salvation, moved Catholic thought toward positions held among Protestants.[8] The new historical scholarship also revealed that revered theologians of the past had manifested a surprisingly respectful attitude toward non-Catholics. A principle that had guided St. Augustine was frequently quoted in these years: "Hate error, love those who err. And discover the truth concealed in every error."[9]

The attention of Catholic historians was turned freshly to the origins of Protestantism. Before World War I, several German Catholic scholars had boldly criticized Denifle's treatment of Luther and pointed to the need for more objective studies.[10] The first favorable Catholic treatment of Luther (especially of his "religious psyche") was published in 1917 by Franz Xaver Kiefl, dean of the Regensburg cathedral. Luther, contended Kiefl, was "the powerful instrument chosen by Providence" to precipitate a cleansing of the Roman Church.[11] In 1929 four German Catholic scholars contributed to a volume containing essays on Luther by Catholics and Protestants. One of the Catholic authors, Anton Fischer, wrote that as a man of prayer Luther is as valuable to Catholics as he is to Protestants: "The praying Luther . . . is a truly ecumenical man. He has something to say and to give to all Christian communities."[12] Such positions spread quietly among Catholic scholars until publication in the late 1930s of a classic study by Josef Lortz revealed the remarkable distance that the Catholic reassessment of the Reformation had progressed.[13]

In the years between the two world wars many Catholic intellectuals were attracted to Thomism and to other medieval systems of thought. The contrasting styles noted in the preceding chapter continued among the neo-scholastics.[14] A key feature of the approach taken by those who followed paths opened by Mercier was respect for the positions of outsiders. That respect, together with the faith and optimism undergirding it, were explained by an American Catholic philosopher in 1927:

> Scholastic metaphysics maintains that reality and history are rational and purposive; that there is a Providence; that every error contains some truth, and furthers its development by the

way of contrast and conflict; that every system has a special function to perform and a definite end to achieve, despite the admixture of many erroneous ideas. All of which means that nothing in the world is absolutely useless or harmless; that modern life and modern philosophy must have a meaning; that it is for us to discover and appropriate the elements of truth they contain.[15]

Such openness prepared some Catholic intellectuals to acknowledge that even Protestantism has "a special function to perform and a definite end to achieve," and it encouraged them to look beneath Protestantism's errors to find "elements of truth."

Catholic appreciation for non-Catholics was also aroused by fresh consideration of the ancient view of the church as the mystical body of Christ. During the second half of the nineteenth century the mystical body theme (revived earlier by Möhler) had provided some Catholic theologians a new context in which to develop current emphases upon the church's hierarchical structure. But by the 1920s, as reflection upon the mystical body spread more widely and assimilated the fruits of biblical and patristics research, the theme was developed among some influential theologians in such a way that it stressed the invisible bonds uniting men to Christ and to one another. By placing more emphasis upon those bonds and less upon hierarchical structure than had been typical in Counter-Reformation thought, they moved Catholic ecclesiology a step toward an orientation that had been long prominent in Protestant doctrines of the church. Moreover, their elaborations of the mystical body concept accented the universal scope and unitive conseqences of Christ's redemptive work. Both emphases were prominent in a widely-read work, *Das Wesen des Katholizismus*, published in 1924 by a German theologian, Karl Adam (1878-1966). Adam wrote that "the Church . . . is a divine creation. For she is the unity of redeemed humanity . . . Mankind—not merely this man and that, not you and I only, but the whole of mankind, the unity of all men— was brought home again from its terrible diaspora, back to the living God."[16] The Roman Catholic Church is the "home" prepared by God for the whole human family; already outsiders are unsuspectingly linked to her. Hence Catholics must refuse to acquiesce in the barriers that keep large portions of humanity from the church and that thereby thwart the divine purpose.

Some leaders of the Roman Church's worldwide missionary program further closed the theological and psychological distance separating insiders and outsiders. After World War I, surging anticolonialism threatened the Catholic Church's tenuous footholds in Asia and stimulated fresh thought about her future role beyond the traditional borders of Christendom. It appeared that Catholicism might be considered a merely western religion and handed the same fate that was befalling unwanted occidental ways. In response to that challenge Popes Benedict XV and Pius XI made concerted efforts to strengthen the Catholic Church outside the West and to end her accustomed reliance there upon western clerical leadership and ecclesiastical forms. Missions specialists such as the Belgian Jesuit Pierre Charles urged that programs of cultural adaptation actualize the Roman Church's claim to be the home intended by God for all peoples, whatever their culture and religion. She must show that she is not a monolith, with room only for western perspectives and traditions. To do so, she must demonstrate both her respect for humanity's rich diversity and her ability to assimilate and perfect the varied religious values dispersed among all cultures.[17] Some Catholics urged that Hindus, for example, should no longer be regarded as God-forsaken, idolatrous pagans. Present among them is what German theologian Otto Karrer called an "unconscious Christianity." Its existence is a sign both of the omnipresence of grace and of human responsiveness to grace: "God's will to bestow grace is universal and the actual contact is effected whenever a man surrenders himself to the holiness which his conscience reveals." To such persons the Catholic has a benevolent mission: "It is our duty to desire for them the plenitude of light and grace according to our capacity to help them as our brothers, children of the *same* Father, reverently, humbly, lovingly."[18]

Only minor adjustments would be needed to adapt this approach to the Catholic Church's mission toward non-Christian religions to the question of her responsibility toward non-Catholic churches. Catholic ecumenism and the new Catholic missiology shared common presuppositions, and each reinforced the development of the other.

The Malines Conversations

In December 1921 several prominent Continental Catholics began a series of meetings with a like group of Anglicans at Malines, Belgium, to discuss points of theological agreement and disagreement. Their "Conversations," more than any other event, marked the stumbling entrance of the Roman Catholic Church into the twentieth-century movement for Christian unity. They revealed to a wide audience the surprising possibility as well as the unsurprising difficulty of irenic Catholic encounter with outsiders inhabiting the non-Roman churches of the West.

The chief Catholic instigator of the Conversations was the indomitable Portal. He and Halifax had been stirred by the appeal for Christian unity issued in August 1920 by the Sixth Lambeth Conference of Anglican bishops. The two friends thought the statement hinted at possible Anglican initiatives to break the deadlock created by the 1896 Catholic rejection of Anglican orders. They asked the widely admired Mercier, now cardinal archbishop of Malines, to host discussions between scholars from the two churches. Unknown to Portal and Halifax, Mercier was already considering the initiation of dialogue between Roman and non-Roman theologians, and he quickly accepted the two men's request. From 1921 to 1926 five sessions, each lasting several days, were held at the episcopal residence in Malines. Although the first session was convened without explicit authorization from Rome or Canterbury, by the time of the second session, in 1923, the participants had received the cautious approval of Pope Pius XI and Archbishop of Canterbury Randall Davidson for their undertaking. During these years they gathered for private discussions in the hope of finding ways by which their churches could be led toward greater mutual understanding and, if agreement proved sufficient, toward union.

In the first four sessions several traditionally disputed dogmatic and canonical issues were discussed, with attention focused especially on the problem of papal authority. A flush of optimism led to consideration also of possible practical steps by which the two churches might eventually unite. Following the fourth session both Mercier and Portal died. Authorities in Rome wished the Conversations (by now widely publicized) to end, so the fifth meeting, in October 1926, proved to be the last.[19]

The decision to terminate the Conversations was prompted by several pressures. English Catholic leaders had lobbyed vigorously against continuation. In their judgment, the Catholic participants had seriously erred in not including English Catholics in the discussions and in not consulting the English hierarchy adequately about issues considered. English Catholics increasingly regarded their Continental brothers as ill-informed intruders into English ecclesiastical affairs, whose high valuation of Anglicanism was based on knowledge of only the small and unrepresentative high-church wing of the Church of England, and whose only sure effect upon the English scene would be to retard the flow of converts from Anglicanism to Catholicism. Especially galling for the few English Catholics who learned of it was a paper Mercier read at the fourth session entitled "The Church of England United, Not Absorbed." Its unnamed author daringly proposed that the Anglican Church be united to Rome on the pattern of the Eastern uniate churches: the alleged patriarchate of Canterbury would be restored; Anglican bishops, priests, liturgy, and canon law would be preserved; and the English Catholic hierarchy would be suppressed.

The Holy See's termination of the Conversations was further prompted by growing doubt that Anglican objections to Catholic teaching could soon be dissipated. In view of more hopeful prospects for union with Eastern Orthodox churches, it seemed best to Roman authorities that Catholic unionist attention and energy be turned eastward.[20]

Among many English Catholics the Conversations occasioned bitter reassertion of a negative judgment of Protestantism in general and of Anglicanism in particular, but among some Continental Catholics they awakened fresh interest in those forms of non-Catholic Christianity.[21] Moreover, for four young men who soon charted the direction of emerging Catholic ecumenism (Lambert Beauduin, Henry St. John, Paul Couturier, and Marie-Joseph Congar), the irenic perspectives of Mercier and his colleagues were a formative influence.[22]

A fundamental conviction of Catholic participants in the Conversations was that corporate reunion, not individual conversion, is the proper route to reconciliation. They agreed that persons in other churches who desire to enter the Roman Church should be received, but they also recognized that the number of such persons never will be large, that fresh antagonisms will be aroused by efforts to proselytize, and that conversion cannot introduce into the Roman Church the corporate riches of the separated churches. Those bodies retain positive value for their own members as well as for the Roman Church. With that acknowledgment an issue of great theological and strategic import for Catholic ecumenism was joined, although it was not to be addressed systematically and publicly for a decade.

However compelling corporate reunion became for Catholics who worked in the spirit of Portal and Mercier, the Conversations and their repercussions had convincingly demonstrated how far the churches were from its realization. The acrimony that the Conversations aroused among English Christians underscored the necessity of resolving a host of difficult psychological and theological issues before attempting to formulate reunion plans. The successors of Portal and Mercier saw that future union must be built upon the patiently-laid foundation of widespread mutual love and understanding—upon what Mercier called a "rapprochement of hearts." Even that would not be easily achieved, but it appeared to lie within reach. With corporate reunion plainly not an imminent possibility, the way was open for concentration upon the crucial preparatory tasks that claimed the energies of Catholic ecumenists for the next three decades.[23]

Mercier's appraisal of the fruits that would issue from an irenic pursuit of rapprochement echoed the conviction of earlier pioneers. In 1925 he asked:

Fundamentally, is the Church of England . . . not still implicitly united to Rome, even today? If people on both sides of the barrier examined more deeply what they really felt, would they not find, with the grace of the Holy Spirit aiding them, that they are wrong in believing themselves irrevocably separated? Is it not conceivable that historical factors, errors of misinterpretation and ill-founded fears have created and maintained superficial differences which have covered up and hidden from our deeper consciousness certain truths in which we believe without realizing it?[24]

In spite of formidable contrary evidence, Mercier was confident that the chasm between Rome and Canterbury was passable. Patient study and charitable dialogue would be rewarded eventually by the discovery of a bridge constructed of a common faith. That agenda and that optimism were bequeathed from Malines to the persons destined to guide the unfolding of Catholic ecumenism through the middle decades of the century. But for the moment further pursuit of Anglican-Catholic unity was stymied. Other realms, however, beckoned.

Encounter with Eastern Orthodoxy

The Bolshevik regime that seized power in Russia during World War I submitted the Russian Orthodox Church to intense persecution. Nearly one million Orthodox Christians left their homeland, most of them fleeing to Western Europe where they introduced Catholics and Protestants to a form of Christianity not widely known in the Occident. In the postwar years other Orthodox churches in turbulent Eastern Europe sought ties with Western churches in the fledgling ecumenical organizations. Catholics and Protestants now were challenged to respond to churches that did not fit the polemical categories they had evolved to cope with each other. Here were fellow Christians—not outsiders. As that lesson was learned, it helped trigger Catholics' and Protestants' mutual discovery of kinship.

Active leadership in shaping an irenic Catholic response to Orthodoxy came from Pope Pius XI in the mid-1920s. Like other Catholics familiar with conditions in Eastern Europe, Pius XI believed that the new regime in Russia soon would fall and that when it did, his church must be ready to lead the Russian Church to restored communion with Rome. Catholics meanwhile should aid their beleaguered Russian brothers and prepare for the day of possible union.[25]

The pope knew that Catholic unionist initiatives would be resented, for many Orthodox churchmen regarded Catholics in their midst as proselytizers bent upon winning them to the Roman fold and imposing Latin ways upon them, thereby divesting them of prized liturgical, canonical, and theological traditions.[26] Pius had no intention of altering the traditional Catholic insistence that the See of Rome had been established by Christ as the center of unity for all Christians. But to that position he joined a winsome spirit of love and respect, strikingly expressed in 1927:

> For reunion it is above all necessary to know and to love one another. To know one another because if the work of reunion has failed so often, these failures have been due in large measure to the fact that neither side has known the other. If there have been mutual prejudices, these prejudices must fall. The errors and equivocations which exist and recur among our separated brethren against the Catholic Church seem simply incredible. But on the other hand, Catholics too have sometimes failed to have a proper appreciation of their responsibility; or, because of ignorance, they have lacked a fraternal spirit. Do we know all that is valuable, good, and Christian within these fragments of the ancient Christian faith? The separated particles of gold-bearing rock themselves contain gold. The ancient Eastern Christian bodies have preserved in themselves a holiness so worthy of reverence that they not only merit all our respect, but our understanding as well.[27]

By his words and deeds Pius sought to assure Eastern Christians that their traditions were so laden with "gold" that they would continue to exist with full integrity should their churches return to communion with Rome. Reunion would benefit both the Orthodox East and the Latin West.[28] To facilitate movement toward that objective Catholics must carefully study the Eastern churches. Their study, he insisted, is to be guided by the expectation of finding treasures among Christian brothers, not of uncovering weaknesses among opponents. The knowledge they gain is to be used in building a wider community of reconciliation, not in attacking rival churches.

The significance of Pius' approach to the Orthodox can scarcely be overstated. Since the time of the Crusades, European expansion had often been accompanied by contempt for all foreign cultures and religions. More recent phases of western colonialism, regarding European cultural and religious superiority as axiomatic, had imposed western ways around the globe. Through much of the Counter-Reformation period the Catholic approach to other churches and other religions had been governed by that mentality, and "Latinization" was one consequence. But as the twentieth century made increasingly evident, western cultural and political hegemony could not withstand the tides of liberation and self-determination rising around the world. Pius XI correctly read the signs of the times and attempted to establish another, more pluralistic basis upon which to build Christian unity. Such a course would not be easy, for it clashed with the forces rising within the Roman Church in recent decades that caused high value to be assigned to ecclesiastical uniformity and theological unanimity.

The pope's most germinal step toward Christian reconciliation was his instruction to the head of the Order of St. Benedict. On 21 March 1924, in the letter *Equidem verba*, he asked this oldest of the religious orders to designate certain monasteries as centers dedicated to seeking the union of separated Eastern Christians, especially those of Russia, with the Church of Rome. The key response from the Benedictines was establishment of a new monastery at Amay, Belgium, in December 1925. From here nascent Catholic ecumenism received greater sustained direction and impetus in the interwar years than from any other quarter.

As she had done so often in the past, the Roman Church had turned to her monastic tradition in order to enlist leadership for movement to a new frontier.

The Benedictine chosen to head the "Monks of Union" at Amay was Dom Lambert Beauduin (1873-1960).[29] Earlier in his career Beauduin had served as a diocesan priest in an innovative ministry among urban workers. Upon becoming a Benedictine monk, he had grown strongly convinced of the need for a revitalized liturgy, and in 1909 he had assumed a pioneering role in the Catholic liturgical revival. During World War I, he had participated actively in the underground resistance against the German invaders of his homeland. As a theological professor in Louvain and Rome he had made ecclesiology his area of specialization. It was Beauduin who had authored the controversial paper, "The Church of England United, not Absorbed," read by Mercier at the fourth session of the Malines Conversations. He also had prompted the pope's decision to request Benedictine pursuit of reconciliation with Eastern Orthodoxy. Boldness, coupled with theological perceptiveness, pastoral sensitivity, a warm personality, and considerable appreciation of the Eastern churches, equipped Beauduin admirably for his pioneering ecumenical role.

Prayer was a central feature of the Monks' work for reunion. Some of the group adopted the Eastern liturgical rite and observed it in a special chapel established for them. Visiting churchmen from the East who wished to know more about Latin Catholicism were hospitably received at Amay. Under Beauduin's tutelage the Benedictines studied the languages, history, literature, art, and especially the theology and liturgy of the Eastern churches. They shared their appreciation of "gold" from the East with a growing audience. The Monks traveled frequently, some of them extensively, to interest other Catholics in the Eastern churches. Their chief means of communication was the journal *Irénikon* (from the Greek word meaning "peaceful"). Its editors declared in the April 1926 inaugural issue that they wished their publication to become "the organ of a great movement for the union of the churches." Thereafter *Irénikon* was published regularly, its pages containing information about other churches, theological and historical studies written by Catholics and Orthodox, and reviews of pertinent books and articles.

Although the focus of the Monks' work was Eastern Orthodoxy (especially the Russian Church), for the first two years they also studied Anglicanism and, to a lesser extent, Continental Protestantism. The expansion of their ecumenical horizon was prompted by Beauduin's long-standing interest in Anglicanism, by growing Orthodox encounter with Protestantism in ecumenical organizations, and by mounting Protestant appreciation of pre-Reformation forms of worship and theology.[30] More fundamentally, Beauduin sensed that because Christ's mystical body extends among all Christians and because the problems of manifesting its unity are distinguishable but not completely separable, the healing of the split between Rome and Orthodoxy was closely linked to the healing that must occur in the West between Rome and Protestantism.

In the early issues of *Irénikon* Beauduin gave an appreciative Catholic approach to the separated Eastern churches its first sustained public elaboration. The influence of predecessors whose major interest had been reunion with Western churches was evident; later, central themes of his approach would be directed by Beauduin's successors to Protestantism.[31] In his articles the preservationist motif was not argued. Its presence was manifested as quiet confidence that eventually the separated churches will be reunited with Rome. But that day was seen to lie in the distant future. Movement toward it is impeded by formidable barriers of mutual prejudice, misunderstanding, and bitterness. Those barriers, Beauduin wrote, must be overcome by a "spiritual reconciliation of hearts and minds." Attitudes and opinions must be transformed on both sides. The crucial first step is for divided Christians who have long lived in isolation to meet one another. As they attempt to understand one another, their mutual ignorance will begin to give way to knowledge, their contempt to respect, and their bitterness to love. When such reconciliation among Christian persons is accomplished, they will no longer accept the ecclesiastical barriers that had kept them apart. Then church leaders will find themselves in a position fruitfully to undertake reunion negotiations, for reunion will already be "three-quarters realized and God will do the rest."[32]

Dom Lambert termed this approach to Christian unity the "psychological method."[33] It rested upon the conviction that division is rooted more in the malleable wills and minds of men than in irreconcilable dogmatic statements and irreversible historical events. When Christians genuinely want to find a way to union, they can do so. Beauduin's recognition of the critical importance of the subjective, non-dogmatic factors separating Christians recovered an insight that lay deep in the church's past and that had been voiced in Erasmus's futile plea for the return of mutual love to the hearts of Catholics and Protestants. Doubtless the twentieth century's discovery of the complexity of the human mind and of the subjective coloring of all religious affirmation and association helped shape Beauduin's perception and helped others accept it.[34]

Beauduin contended that as separated Christians develop mutual love and respect, they will at last be able to approach controverted theological issues constructively. Then the Catholic partner in dialogue must recognize frankly the inadequacy of customary formulations of Catholic teaching. Eastern Christians find them unpalatable because of their association with painfully remembered past disputes and their insensitive advocacy by Catholic apologists. The Catholic must understand the debated doctrines profoundly enough to be able to explain them disengaged from their objectionable historical dress and harmonized with the whole of Catholic teaching. Thereby they will become more acceptable to the non-Catholic. This transformation of theological expression, Beauduin argued, flows not from disrespect for Catholic truth but from full loyalty to it: "It is a question of not betraying the truth, of presenting it with all its supernatural power, and of not thwarting its spread in souls by incomplete and too hasty statement."[35]

Beauduin's own major attempt at theological explanation and restatement was undertaken in three articles treating the First Vatican Council's definition of papal infallibility. He acknowledged that numerous misunderstandings surrounded the Council's teaching and that for many non-Catholics it seemed so to distort the gospel as to make reunion with Rome impossible. For the sake of unity, therefore, this central truth preserved by the Roman Church must be explicated anew. Dom Lambert disavowed any intention of changing immutable truth; rather he wished to find "especially appropriate formulae" for it, through which the church's teaching "progresses without changing, evolves while remaining identical with itself."[36] Beauduin proceeded to this delicate ground by rejecting specious interpretations of the conciliar definition and by showing how it should be understood in relation to traditional Catholic belief. The papal teaching authority, he argued, guarantees rather than replaces the normal teaching authority of bishops in communion with Rome; and it safeguards rather than thwarts the gifts of the Spirit among the faithful. Papal infallibility is not intended to produce domination by the bishop of Rome. It is a power given by Christ to preserve the revelation upon which the church lives. And it is a "service of humility and of charity" intended by him to maintain and nourish the rich graces bestowed among all the faithful.[37]

The Belgian monk's argument for theological reformulation

reflected the effort of avant-garde theologians of his generation to reckon with the developmental character of Catholic dogmatic affirmation and to draw proper conclusions from the fact that throughout history the church has given Christian truth a variety of legitimate expressions.[38] For Beauduin this perception meant not only that more apt theological language must be found for conversation with Eastern Christians, but also that his church must admit the possibility of a future convergence of non-Catholic and Catholic understandings of Christian truth. The possibility is supported by past precedent, Dom Lambert claimed, for history shows that some Roman dogmatic definitions that initially clashed with positions of other churches later were "elucidated" by the Roman magisterium in such fashion as to make evident their fundamental agreement with the non-Catholic positions. For example, the Catholic definition in 1274 of the Holy Spirit's procession initially appeared incompatible with the corresponding Orthodox teaching. However, in 1439, at the Council of Florence, Pope Eugene IV declared that the two are different expressions of "the same and unique truth." Beauduin suggested that the decrees of Trent and the First Vatican Council might eventually be understood in such ways that they will be seen similarly to converge with the positions of other Christians.[39]

The popes had already admitted that liturgical and canonical pluralism could be allowed were the Eastern churches to return to communion with Rome. Now Beauduin was arguing for a significant measure of dogmatic pluralism as well.

Lambert Beauduin was a prophet who pointed in unfamiliar directions, raised provocative questions, and outlined seminal answers that others would explore more thoroughly. But his innovations antagonized fellow Catholics. Some Benedictines were dissatisfied with the activism and independence of the Monks of Union, and some Jesuits were offended by Beauduin's disparagement of Counter-Reformation piety. Officials in Rome expected the Monks to focus more exclusively upon the winning of Russian Orthodox to Catholicism and to be guided by a more traditional missionary approach. Their displeasure was heightened by the defection from Catholicism of several persons associated with Amay. Three times Roman authorities threatened to suppress *Irénikon*. In

December 1928 Dom Lambert, aware of the growing conflict between his views and those of Vatican officials, relinquished his position as prior and was required to leave the monastery. Beauduin's authorship of the controversial paper read by Mercier at Malines was disclosed in 1930, and in January 1931 he was ordered to Rome to answer a series of charges. Now Beauduin felt the full sting of what a recent biographer has described as the "unprincipled duplicity, the truly Machiavellian tactics" used against him.[40] In 1932 he was sentenced for two years to an isolated monastery far from Amay. While here he wrote a friend that "there are different ways of working for union, and I believe that the most opportune for the moment is to pray and to suffer for it." [41] The next seventeen years were spent at several religious communities in France, from which he was able to make a quiet contribution to the ecumenical and liturgical ferment within French Catholicism. Not until 1951 was his exile ended and he allowed to rejoin his community (since 1939 located at Chevetogne, Belgium). In Beauduin's prolonged absence the remaining Monks of Union, notably Dom Clément Lialine, continued the work into which he had led them, though they ventured less frequently into controversial areas.[42]

Other Catholics also were prompted by the Orthodox presence in Western Europe to seek Catholic-Orthodox rapprochement. The Apostolate of Reunion was organized in Holland in 1927, building upon a venture started seven years earlier. Unionist circles in Louvain and Brussels met periodically for study. In 1923 a seminary for Russian students was established in Lille, France. The seminary later closed, but a Dominican study center named Istina (the Slavic word for "truth") and directed by Christophe J. Dumont, continued to engage the sizeable community of Russian émigrés settled there. In 1936 it relocated in a Paris suburb.[43] The French capital had become a focal point of Catholic-Orthodox conversation largely because of the presence since 1925 of the Theological Academy of St. Sergius. The Russian Orthodox school had gathered a distinguished faculty, and some St. Sergius professors had become actively involved in dialogue with Protestant and Catholic scholars. At some discussions in which Russian Orthodox theologians participated, both Protestant and Catholic theologians were present. Here they learned to talk respectfully and constructively with one another.[44] Some Orthodox theologians also spoke and wrote appreciatively in Catholic circles about developments in Protestantism.[45] In England a Benedictine monk, Dom Bede Winslow (1888-1959), stimulated Catholic interest in the Christian East, and in 1936 he established and became first editor of the *Eastern Churches Quarterly*.[46] Winslow and other English Catholics attracted to the Orthodox soon found themselves in unaccustomedly close association with Anglicans of a similar interest. In several European lands a new link stretched between the major factions of Western Christianity.

* * *

The unitive labors of Beauduin, Winslow, and their small circle of Catholic co-workers addressed a fundamental need of the time. Momentous events and forces—war, revolution, emigration, depression, industrialization, nationalism—were undermining institutions and ideas that long had provided stability and meaning. Instinctively men searched for roots and cohesion. The paths of some led toward religion. Theologians and pastors responded to the anxious queries of their contemporaries and of their own souls in a variety of ways. One response common to Beauduin and other influential Catholics, Orthodox, and Protestants was reconsideration of the doctrine of the church, for they judged that should the church be actualized as its founder intended, men would discover within its fellowship the fulfillment of their deepest longings for authentic selfhood and brotherhood.

Among the handful of Catholics who labored at the task of reconceiving and repatterning the Christian community in light of both ancient and current Catholic wisdom, a common ecclesiological perspective emerged. Three features of it should be noted. Its proponents believed the mystical body theme to be a more adequate expression of the intrinsic nature of the church than the ecclesiological statements that had dominated theological manuals and catechisms for centuries. They did not directly attack the objectionable traditions but preferred, in a style reminiscent of Pope Leo XIII, to turn quietly to earlier, more fertile reaches of the Christian past to find the principal motifs of their positions. In the new ecclesiological outlook, too, a pastoral intention and tone replaced the usual juridical, abstract character of most inherited treatises on the church. Care was taken to show that the wounds inflicted by contemporary society are healed through participation in the life of the Christian community. A third feature of the new ecclesiology was its enlargement of Catholic horizons to universal dimensions. Because God intends all persons for the church, Catholics must learn to respect all outsiders—whether Christian or non-Christian—and to seek bonds of community with them.

Catholic ecumenical initiatives in the first half of the twentieth century were shaped under the influence of these human needs and theological perceptions. With varied accents such initiatives proclaimed a single message: only through the church established by Christ will non-Catholic Christians find the healing graces that bind them most closely to the human family and nurture most completely the unique gifts with which each has been blessed. Intrinsic to this conception of the ecumenical task was its linkage to the larger task of molding the entire human community according to the Creator's design and—whether recognized or not—according to the deepest aspirations of each heart.

NOTES

1. Quoted by Otto Karrer, *Religions of Mankind*, trans. E. I. Watkin (New York: Sheed and Ward, 1936), p. 251. Karrer adds (p. 253) that "fundamentally, the Florentine definition is no more than a paraphrase of earlier pronouncements, the definition of the Fourth Lateran Council and a number of primitive utterances." The original Latin text appears in H. Denziger and A. Schönmetzer, eds., *Enchiridion Symbolorum* (1965), 1351.

2. The major secular and religious champions of those bonds are provocatively studied in W. Warren Wagar, *The City of Man* (Baltimore: Penguin Books, 1968).

3. J. H. Randall, *A World Community: The Supreme Task of the Twentieth Century* (New York: Stokes, 1930), p. xi.

4. Beauduin, "Le Cardinal Mercier et la réunion des églises d'Orient," *Irénikon* 5 (1928): 227. Similar statements were made in this period by French and German Catholics, e.g., J. Calvet, *Le problème Catholique de l'union des églises* (Paris: J. De Gigord, 1921), pp. 90-100, and Karl Adam, *The Spirit of Catholicism*, trans. Dom Justin McCann (New York: Macmillan, 1929), pp. 5-6.

5. *Caritate Christi*, in T. M. McLaughlin, ed., *The Church and the Reconstruction of the Modern World: The Social Encyclicals of Pius XI* (Garden City, New York: Doubleday Image Books, 1957) pp. 286-7. See also *Quadragesimo anno* (1931), *Church*, p. 252; and *Divini redemptoris* (1937), *Church*, p. 395.

6. Maritain, *True Humanism*, trans. M. R. Adamson, 6th ed. (London: Geoffrey Bles, 1954). This important volume was first published in 1938. It and other manifestations of the "emergence of Christian humanism" are discussed by Charles Moeller, "The Church in the Modern World," *One in Christ* 2 (1966): 353-5. Actual instances of the type of collaboration called for by Pius and Maritain are considered in the following chapter.

7. Jacques Maritain, Peter Wust, Christopher Dawson, *Essays in Order* (New York: Macmillan, 1931), p. xvi. Dawson here quotes Wust.

8. Roger Aubert, "La théologie catholique au milieu du XXe siècle, II," *La revue nouvelle* 18 (1953): 44-6; Gustave Thils, *Orientations de la théologie* (Louvain: Editions Ceuterick, 1958), pp. 43-9.

9. Cited in Karrer, *Religions*, p. 8.

10. In 1906 Hermann Mauert had complained of the absence in Denifle's study of "the just, all-around careful weighing, objective probing of the non-partisan judge, and in this case of the calm, collected historian." Mauert. *P. Heinrich Denifle, O. P.* (Freiburg, 1906), p. 35; cited in Leonard Swidler, *The Ecumenical Vanguard: The History of the Una Sancta Movement* (Pittsburgh: Duquesne University Press, 1966), p. 20. A similar position had been taken by Sebastian Merkle; see Jedin, "Changes," p. 88, and Erwin Iserloh, "Luther in Contemporary Catholic Thought," Hans Küng, ed., *Do We Know the Others?* Concilium, vol. 14 (New York: Paulist Press, 1966), pp. 9-11.

11. Kiefl, "Martin Luthers religiöse Psyche," *Hochland* 15 (1917-1918): 9. His article was one of many stimulated by the 400th anniversary of the beginning of the Reformation. See Stauffer, *Luther*, pp. 37-8.

12. Fischer, "Was der betende Luther der ganzen Christenheit zu sagen hat," in Alfred von Martin, ed., *Luther in ökumenische Sicht*, p. 187. See Stauffer, *Luther*, pp. 38-9, and Swidler, *Ecumenical Vanguard*, pp. 22-4. Lest the impression be created that all liberal Catholics treating Luther were moving in the same direction, mention should be made of Jacques Maritain, *Three Reformers: Luther, Descartes, Rousseau* (New York: Charles Scribner's Sons, 1929); here Luther is bitterly exposed as "the father of modern individualism" (p. 198).

13. Lortz's study will be considered in Chapter 5.

14. Their divergent courses are summarized by Fernand van Steenberghen, "La philosophie néo-scholastique," in R. Vander Gucht and H. Vorgrimler, eds., *Bilan de la théologie du XXe siècle* (Tournai-Paris: Casterman, 1970), pp. 314-23.

15. John S. Zybura, "Status and Viewpoint of the New Scholasticism," in Zybura, ed., *Present-Day Thinkers and the New Scholasticism:*

An International Symposium, 2nd ed., rev. (St. Louis: B. Herder Book Co., 1927), pp. 503-4. The words of A. D. Sertillanges, a leading French Dominican specialist on St. Thomas, made a related point somewhat more colorfully: "The very errors of great men can contribute to the profit we expect to reap from associating with them . . . Their errors are not vulgar errors, but excesses; in their very mistakes they are not without depth and keenness of vision; following them cautiously one is sure to go a long way and one can avoid their blunders . . . The man who wants to acquire, from his author, not fighting qualities, but truth and penetration, must bring to them this spirit of conciliation and diligent harvesting, the spirit of the bee. Honey is made of many flowers." *The Intellectual Life: Its Spirit, Conditions, Methods*, trans. Mary Ryan (Westminster, Maryland: The Newman Bookshop, 1947), pp. 117-20. A similar point of view had been prominent in the thought of F. D. Maurice, a nineteenth-century Anglican theologian who exerted great influence upon leading figures in the ecumenical movement; see Alec Vidler, *The Theology of F. D. Maurice* (London: SCM Press, 1948), p. 89.

16. Adam, *Spirit*, pp. 32, 33, 35. See Stanislas Jaki, *Les tendances nouvelles de l'ecclésiologie* (Rome: Casa Editrice Herder, 1957); Congar, *L'église*, pp. 428-35, 461-5; and Aubert, "La théologie catholique durant la première moitié du XXe siècle," in Vander Gucht and Vorgrimler, eds., *Bilan*, pp. 444-6.

17. Charles' missiological principles are developed in *Les dossiers de l'action missionaire*, 2nd ed. (Louvain: Editions de l'Aucam, 1938-9); the first edition of this work appeared in 1926. See also A. Rétif, "L'avènement des jeunes églises," S. Delacroix, ed., *Histoire universelle des missions catholiques*, 3 vols. (Paris: Librairie Grund, 1957), 3: 126-46; K. S. Latourette, *A History of the Expansion of Christianity*, 7 vols. (New York: Harper and Brothers, 1945), 7: 5-65.

18. Karrer, *Religions*, pp. 261, 278 (Karrer later became an important theological figure in Catholic ecumenical initiatives in Germany). The interaction of the four currents issuing from this "intellectual revival" and their relation to emerging Catholic ecumenism constitute a major chapter of the Catholic intellectual history of the period, but unfortunately it has not yet received the attention it merits. Two key figures in whom most of the currents converged were Pierre Charles and Emile Mersch; see Paul M. Minus, Jr., "The Contemporary Catholic Reconsideration of Protestantism in French-speaking Europe," (Ph. D. diss., Yale University, 1962), pp. 82-9.

19. The most comprehensive treatment of the Conversations is Jacques Bivort de la Saudée, *Anglicans et Catholiques*, 2 vols. (Brussels: Ad. Goemaere, 1949). More recent studies are indicated in the notes that follow.

20. A. Simon, "Le Cardinal Mercier et l'union," in J. Coppens et al., *Union et désunion des chrétiens*, pp. 109-37; Henry St. John, *Essays in Christian Unity* (London: Blackfriars Publications, 1955), pp. 25-30;

Roger Aubert, "Cardinal Mercier, Cardinal Bourne and the Malines Conversations," *One in Christ* 4 (1968): 372-9; Aubert, "Les Conversations de Malines. Le Cardinal Mercier et le Saint-Siège," *Bulletin de la Classe des Lettres et des Sciences Morales et Politiques*, Academie Royale de Belgique, 5th series, 53 (1967-3): 87-159; Sonya A. Quitslund, *Beauduin: A Prophet Vindicated* (New York: Newman Press, 1973). pp. 56-79; R. J. Lahey, "The Origins and Approval of the Malines Conversations," *Church History* 43 (1974): 366-84.

21. In 1928 a Belgian Catholic scholar noted that "since the Conversations of Malines and the movement for the reunion of the churches the study of the Anglican Church is the order of the day." J. Coppens, Review of *Anglicaansche Bekeerlinger*, by A. Janssens, in *Ephemerides Theologicae Lovanienses* 5 (1928): 478. A favorable response to the Conversations has been found among a few English Catholics by Hughes, *Absolutely Null*, p. 234.

22. Beauduin, "Le Cardinal Mercier," *Irénikon* (1928) 5: 226-30; St. John, *Essays*, pp. xv-xvi, 30; Maurice Villain, *L'Abbé Paul Couturier*, 3rd ed., Eglise Vivante (Tournai: Casterman, 1959), pp. 41-2; Congar, *Chrétiens désunis: Principes d'un "oecumenisme" catholique*, Unam Sanctam 1 (Paris: Editions du Cerf, 1937), pp. 207-12. Congar's original dedication of this highly significant volume was omitted from the translated edition published in England in 1939; had it been included in the English edition, it would have read: "To the noble spirit of Cardinal Mercier. To all those of the Malines Conversations. In memory, in hope!" Its omission reflected the continued disfavor of English Catholics toward the Conversations.

23. Lambert Beauduin, "Notre travail pour l'union," *Irénikon* 8 (1930): 385-401; Jean Guitton, "Vérité et charité," in J. Cadier et al., *Unité chrétienne et tolérance religieuse* (Paris: Editions du Temps Present, 1950), pp. 216-22; St. Jean, *Essays*, pp. 25-30. A slogan coined in the period expressed the spirit with which those tasks were approached: "To unite it is necessary to love one another; to love one another it is necessary to know one another; to know one another it is necessary to meet one another." These words, inaccurately attributed by some to Mercier, probably were first written by Paul Couturier. See Minus, "Catholic Reconsideration," pp. 58-60.

24. Roger Aubert, "The History of the Malines Conversations," *One in Christ* 3 (1967): 66.

25. Roger Aubert, "Un homme d'église, Dom Lambert Beauduin," *La revue nouvelle* 31 (1960): 236; Nicholas Zernov, *The Russian Religious Renaissance of the Twentieth Century* (London: Darton, Longman and Todd, 1963), pp. 254-5; Irene Posnoff, "Russian Catholics and Ecumenism in the Twentieth Century," in A. H. Armstrong and E. J. B. Fry, eds., *Re-discovering Eastern Christendom* (London: Darton, Longman and Todd, 1963), pp. 135-53.

26. That distrust was voiced angrily by an Orthodox delegate at the

1925 Universal Conference on Life and Work at Stockholm: "Proselytism of a purely pharisaical type has become a kind of disease of the new Romanism, and the conversion of the whole universe to the foot of the Roman Chair has become the bright vision and the sweet dream of the contemporary papacy. From these visions not one church is excepted, not one Christian confession; they are all represented as the obligatory field for Christian missionary practice, just as though they formed a purely heathen domain." Cited in Yves Congar, *After Nine Hundred Years* (New York: Fordham University Press, 1959), pp. 112-3. This portrait of the "new Romanism" is perhaps accounted for partly by Pius XI's determined effort to emphasize the ties binding worldwide Catholicism to Rome: see Rétif, "L'avènement des jeunes églises,"pp. 131-38. As late as the Second Vatican Council, it was reported by a Catholic source that at least one Roman Catholic working among the Orthodox believed Rome had given secret instructions overruling public papal statements and ordering the "Latinizing" of Eastern churchmen who entered the Roman Catholic Church. See "Latin or Catholic?" in Maximos IV Sayegh, ed., *The Eastern Churches and Catholic Unity* (New York: Herder and Herder, 1963), p. 182.

27. George H. Tavard, *Two Centuries of Ecumenism*, pp. 120-1. The original Italian statement appears in "Discorsi Agli Universitari," *Studium* (Rome, 1932), p. 28.

28. Aubert, *Saint-Siège*, p. 107; Gregory Baum, *Progress and Perspectives: The Catholic Quest for Christian Unity* (New York: Sheed and Ward, 1962), pp. 31-3.

29. Useful studies of Beauduin include Quitslund, *Beauduin*; Dom Olivier Rousseau, "In memoriam: Dom Lambert Beauduin (1873-1960)," *Irénikon* 33 (1960): 3-28; Aubert, "Un homme d'église," *La revue nouvelle* 30 (1960): 224-49; Louis Bouyer, *Dom Lambert Beauduin: un homme d'église*, Eglise Vivante (Tournai: Casterman, 1964); Ruth Slade, "Dom Lambert Beauduin: A Pioneer of Catholic Ecumenism (1873-1960)," *Eastern Churches Quarterly* 14 (1961-62): 224-33; Dom Maieul Cappuyns, "Dom Lambert Beauduin: Quelques documents et souvenirs," *Revue d'histoire ecclésiastique* 61 (1966): 424-54, 761-807.

30. The two latter developments were noted periodically in *Irénikon:* e.g. (1926) 1: 148-9, 165-73, 178-9, 373-8, 389-90.

31. Both Paul Couturier and Marie-Joseph Congar, who in the late 1930s helped significantly to mold a new Catholic approach to Protestantism, were considerably influenced by Beauduin and the Monks of Union. See Villain, *Couturier*, pp. 39-44, and Congar, *Chrétiens désunis*, p. xviii.

32. Beauduin, "Le vrai travail pour l'union," *Irénikon* 3 (1927): 9.

33. Beauduin, "Notre travail pour l'union," *Irénikon* 8 (1930): 393.

34. Interest in the "non-theological factors" involved in the disunity and unity of Christians also arose among some Protestant ecumenical leaders prior to World War II and became prominent following the war.

See John E. Skoglund and J. Robert Nelson, *Fifty Years of Faith and Order* (St. Louis: Abbott Books, 1964), pp. 76, 88-9, 104. A pioneering study of those factors was H. Richard Niebuhr, *The Social Sources of Denominationalism* (New York: Henry Holt and Co., 1929).

35. "Vrai travail," p. 7.

36. "L'infallibilité du Pape et l'union," *Irénikon* 3 (1927): 450.

37. "L'infallibilité," *Irénikon* 5 (1928): 97, 98. See also Ibid., 231-8.

38. Earlier Catholic discussion of doctrinal development is analyzed in Owen Chadwick, *From Bossuet to Newman: The Idea of Doctrinal Development* (Cambridge: University Press, 1957). Provocative contributions to the debate about doctrinal development made in Beauduin's time by such figures as Maurice Blondel, Ambroise Gardeil and Pierre Rousselot are discussed in Aubert, "La théologie catholique," Vander Gucht and Vorgrimler, *Bilan*, 1: 442-3; Schoof, *Survey of Catholic Theology*, pp. 188-94; and (on a closely related issue) Roger Aubert, *Le problème de l'acte de foi: Données traditionnelles et résultats des controverses récentes*, 3rd ed. (Louvain: E. Warny, 1958), pp. 267-575.

39. "Vrai travail," p. 8. Beauduin might have pointed out a similar instance of theological reconciliation proposed by Athanasius in the late stages of the fourth-century Arian controversy; see Henry Chadwick, *The Early Church*, The Pelican History of the Church (Baltimore: Penguin Books, 1967), 1: 144. The American Jesuit theologian Avery Dulles has recently suggested that "the unity within difference permitted by the Florentine Decree of Union might prove paradigmatic for Protestant-Catholic relations." His discussion of the issue is considerably more nuanced than Beauduin's brief and suggestive comment. See Dulles, *The Survival of Dogma* (Garden City, New York: Doubleday and Co., 1971). p. 167.

40. Quitslund, *Beauduin*, p. 111.

41. Ibid., p. 185.

42. Lialine's ecumenical stance was developed in a series of four articles in *Irénikon:* "De la méthode irénique," 15 (1938): 3-28, 131-53, 236-55, 450-59.

43. Minus, "Catholic Reconsideration," pp. 48-52; Hiley Ward, ed., *Documents of Dialogue* (Englewood Cliffs, New Jersey: Prentice-Hall, 1966), p. 46; *Eastern Churches Quarterly* 9 (1951-52); 371-2.

44. The Russian philosopher Nicholas Berdyaev chaired such a group in Paris during the late 1920s. See Zernov, *Russian Religious Renaissance*, pp. 277-8. The inauguration in 1932 of an annual Protestant-Catholic-Orthodox retreat near Paris for theological discussion was reported in *Irénikon* 12 (1935): 649-50.

45. The exercise of this interpretive role can be seen, for example, in several articles written by Orthodox theologians for *Irénikon:* 6 (1929): 786; 14 (1937): 248; 15 (1939): 34.

46. E. J. B. Fry, "Memoir of Dom Bede Winslow," in Armstrong

and Fry, eds., *Eastern Orthodoxy*, pp. 1-10; Donald Attwater, "The Early Days of the *ECQ*," Ibid., pp. 11-14. In 1966 the *Eastern Churches Quarterly* turned its attention to a wider range of ecumenical issues and changed its name to *One In Christ*.

IV
Meeting a
"New" Protestantism

Catholics who began to view non-Catholics more appreciatively during the interwar period found that they could alter traditional negative judgments of Eastern Orthodox Christians with relatively little difficulty. Because Orthodox doctrine and devotion closely resembled Catholic counterparts, "particles of gold-bearing rock" could be readily identified. Anglicans presented a more difficult problem. The Catholic impressed by the Church of England's substantial pre-Reformation heritage might claim the existence of gold there, but the Catholic more impressed by her Protestant heritage believed he had ample justification for scorning that body.

Few Catholics suspected the presence of valuable ore among the generality of Protestants. For four hundred years the prevailing posture toward Protestantism had rested upon two complementary (but scarcely complimentary) judgments: Protestant "sects" were doctrinally and spiritually impoverished imitations of the true church; individual Protestants were pitifully and dangerously benighted perpetuators of heresy. The accents upon those judgments had changed in response to shifting climates in both Catholicism and Protestantism. During the 1920s and '30s the Catholic allergy to modernism still tailored most assessments of Protestantism. An American Catholic's statement was typical: so devoid of Christian substance have the Protestant sects become that among them "it does not much matter what one believes providing one fulfills the duties of fraternalism and humanitarianism."[1]

The most thorough Catholic study of Protestantism that appeared between the two world wars was written by Charles Journet

(b. 1891), a Swiss theologian who later became a cardinal. He charged that the liberal Protestantism of his land was based upon three misunderstandings of Christianity. Protestants had become more interested in man's religious consciousness than in divine revelation. They no longer acknowledged sacramental mediation of the divine presence. And they rejected the single ecclesiastical order instituted by Christ in favor of countless polities devised by man.[2]

Had Journet been in closer touch with Protestant theological centers, he would have discovered that critiques surprisingly similar to his own were being voiced among some of them. For in the two decades that followed World War I, an influential minority of Protestants forsook the religious liberalism that long had reigned and sought to recover earlier understandings of the church—especially of her faith, liturgy, and unity. Through their labors Protestantism was nudged toward positions that had characterized both the reformers and pre-Reformation Catholicism. Among the persons committed to shaping a "new" Protestant outlook, as well as among Protestants alarmed at the rampant secularization of society, Catholics met patterns of thought and action unexpectedly akin to their own. The Catholics who were eager to discover hidden bonds between themselves and non-Catholics grasped the opportunities for friendship and dialogue that had emerged. Soon their new associations prompted them to reassess and amend the Roman Church's traditional negative judgment of Protestantism.

The Ecumenical Organizations

Following World War I, ecumenical pioneers' advocacy of Christian unity won the support of a widening circle of churches and engaged them in an increasing array of collaborative activities. Protestants dominated the early interchurch ventures but welcomed the participation of the several interested Eastern churches. Among some Protestant bodies commitment to unity resulted in consideration of organic union. Many denominations entered local, national, and international councils through which they engaged cooperatively in common tasks. The three international councils formed in the 1920s (and merged later in the World Council of Churches) provided the principal rallying points for the young ecumenical movement. The International Missionary Council became an organ for interchurch cooperation in traditional mission fields. The Universal Christian Council of Life and Work encouraged churches to formulate and implement common Christian perspectives on urgent social and political problems. And the World Conference on Faith and Order sponsored study of doctrinal issues important to the pursuit of church union.

Roman Catholics had not been asked to attend the first major ecumenical conference of the century at Edinburgh in 1910, but the leaders of subsequent assemblies decided that the Roman Church should be invited and should be asked to join whatever continuing organizations emerged from them. These ecclesiastical statesmen believed (not without opposition) that the ecumenical movement must deliberately attempt to include all Christian churches, even the one with which most sharply disagreed. Hence in 1914 and 1919 ecumenical leaders approached Pope Benedict XV to invite Roman Catholic attendance at the initial Faith and Order Conference. Benedict received them cordially but refused to allow the participation of his church. He did encourage the non-Roman churches to persevere in their quest for unity, for it could lead them, he stated, to "see the light and become reunited to the visible Head of the Church, by whom they will be received with open arms."[3]

Although the Roman Church took no official part in the early international conferences, some Catholics manifested lively (and at times veiled) interest in them. A few unofficial Catholic observers attended the Universal Christian Conference on Life and Work at Stockholm in 1925.[4] American Catholic theologians served on a preparatory committee for the 1927 Lausanne Faith and Order assembly.[5] Catholic priests attended that gathering as observers—with the approval of the local bishop but contrary to a directive from the Holy Office.[6] Several Catholic scholars contributed to the preparatory volumes for the 1937 Oxford Life and Work conference; their "valuable, though unofficial collaboration" was acknowledged in the conference report. The Vatican did not grant the request of conference officials that a Catholic theologian be allowed to attend.[7] Catholic theologians participated in preparatory discussions for the 1937 Edinburgh Faith and Order confer-

ence, and a German Catholic theologian contributed an essay to
the pre-conference study book.[8] Four English Jesuits and one
Catholic layman attended that gathering as unofficial observers.
To preserve their anonymity the conference report indicated that
Catholics were present but it did not reveal their names. Fraternal
messages from the prior of the Monks of Union and the local
Catholic bishop were read to the conference.[9]

Some Catholic journals included reports on the international
ecumenical conferences of the 1920s and 1930s, and several mono-
graphic studies of the conferences were published by Catholic authors.[10] Catholic commentary before 1928 usually echoed Pope
Benedict's statement: even though their church could neither accept the assumptions underlying ecumenical ventures nor participate officially in them, Protestants' interest in unity was welcome, for it could lead them eventually to discover the papal
center of the unity intended by God for all men. Dom André de
Lilienfeld, one of the Monks of Union, went further than most
Catholic observers when he asserted in July 1927 that the ecumenical movement was "born under the inspiration of God."[11]

Six months later Pope Pius XI's considerably harsher assessment was published. On 6 January 1928, in the encyclical
Mortalium animos, he officially repudiated the young ecumenical
movement and forbade Catholic participation in it. The pope
warned Catholics attracted to the movement that it was led by
"pan-Christians" seeking to federate churches on the precarious
bases of charity and doctrinal compromise. Pius' judgment was
emphatic: "It is clear that the Apostolic See can by no means take
part in these assemblies, nor is it in any way lawful for Catholics
to give to such enterprises their encouragement or support; if they
did so, they would be giving countenance to a false Christianity
quite alien to the one Church of Christ." The only route to Christian unity, he insisted, is non-Catholics' acceptance of all Catholic
dogmas and return to the Roman Church. Like his predecessor,
Pius affirmed that if non-Roman Christians "humbly beg light
from heaven, there is no doubt but that they will recognize the one
true Church of Jesus Christ, and entering therein, will at last be
united with us in perfect charity."[12]

Here was a bald statement of the preservationist motif, delivered without even a faint hint of need or willingness to amend Catholic ways for the sake of unity. Although the encyclical unequivocally enjoined official Catholic participation in the major interchurch conferences and organizations, Catholics did not agree on its further intention. A French Jesuit suggested that it had been aimed at Catholics outside France who had fraternized with Protestants on the basis of a supposed equality of churches.[13] In Germany a Catholic theologian associated with the Society for Ecumenical Work, an organization of Protestants and Catholics formed several months earlier, declared that *Mortalium animos* had not intended to proscribe all Catholic participation in ecumenical activity; the fact that the Society continued as before apparently confirmed his analysis.[14] An American Jesuit interpreted the encyclical as a corrective intended for Catholics who had been led to false hopes by the Malines Conversations.[15]

Dom Lambert Beauduin wrote that the pope had not intended to end Catholic initiatives for unity. His purpose had been to state their ultimate goal and to reject a doctrine-compromising federation of churches as a means acceptable to Catholics. Beauduin maintained that although Catholics' participation in ecumenical conferences had been forbidden, they, like Benedict XV, should not disapprove such meetings among non-Catholics. Dom Lambert also urged that Catholics not cease their labors for greater mutual knowledge and love between Catholics and other Christians, for in *Mortalium animos* Pius XI had not rescinded his earlier measures to facilitate rapprochement.[16]

Reactions among participants in the ecumenical movement were less varied. An official statement of the Reformed Church of Hungary doubtless bespoke the mind of many Protestants: revealed in the intransigent narrowness of *Mortalium animos* is "that spirit which has been the prime cause of all division."[17] Ecumenical leaders were afforded some consolation by the knowledge that their efforts had stirred enough interest among Catholics to prompt so strong a papal statement. They agreed that the pope had misunderstood and caricatured their pursuit of Christian unity.[18] Later commentators have noted that Pius and his advisers appear to have been influenced by observation of interreligious (as distinguished from interdenominational) conferences then in vogue and by lingering Roman reactions to earlier stages of ecumenical development. It is also likely that Vatican officials saw the bogey of modernism stalking the large ecumenical assemblies, especially the Stockholm Life and Work conference.[19]

Given the distance created by the four hundred-year-old separation (and its accentuation in recent decades), it is surprising neither that *Mortalium animos* found the young ecumenical movement so wanting nor that ecumenical leaders found the pope's interpretation of their labors so unacceptable. They now had a plain statement of how the Roman Church—under Pius XI—viewed their quest for unity. They could not properly have expected the pope to compromise fundamental positions of his church in order to embrace a still evolving ecumenical perspective. But they justifiably could have expected his pronouncement to be accompanied by more evidence of the love, knowledge, and respect that he and other Catholics had declared indispensable for the pursuit of unity.

As the ecumenical movement matured in the next decade, some Catholics concluded that their church must alter her hostile stance, and, as we have seen, a few hardy frontiersmen ventured into active, albeit unofficial, roles in relation to the Edinburgh and Oxford conferences.

Vigorous public advocacy of a more positive Catholic approach to the ecumenical organizations first was made in 1937 by Marie-Joseph Congar, a young French Dominican theologian. Congar explained that salutary changes had occurred in ecumenical circles since *Mortalium animos.* No longer so strongly attracted to liberalism, Protestant ecumenical leaders manifest a more authentic "interior faith" and a recognition that "the Church is not merely a society for moral uplift . . . [rather] she belongs to an entirely different world and . . . her sole concern is the receiving of the Word of God by faith." Despite those developments, Congar judged that the Roman Church should not participate officially in ecumenical agencies and assemblies, for her participation would be misinterpreted as assent to non-Catholic ecumenical assumptions and thus as a surrendering of her unique vocation of "presenting and proclaiming the real meaning of unity and catholicity." The Roman Church instead should offer "theological assistance" through "some more or less permanent advisory contact of Catholic theologians."[20] Congar's proposal may have influenced an important decision made two years later when, in response to an inquiry from the chairman of the Provisional Committee of the World Council of Churches, authorities in Rome gave official permission for Catholic theologians to engage in periodic confidential conversation with ecumenical leaders.[21] The door slammed tight in 1928 was now ajar.

Neo-Orthodox Theology

The changed climate detected by Congar within Protestantism resulted largely from the mounting impact of "dialectic" or "neo-orthodox" theology. Its leaders, notably Karl Barth (1886-1968), sharply attacked liberal theology and sought to recover earlier (especially Pauline and Reformation) modes of theological affirmation. Central to the new orthodoxy was the conviction that the Word of God, not man's paltry words, must determine the church's thought and life. Christians should search the Bible and past doctrinal formulations to discover what they teach of divine revelation, and the church must constantly examine herself to test whether or not she is living according to God's Word.

As early as 1928 a few European Catholic theologians saw that the new theology was leading Protestant thought into greener pastures. A bellwether decision was made that year by Dominicans of the Paris province: henceforth studies of Protestant and Orthodox theology were to be included regularly in their influential scholarly journal, the *Revue des sciences philosophiques et théologiques*. The first of the studies analyzed Emil Brunner's *Der Mittler*. Its author regretted that the Swiss Protestant's work erred at certain points, but he concluded that Brunner nevertheless had demonstrated that he "adores the same Jesus Christ as we—God and Redeemer."[22] The same year a German Catholic theologian, Robert Grosche, heard Barth lecture and, under the impact of that experience, took steps to establish a scholarly journal in which Catholic theologians could respond to the new Protestant theology. Five years later his *Catholica Vierteljahrschrift für Kontroverstheologie* appeared, and until its suppression by the Hitler regime in 1939, *Catholica* remained a key organ for serious Catholic dialogue with Protestant thought.[23] In 1936 Dom Olivier Rous-

seau of Amay concluded that in the theological movement spear-
headed by Barth "all Protestantism has taken a step forward," and
that through it the prospect of fruitful Protestant-Catholic theological encounter had been substantially brightened.[24]

A major reason for lively Catholic interest in Barth and his
school was succinctly stated by an astute Protestant observer in
1933: "The new quest for the church, the return to the old confessions, the demand for authority, the emphasis upon objectivity, appears to the Roman Catholics like a loan which Barthian theology
has made from Roman Catholic theology. They rejoice in the hope
that these discoveries may work further by their own innate logic
and foster an appreciation for still other Catholic truths."[25] The
expanded area of shared theological ground allowed Catholics to
recognize, moreover, that Barth was grappling with issues crucial
for Catholics and Protestants alike, and that he was doing so with
uncommon penetration and erudition. But he also was sharply crit-
icizing important Catholic teachings (especially what he regarded
as undue exaltation of man in Catholic treatments of the doctrines
of *analogia entis* and *imago dei*), and his Catholic interlocutors
knew that Barth's critiques required cogent responses. The day of
glib manufacture and destruction of theological straw men was
rapidly passing.

The Liturgical Movement

Another feature of Protestantism viewed sympathetically by
Roman Catholics in the interwar period was the attempt to recover
earlier forms and understandings of the church's corporate life,
especially of her worship. The liturgical revival spread initially
among small circles of Protestant churchmen in Germany, England, Sweden, Switzerland, and Holland. The conviction shared
most widely was that the eucharist must again become central in
the life of the Christian community. Some went so far as to re-
claim for Protestantism pre-Reformation patterns such as private
confession and a breviary. Persons in the varied "high church" circles recognized that practices they wished to recover had been
maintained in the Roman Catholic Church—but compromised,
they believed, by Roman legalism and dogmatism. What they
sought, claimed Swedish Archbishop Nathan Söderblom, was an

"evangelical catholicity."[26] An unreformed Roman Catholicism was no closer to that goal than an unreformed Protestantism.

The Protestant liturgical revival quickly attracted Catholic interest. In the first major analysis of the German High Church Union, published in 1923, Belgian Jesuit Pierre Charles (later to become a distinguished missiologist) declared that although Protestantism is "an impoverished and sterile religion," Catholics must manifest "unlimited charity" toward eager Protestant seekers of light. Three years later a German Jesuit, Max Pribilla, wrote of the Union that it is a "small flock . . . but a high Christian idealism and a spirit of reconciliation born of love permeates its members."[27]

Common Catholic-Protestant interest in liturgical recovery and its consequences for reunion was more pronounced in Germany than elsewhere. Several German liturgical organizations founded by Protestants (mostly Lutherans) welcomed Catholic members. The most active was the High Church Ecumenical Federation, formed in 1924.[28] The first issue of its periodical, *Una Sancta*, declared the Federation's aspiration: "We turn . . . to all those, and not least to our Roman Catholic fellow-Christians who, penetrated with a truly worldwide ecumenical conviction, wish to work with us to free the Christian spirit everywhere from confessionalistic narrowness and particular seclusion and attain the breadth of real 'catholicity.' "[29] Catholics contributed articles to *Una Sancta*, and by 1927 two Catholics had joined the editorial board of the journal.

On 11 April 1927, however, a decree of the Holy Office forbade Catholics either to belong to the Federation or to write for its publication. The ban, apparently resulting from fear that the influence of Friedrich Heiler (a Lutheran scholar and Federation leader who had converted from Roman Catholicism) would be detrimental to the faith of Catholics active in the organization, precipitated changes for both the Federation and *Una Sancta*. The goals and membership of the Federation continued in a new organization, the Society for Ecumenical Work. The successor to *Una Sancta* was *Religiöse Besinnung*, but it was established without official relationship to the Society. For several years the new journal published articles by Protestant and Catholic authors. As we have seen, the Society was unshaken by *Mortalium animos* the following January. Catholics continued to participate, and later in 1928, when co-chairmen were elected, one was Protestant and the other Catholic. But in the early 1930s oppressive economic and political conditions in Germany ended the activities of the Society and caused publication of *Religiöse Besinnung* to cease.[30]

In the final issue of the journal its Protestant editor, Karl Thieme, dramatically proposed a way toward Protestant reunion with the Roman Church. His proposal resembled Beauduin's earlier appeal for an Anglican Church united with Rome. But for the first time the possibility of a uniate Protestantism was publicly raised by a Protestant.

> Here, then, is the question which we now put to the Roman Catholic Church. There are German Evangelical Christians, there are Christian families, there are also probably whole believing congregations with their shepherds, all of whom are forced by their consciences to ask for admittance into the one, eternal Church. But they are compelled by those same consciences, by their understanding of the welfare of the Church, and by the anxiety with which their brethren watch the course they are now taking, to insist upon conditions already accorded Slavic Christians—to request there under the guidance of their own shepherds that they may, in their own beloved language, render God service and worship according to the ordinances of the Catholic Church. Will this plea be granted or repudiated?[31]

The question of a Protestant uniate body was considered at a meeting of German Protestant and Catholic theologians and liturgical leaders held in 1934 under the sponsorship of Nicolaus Bares, the Catholic bishop of Berlin. Their discussion of grace, justification, the church, and the sacraments revealed a high measure of agreement. Some expressed hope that Rome would make disciplinary concessions (such as the use of a vernacular mass and reception of communion in both kinds) to groups of Protestants already inclined doctrinally to embrace the Roman Church. Successful completion of reunion on that basis, they believed, might attract other Protestants to Rome.[32]

Persons who took this position gave an intelligible, seemingly plausible answer to the question of how Protestants and Catholics could unite. The uniate pattern had been accepted by some Eastern Christians; with modification it might prove viable for Protestants. However, even the mounting pressures toward unity generated by Hitler failed to convince most German Catholics and Protestants that their churches were sufficiently close in faith and polity to warrant serious consideration of this route to reunion. Earnestly though the uniate adaptation might be argued, for the overwhelming majority of Protestants it seemed an unacceptable capitulation to Rome. Those convinced of the need for greater unity preferred to journey over other roads being mapped by the ecumenical movement.

Facing Common Threats Together

The recurring crises of twentieth-century society convinced growing numbers of Catholics that they must collaborate with like-minded persons if cherished values and institutions were to be preserved. The number who actually collaborated in the first third of the century was small, but under the pressures of increased papal encouragement and a threatening political climate patterns of cooperation were forged in several lands that came to be widely accepted during World War II.

Even before World War I some English Catholics had been active in ecumenical efforts to avert international conflict. Catholics were members of an English interdenominational committee that invited 130 German churchmen to England in the summer of 1908. The following summer a like group of Englishmen visited Germany. The Anglo-German exchange helped prompt an analogous interest in the United States. There in 1914 the philanthropist Andrew Carnegie gave two million dollars for peace efforts by the churches, on the condition that the foundation administering his gift, the Church Peace Union, include representatives of Protestant, Catholic and Jewish bodies.[33]

English Roman Catholics also worked with non-Catholic Christians to influence the English social order by Christian ethical teaching. From 1911 to 1914 they participated in annual consultations sponsored by the Interdenominational Conference of Social Service Unions. Following World War I, the scope of the Conference was enlarged and plans laid for a 1924 "Conference on Christian Politics, Economics and Citizenship." Catholics initially contributed to the intensive preparations for "Copec," but when they saw that the Catholic position on issues such as marriage and the family was not compatible with positions taken by persons of other churches, they decided that they could not participate in the Conference.[34]

After World War I, Continental churchmen who had worked ecumenically to prevent that conflict determined to do all in their power to help preserve the tenuous peace that followed the Armistice. Some of them formed the International Fellowship of Reconciliation (1919), which drew Catholics into its activities, including several men who became leaders of the Fellowship. One Catholic leader, Kaspar Mayr, was co-organizer of the European Youth Peace Crusade in 1932. For two months Catholic and Protestant youth traveled through Belgium, Holland, Germany, France, and Switzerland to win support for a pacifist position. On Easter Sunday they converged in Geneva to present their message to the World Disarmament Conference then meeting in the Swiss city.[35]

In the two decades after World War I, American Catholics slowly emerged from their enclaves in a traditionally Protestant land to take an ever more prominent role in public affairs. Only occasionally did they collaborate with non-Catholics in attempts to influence the quality of American life. An early instance occurred in 1923 when the National Catholic Welfare Conference, the principal coordinating body among American Catholics, declared jointly with comparable Protestant and Jewish agencies that the twelve-hour work day then normal among steel workers was "morally indefensible." Partly because of the public sentiment aroused by the interfaith proclamation, the steel industry established an eight-hour work day.[36]

Increased Catholic visibility in American society accentuated the uneasiness of Protestants who feared that Catholic acceptance of Vatican authority potentially would subvert the institutions and spirit of American democracy. The 1928 political campaign of Al Smith, the first Roman Catholic to seek the presidency, occasioned a bitter airing of the place of Catholics in American life.

The intense emotions that surfaced convinced cool-headed Protestants and Catholics that they must find ways to combat the religious intolerance and suspicion flourishing in the United States. Because anti-Semitism also had intensified, some judged the time opportune to establish an organization of Protestants, Catholics, and Jews to promote more respectful relations among the three groups and to facilitate their collaboration against common foes. In 1928 the National Conference of Christians and Jews was established. Within four years the NCCJ's first national consultation, on "American Community Relations," was held in Washington, D. C. By 1934 the organization's program had touched two hundred American cities. Participants in NCCJ activities normally avoided direct discussion of doctrinal issues they knew to be divisive. They did, however, help create a climate in which such discussion later became possible.[37]

Sensitive Catholics and Protestants on both sides of the Atlantic began to accept responsibility for redressing the wrongs increasingly perpetrated against European Jews. In 1926 American Protestants and Catholics were invited to contribute to an "American Christian Fund for Jewish Relief" intended for victims of persecution in eastern and central Europe. A Protestant clergyman and a Catholic layman served as co-chairmen of the Fund.[38]

The more critical arena of Christian response to mounting anti-Semitism was Germany. In the 1930s most Christians there did little to challenge the policies of Hitler's Third Reich, but a courageous minority of Catholics and Protestants publicly expressed disapproval of nazism's undisguised contempt for Jews and of its attempt to control the churches.[39] Catholic leadership came especially from Cardinals Von Galen and Faulhaber. In 1935 the latter expressed a conviction that was to spread rapidly among German Christians: "Catholic and Protestant are separated by many important matters of dogma, but there are great central convictions common to both and now subject to the sharpest attack. What we face today is a conflict not between the two halves of Christianity, but between Christianity and the world."[40] In the next decade that conflict drove Protestants and Catholics to a conscious solidarity far surpassing any known in the past.

New Categories and Attitudes

As Roman Catholics began to meet a new breed of Protestant, some sensed the inadequacy of inherited theological and psychological responses to individual Protestants and their churches. Several Catholic theologians deeply involved in the ferment within their church began to articulate responses that more accurately reflected and measured the unexpectedly rich reality they confronted.

The first major step was taken in 1924 in Karl Adam's influential book, *Das Wesen des Katholizismus* (translated into English as *The Spirit of Catholicism*).[41] Even this important transitional volume did not point in fresh directions without also demonstrating the continuing power of the traditional Catholic posture toward Protestantism. Most striking among Adam's links with the polemical past was his claim that modern man's rootlessness is a consequence of the Reformation's break with Roman Catholicism.

Adam nevertheless found encouraging developments among Protestant churches, particularly the "high church" movement within German Protestantism. More important than his remarks about specific facets of Protestantism was the theological basis he established for allowing an expression of Catholic respect for Protestantism. The "grace of Christ," he contended, reaches far beyond the visible boundaries of the Roman Catholic Church; it operates "not only in the Christian communions, but also in the non-Christian world, in Jews and Turks and in Japanese."[42] This grace works through divinely-sown "seeds of truth" dispersed among humanity. From the Roman Church, non-Catholic churches have received the effectual seeds of baptism and the preaching of Christ. Although dislodged from their rightful place, they have retained their capacity to be instruments of Christ's grace. Where grace is received in good faith by non-Catholic Christians, it enables them to live saintly lives and to move toward eternal salvation.

Adam maintained that such persons are linked invisibly to the "soul" of the Catholic Church. The growth of grace among them will bring an increase of faith and love, as well as a desire to enter visibly the church to which they are already unknowingly joined.

Protestants' religious renewal therefore directly enhances the likelihood of reunion. Adam's hope was openly confessed:

> There is a special possibility of such reunion with the Catholic Church wherever Protestantism has remained faithful to Christ and believes truly in the Incarnate God. And it is because we believe that very many non-Catholics are already thus invisibly united with the Church, that we do not abandon our conviction that this invisible union will one day be made visible in all its beauty. The more consciously and completely we all of us exhibit the spirit of Christ, the more certainly will that hour of grace approach.[43]

In 1929 a fresh theological appraisal of Protestantism was essayed by a Jesuit professor teaching in Namur, Belgium. Emile Mersch (1890-1940), who became a leading interpreter of the doctrine of the mystical body of Christ, published his three-part study in the scholarly Jesuit journal of Louvain, *Nouvelle revue théologique*. Like Adam, Mersch did not question that the true church established by Christ is the Roman Church. And like Adam he identified Protestantism's fundamental theological error as a misunderstanding of God's activity among men: Protestantism denies that "our substance, our acts, our knowledge, our ecclesiastical unity and its authority are truly united to the divine action and intrinsically divinized." That denial means that Protestants' faith is a mixture of two "opposing tendencies . . . faith in the incarnate God and unbelief toward this same incarnate God as he is continued in Catholicism."[44]

Mersch's positive evaluation of Protestantism was more comprehensive and daring than Adam's. The Catholic, he maintained, must admit that other Christian bodies possess "authentic Christian elements," even though among some they are minimal and scarcely recognizable. Wherever these "gifts from heaven" exist, they retain their "transcendent value" and merit loving veneration. They are present in Protestantism. The Catholic therefore must alter his inherited judgment and acknowledge that "Protestantism, because of them, and in spite of everything, is holy."[45]

The "unbelief" now existing within Protestantism should not

be regarded as permanent. It will dissipate as Protestants' spiritual life intensifies and their authentic Christian elements unfold. When that process has occurred, their Christianity will be "whole" and their lives as Christians fulfilled. Then they will recognize the Roman Church as the home God has prepared for all his people, and to her they will return.

Protestants' return will be of great value for them, but what will be its effect upon the Roman Church? Mersch ventured on fresh ground by stating cautiously that Protestants can contribute significantly to Catholicism, not in the realm of "essentials," but in the realm of "secondary though important perfectings." He explained that all the diverse cultures and peoples of the world will be brought to their divinely intended fulfillment by incorporation into the church. Until that process is finished the church is incomplete and Christ's full power is unexpressed: "The Catholic Church will be perfectly Christian only when the incorporation of all nations into the unique body of Christ will permit her to make explicit all the divinizing virtualities of the Savior."[46] The return of Protestants will provide an occasion for such perfecting and explicitation. Protestants will not bring the Roman Church something essential that she now lacks; they will afford her the opportunity to make explicit what already has been given to her.

Mersch encouraged Catholics to rejoice at the existence of Christian belief and practice wherever they are found. The Catholic Church's love of such "elements" among other Christians leads her to seek their return to herself and thus to Christ. Catholics can best contribute to Protestantism's return and fulfillment by ridding themselves of the provincialism and narrowness that separate them from other persons. Such cleansing will make them more convincing representatives of the inclusiveness of God's love toward humanity—and thus more genuinely Catholic. Their effective prosecution of the ecumenical task demands a transformation of the quality of life actually lived by Catholics.

Mersch and Adam gave the Catholic rediscovery of Protestantism a rudimentary theological conceptualization. In Mersch's writing especially four key notes had been struck that later would command extensive consideration: the presence of true Christian "elements" in Protestantism was acknowledged; the possibility of some enrichment of the Roman Catholic Church by Protestants was admitted; Protestant reunion with the Catholic Church was conceived principally as a fulfillment of the Protestant's faith; and a more authentic Catholicism among Catholics was recognized as their main contribution to the furtherance of reunion.

In the 1920s and 1930s other European Catholic intellectuals challenged the widespread hostile attitudes and negative behavior of their co-religionists toward Protestants. Scattered attempts were made in articles and in several books to apply to Protestants the knowledge and love that Pius XI, Beauduin, and others had urged toward the Orthodox.

One of the earliest attempts to reshape Catholic attitudes was made by the German Jesuit theologian, Max Pribilla (1874-1956). In addition to the two volumes noted earlier, he frequently wrote articles on ecumenical subjects for German journals, especially for the Jesuit publication, *Stimmen der Zeit*, which he later edited. Throughout his writings, Pribilla insisted that Catholics' major contribution to reunion is to show Protestants "as brothers in Christ, the love to which they have a claim."[47]

That love also was championed and its implications explored in *La vie intellectuelle*, a journal founded by Dominicans of the Paris province in 1928. In one of the first articles advocating a fresh approach to Protestantism, a Dominican priest in Norway urged that Catholics not content themselves with well-worn Counter-Reformation apologetics but seek to discover the real reasons for the Reformation's break with the Roman Church and the real opinions of present-day Protestants about Roman Catholicism.[48] A Catholic laywoman argued in a later issue that liberal Protestantism's polemical stance against Catholicism and its disdain for dogma still weigh heavily in Protestant circles and make useless any Catholic attempt to explore traditionally disputed theological matters. The Catholic in search of rapprochement must first seek to understand the Protestant's "state of mind—so different from our own."[49]

The non-doctrinal, psychological dimensions of Christian separation were analyzed in a series of articles on French Protestantism appearing in *La vie intellectuelle* from 1935 to 1938. The editor of the series, Marie-Joseph Congar, stressed that before Protestants and Catholics can engage in productive dialogue, each side must rid itself of the prejudices, passions, and ignorance that have accumulated for generations and that make communication nearly impossible. Catholics must engage in uncommon effort to understand Protestants firsthand, without the distorting intervention of ideological preconceptions.

> Let us first try *to understand them*, to meet them and put ourselves in their "presence," not as though we were faced with a system, nor yet as if we were face to face with a case, known in advance and clarified, but as though we were in front of a unique human being, our neighbor, whom no abstract view could exhaust or explain but who, in unique circumstances, has followed his own predestined course and unique impulses, and traveled ways that are all his own. To stand before him as a brother in friendly understanding and with a reverent and discreet curiosity, trying to look upon him as his mother might and, above all, *to understand him.*[50]

Their attempt at understanding will teach Catholics that Protestants are "brothers in Christ." And, Congar asserted, it will lead eventually to greater charity on both sides, to a fuller grasp of God's truth by Protestants, and to incorporation within the Catholic Church of "much of both value and profundity" existing within Protestantism.

The valued items that Congar had discovered among Protestants were explicitly identified: "The zeal, biblical sense and prophetic expectancy, the reliance upon the transcendence of God over any human possibilities, the intimacy and stark simplicity of faith, the honesty, all these represent the best in the Christian heritage of the Reformation."[51]

Very few Catholics yet had sufficiently open minds toward Protestantism or adequate knowledge of it to be able to confirm Congar's discoveries. But a resourceful handful agreed that ore had been struck, that it must be assayed carefully, and that news of its presence must be spread.

* * *

Because Congar's Catholic contemporaries were the heirs of a tradition that made changelessness a hallmark of their church and a warrant of her claims, they were prone to assume that the accustomed repudiation of Protestants and Protestantism was a fixed consequence of Catholic faith. Some perhaps also found it a convenient justification for hostile thoughts and deeds toward Protestants. The force of such pressures bore heavily upon Congar and his co-workers, and their refusal to yield to them bespeaks the power both of countervailing pressures and of their own intellects and wills.

Yet the pioneers' break with the past was not complete. Even as they edged Catholics toward the ecumenical era they retained ties with the Counter-Reformation era. One mark of the past upon the irenic approach to Protestantism should be especially noted. Appreciation of Protestantism was keyed to developments that appeared to be making Protestantism more Catholic and less Protestant. Protestantism tended to be valued not for its distinctive or complementary features, but for those fresh features that made evident its growing resemblance to Catholicism. What was stressed about the new relationship emerging between Protestantism and Catholicism was the evolution among Protestants that appeared to foreshadow a mass return to the Roman Church.

This emphasis eased the interpretative task of the early Catholic ecumenists, for their fellow Catholics were wont to be told of Protestants' change and of the desirability of their return. The lingering traditional mindset also affected the evaluations of Protestant churches that were made (first instinctively, later more deliberately) by Catholic ecumenists. The Roman Church was considered the touchstone by which to evaluate churches evolving toward her: those bodies resembling her more rated higher than those resembling her less. This asymmetrical basis of interchurch relationships was an appropriate transitional position for the Roman Church during the early years of her initiation to ecumenism. It would become the task of Catholic leaders in the post-Vatican II period to determine if the earlier position were a permanent expression of faith or a stage on the way toward a fuller grasp of the requirements of Christian truth.

NOTES

1. William I. Lonergan, "Rome, Malines and America," *America* 38 (1928): 409.

2. Charles Journet, *L'esprit du Protestantisme en Suisse* (Paris: Desclée, de Brouwer, 1925).

3. Cited in Tissington Tatlow, "The World Conference on Faith and Order," in Rouse and Neill, eds., *Ecumenical Movement*, p. 416. A similar papal response was made to the attempt of Archbishop Söderblom and other Life and Work leaders to involve the Roman Church officially in the 1925 Stockholm Conference; see Nils Karlstrom, "Movements for International Friendship and Life and Work, 1910-1925," in Ibid., pp. 526, 528, 538-40.

4. Ibid., p. 549.

5. Oliver S. Tomkins, "The Roman Catholic Church and the Ecumenical Movement," in Ibid., p. 681.

6. Ibid., p. 682. Swidler states that seventeen priests attended; *Ecumenical Vanguard*, p. 149. The Holy Office directive is translated in G. K. A. Bell, ed., *Documents on Christian Unity: A Selection from the First and Second Series, 1920-1930* (London: Oxford University Press, 1955), pp. 187-8.

7. Tomkins, "Roman Catholic Church," p. 685; W. A. Visser 't Hooft, *Memoirs* (London: SCM Press, Philadelphia: Westminster Press, 1973), p. 69.

8. Roderick Dunkerley, ed., *The Ministry and the Sacraments* (London: SCM Press, 1937), pp. vi, 47-65.

9. Tomkins, "Roman Catholic Church," p. 686; Aubert, *Saint-Siège*, p. 141; Ruth Slade, "Angleterre," in *Situation oecuménique dans le monde* (Paris: Cerf, 1967), p. 126.

10. The earliest articles written about the ecumenical conferences include Pierre Battifol, "Une évolution du Protestantisme: l'oecuménisme," *La documentation catholique* 8 (1922): cols. 259-72; Comte Gonzague de Reynold, "Réflexions d'un catholique pour le Congrès de Christianisme pratique à Stockholm," *La revue catholique des idées et des faits* 30 (1925): 5-7; Thomas Moore, "Foi et ordre," *Etudes* 192 (1927): 188-201; G. Phillips, "Le mouvement non-catholique pour l'union des églises," *Revue ecclésiastique de Liège*, 21 (1929/30): 289-95; D. Lathoud, "Le mouvement vers l'union des églises," *La vie intellectuelle* 1 (1926): 546-51; Max Pribilla, "Um die Wiedervereinigung im Glauben," *Stimmen der Zeit* (1925): 109. Charles Journet, *L'union des églises et le christianisme* (Paris, 1927) dealt with the Stockholm Conference. Pribilla's *Um Kirchliche Einheit—Stockholm, Lausanne, Rom* (Freiburg, 1929) examined the two conferences and the relation of Rome to the ecumenical movement. Otto Iserland, ed., *Die Kirche Christi* (Einsiedeln and Cologne, n.d.) considered issues treated by the 1937 Oxford conference and was intended by its Continental Catholic authors to be an unofficial companion piece to the official literature of that conference. Congar's *Chrétiens désunis* (1937) included discussion of several of the conferences.

11. *Irénikon* 3 (1928): 208.

12. *Encyclical Letter (Mortalium Animos) on Fostering True Reli-*

gious Union, in Bell, ed., Documents, pp. 194, 200. The original Latin text is in Acta Apostolicae Sedis 20 (1928): 5-16.

13. Yves de la Brière, "L'encyclique Mortalium animos sur l'unité chrétienne," Etudes 194 (1928): 353-7.

14. Johannes Albani's assessment of the encyclical was reported in Religiöse Besinnung 1 (1929): 187, and is cited by Swidler, Ecumenical Vanguard, p. 118-9.

15. "The Encyclical on Unity," (unsigned editorial), America 38 (1928): 383.

16. Beauduin, "L'encyclique Mortalium animos du 6 janvier, 1928," Irénikon 5 (1928): 83. That some Catholics interpreted the encyclical as a rebuke to the Monks of Union is suggested by the fact that Irénikon soon lost approximately 500 subscribers. Olivier Rousseau, "Un difficile printemps," in Semences d'unité, Eglise vivante (Casterman, 1965), p. 23.

17. Leonard Hodgson, ed., Convictions (New York: Macmillan, 1934), p. 120. With more restraint the 1930 Lambeth Conference expressed regret that "in the Encyclical the method of 'complete absorption' has been proposed to the exclusion of that suggested in the Conversations, as, for example, in . . . 'L'Eglise Anglicane unie, non absorbée.' " Cited in Quitslund, Beauduin, p. 76.

18. Visser 't Hooft, Memoirs, p. 66; Tomkins, "Catholic Church," pp. 683-4; W. A. Visser 't Hooft, No Other Name (Philadelphia: Westminster, 1963), p. 109.

19. Tomkins, "Catholic Church," pp. 683-4; Pribilla, Um Kirchliche Einheit, pp. 202-40 (here Pribilla contended that the encyclical had been influenced by continuing hostility to the "branch theory" which had been repudiated by the Holy Office in 1864 and which Roman officials still regarded as the theoretical underpinning of the ecumenical movement); George H. Tavard, The Catholic Approach to Protestantism (New York: Harper, 1955), pp. 105-7; Congar, Chrétiens désunis, pp. 149-68. It should be noted that the 1928 papal action is one of many discussed in this volume whose complete background will remain unknown until the pertinent Vatican archives are opened to scholars.

20. Cited from the English translation: Divided Christendom, pp. 134, 142, 144.

21. Tomkins, "Catholic Church," p. 686.

22. Gaston Rabeau, "Bulletin des théologies chrétiennes non-catholiques," 19 (1928): 824.

23. Robert Grosche, "La situation oecuménique en Allemagne," Istina 7 (1960): 12; Swidler, Ecumenical Vanguard, pp. 124-6. Grosche's journal resumed publication in 1954. Catholica's original statement of purpose declared its wish "to speak to the Evangelical Christians of today: not in order to arrive at an abstract or 'superchurch' Una Sancta via illegitimate compromises, but simply to present to Evangelical Christians the teachings of the Ecclesia Catholica in these days which are so demanding of Catholics and Protestants."

24. "Réflexions sur des symptômes unionistes," *Irénikon* 12 (1936): 158.

25. Adolf Keller, *Karl Barth and Christian Unity*, trans. Werner Petersmann, Manfred Manrodt, and A. J. MacDonald (London: Lutterworth Press, 1933), p. 213. A summary of the early Catholic debate with Barth is found in pp. 207-24 of Keller's volume. The second stage of that debate is reflected in Jérôme Hamer, *Karl Barth* trans. D. M. Maruca from the 1949 French original (Westminster, Maryland: The Newman Press, 1962). More recent Catholic consideration of Barth will be treated in chapter 8.

26. Congar, *Chrétiens désunis*, p. 194; Bengt Sundkler, *Nathan Söderblom: His Life and Work* (London: Lutterworth Press, 1968), pp. 262-7.

27. Charles, *La robe sans couture: un essai de Luthéranisme catholique: la haute église allemande: 1918-1923*, Museum Lessianum, Section théologique, 8 (Bruges: Charles Beyaert, 1923), pp. x, 19; Pribilla, *Um die Wiedervereinigung*, (Freiburg, 1926), p. 14.

28. In March 1927 the Federation's name was changed to the Ecumenical Federation. Swidler, *Ecumenical Vanguard*, pp. 76, 115. See also Kurt Schmidt-Clausen, "Les courants catholicisants dans le Protestantisme allemand," *Istina* 7 (1960): 43-58, and Andrew L. Drummond, *German Protestantism Since Luther* (London: Epworth Press, 1951), pp. 260-1.

29. "Was Wir Wollen," *Una Sancta* 1 (1925): 1-2.

30. Swidler, *Ecumenical Vanguard*, pp. 114-22.

31. "Una Sancta Catholica," *Religiöse Besinnung* 5 (1932-33): 58 (cited in Swidler, *Ecumenical Vanguard*, pp. 122-3).

32. Swidler, *Ecumenical Vanguard*, pp. 135-7.

33. Vera Brittain, *The Rebel Passion* (Nyack, New York: Fellowship Publications, 1964), pp. 28-9; Nils Karlstrom, "Movements for International Friendship and Life and Work, 1910-1925," in Rouse and Neill, eds., *Ecumenical Movement*, pp. 512-3; Charles S. MacFarland, *Pioneers for Peace Through Religion* (New York: Fleming H. Revell, 1946), pp. 17-23.

34. Tomkins, "Catholic Church," p. 682.

35. Brittain, *Rebel Passion*, pp. 128-9, 139-42, 130-1; Lillian Stevenson, *Towards a Christian International: The Story of the International Fellowship of Reconciliation*, new and enlarged edition (London: IFOR, Drayton House, 1941), pp. 19-20, 48-9. Max Metzger, another Catholic leader of the IFOR, is discussed in the following chapter.

36. William A. Brown, *The Church: Protestant and Catholic* (New York: Charles Scribner's Sons, 1935), pp. 359-60.

37. Lerond Curry, *Protestant-Catholic Relations in America* (Lexington: University of Kentucky Press, 1972), pp. 20-35; Everett R. Clinchy, *All in the Name of God* (New York: The John Day Co., 1934), pp. 140-1; John J. Kane, *Catholic-Protestant Conflicts in America*

(Chicago: Regnery, 1955), pp. 209-10.

38. Lerond Curry, "Protestant-Catholic Relationships in America in the 1920s," (M. A. thesis, Florida State University, 1964), p. 115.

39. Adolph Keller, *Christian Europe Today* (New York: Harper, 1942) and Stewart W. Herman, Jr., *It's Your Souls We Want* (New York: Harper, 1943) report early attempts by Catholics and Protestants to cope with the Nazi menace. Other volumes in English that reflect the postwar effort to reach a more accurate and comprehensive understanding of the complex events among the German churches in the Nazi period include Arthur C. Cochrane, *The Church's Confession Under Hitler* (Philadelphia: Westminster Press, 1962); Guenther Lewy, *The Catholic Church and Nazi Germany* (New York: McGraw-Hill, 1964); and J. S. Conway, *The Nazi Persecution of the Churches, 1933-45* (London: Weidenfelf and Nicolson 1968). Historical scholarship on this period is helpfully analyzed in the latter volume, pp. xiii-xxxi.

40. Samuel McCrea Cavert, "From Stockholm to Oxford," *Christian Century* 52 (1935): 1343.

41. By 1963 *Das Wesen* had been translated into eleven languages (Chinese, Dutch, English, French, Hungarian, Italian, Japanese, Latin, Polish, Portuguese, and Spanish); the original English edition had gone through eleven printings; and the American paperback edition was in its twelfth printing.

42. *Spirit of Catholicism*, trans. Dom Justin McCann (New York: The Macmillan Co., 1929), p. 168. In this sentence one sees an instance of the linkage between fresh thought about the Catholic ecumenical task and fresh thought about the Catholic missionary task. Adam's admission of the presence of grace and of the possibility of salvation beyond the Roman Church continued a theological discussion that had risen in the early church and that had been intensified since the middle years of the nineteenth century. See Hocedez, *Histoire*, 3:240-53, and Congar, *Chrétiens désunis*, pp. 287-8.

43. *Spirit*, p. 175.

44. Mersch, "Religion, christianisme, catholicisme, III" 56 (1929): 221-2. Mersch's three articles later were translated and included in his *Morality and the Mystical Body*, trans. Daniel F. Ryan (New York: P. J. Kenedy & Sons, 1939), pp. 3-58.

45. "Religion," p. 221.

46. Ibid., pp. 223, 224.

47. "Söderblom und die ökumenische Bewegung," *Stimmen der Zeit* 122 (1932): 305. Other articles by Pribilla in *Stimmen der Zeit* in the same period include "Um die Wiedervereinigung im Glauben," 109 (1925); "Die Kirche von Anbeginn," 217 (1929); and "Ökumenisch," 119 (1930).

48. H. D. Bechaux, "La recherche de l'unité chrétienne," 1 (1929): 740-6. *La vie intellectuelle* reflected the openness increasingly characteristic of some circles of the Catholic intelligentsia. The spirit animating the

new journal had been expressed on the first page of its inaugural issue: "We shall praise the good wherever we find it."

49. G. Swarts, "L'attitude intellectuelle du protestantisme moderne," 14 (1932): 375. Other articles on Protestantism that appeared in the journal are discussed in Minus, "Catholic Reconsideration," pp. 89-104.

50. Congar, *Dialogue Between Christians*, p. 298. English translations of Congar's four articles in the *La vie intellectuelle* series are included in *Dialogue*, pp. 289-311. In addition to the influence of antecedents discussed in the previous chapter, Congar's non-doctrinal approach to the study of Protestantism reflected influence by the "Konfessionskunde" method, which arose in Germany and encouraged comprehensive study of the total life of a religious group. See Ibid., pp. 144-51.

51. Ibid., pp. 290, 311. Three additional books from the interwar period not already mentioned expressed similar themes: Marius Besson, *Après quatre cents ans*, 4th ed. (Geneva: Librairie Jaquemond, 1934); Arnold Rademacher, *Die Wiedervereinigung der christlichen Kirchen* (Bonn, 1937); Pierre Chaillet, ed., *L'église est une: Hommage à Moehler* (Paris: Bloud et Gay, 1939).

V
Four Modern Pioneers
of Ecumenism

A reshaping of the traditional Catholic approach to Protestantism was made possible by profound alterations occurring simultaneously among the churches and in the wider society. But those changes, necessary as they were, did not provide the precise formulations of thought or compelling movements of the spirit capable of convincing Catholics that Protestants are their brothers in Christ. As with all pivotal points in history, bold individuals had to appear with words and deeds appropriate to the moment and able, consequently, to turn other minds and hearts in a new direction.

Marie-Joseph Congar, Paul Couturier, Max Josef Metzger, and Joseph Lortz were preceded by equally courageous pioneers who anticipated their vision and who would have rejoiced at their accomplishments. But, unlike the others, the four European priests lived in a time ripe for ecumenical breakthroughs. By the beginning of World War II, each had contributed an indispensable foundation upon which Catholic ecumenism would rise.

Yves Marie-Joseph Congar (b. 1904)

Contributions of the French Dominican theologian to the unfolding of a Catholic ecumenical posture have already been noted, and in subsequent chapters we shall often refer to his wide-ranging and influential labors. More than any other person Congar has both made ecumenism a central concern of Roman Catholicism and determined its characteristic features. He has fittingly been called "the father of ecumenism in the Catholic Church."[1]

Early in life Congar was pointed toward his ecumenical vocation. At the outbreak of World War I, German soldiers burned the

Congar family's parish church near Sedan, France. For the next six years the dispossessed Catholic congregation worshipped in the Protestant chapel located next to the Congar garden. Protestant kindness fired in the sensitive young man "a desire to make some return to the Protestants for all I had received from them."[2] During the next fifteen years that desire was nurtured and matured by formative experiences such as theological study at Le Saulchoir, the progressive seminary of the Paris Dominicans; visits to Lutheran landmarks in Germany and to the Monks of Union in Belgium; attendance at lectures by Protestant theologians in Paris; and participation in a theological discussion group of Catholics, Orthodox, and Protestants hosted by Nicholas Berdyaev.

By 1937 Congar was both immersed in the new intellectual currents flowing through Catholicism and acquainted with major developments among non-Roman churches. In July of that year he published his first book, *Chrétiens désunis: principes d'un "oecuménisme" catholique* (translated and published in England two years later as *Divided Christendom: A Catholic Study of the Problem of Reunion*). Here the fruits of predecessors' labors were gathered, systematized, and given a distinctive stamp by the thirty-three-year-old priest. More than any other volume, it became the theological *magna charta* of Catholic ecumenism in the years before Vatican II. Indeed, at many points the Council's *Decree on Ecumenism* echoes *Chrétiens désunis.* Probably no other book has played as formative a role shaping the ecumenical perspective of any church.

Congar undertook three principal tasks in *Chrétiens désunis:* to explain the Catholic Church's unity and catholicity; to analyze the non-Roman churches; and to develop a basis and strategy for uniting those churches to the Roman Catholic Church.

The theological underpinning of Catholic ecumenism is provided, Congar maintained, by a proper understanding of the church's unity and catholicity. To a degree unusual among modern theologians he sought to reveal the religious depths of the two traditional "notes" of the church. According to the Scriptures the church's unity is grounded in the life of the triune God. God's life can be described as perfect self-knowledge and perfect self-love. A measure of that knowledge and love is planted mysteriously into men by baptism, and thereafter, given proper spiritual nourishment, it unfolds as faith and charity. God's life thereby becomes the common life of the many within the church. Because she participates in God's life, the church is one as he is one. Because God transmits his life to men through that church alone, there is but one true church. And because the church's unity is constituted by God's irrevocable gift of his own life, her unity is neither broken nor diminished when individuals secede from her: "one is or is not in the unity of the church; one takes nothing of it when leaving it."[3]

Congar's interpretation of the church's interior life as a participation in the divine life evidenced kinship with theologians like Adam and Mersch who had viewed the church as Christ's mystical body. Some of his contemporaries, however, so accented the interior, mystical aspect of the church that they obscured the importance of her visible structure. Congar's ecclesiological statement was a major attempt in the interwar period to place the two aspects of the church in proper balance.[4] He did so by explaining that God's life is transmitted "in a human form and in an imperfect condition" adapted to the limitations of man's earthly life. Mundane realities such as water, dogmas, a priestly hierarchy, and canon law have been chosen by Christ for crucial roles in lifting men to the divine life. They have been preserved by the body which has as her "visible head . . . and regulator of her social life, the Bishop of St. Peter's see at Rome." Her possession of these instruments makes the Roman Church "a vast sacrament in which everything is a sign and a means of an inward unity of grace."[5] The instruments are indispensable now, but when history ends and earthly limitations disappear, men will participate directly in God's life without them.

If the unity of the church refers primarily to what she is given by God, the catholicity of the church refers primarily to what she receives from men. In relation to the second note especially Congar conceived the Catholic ecumenical task. The catholicity of the church is the capacity of her "principles of unity" (sacraments, dogma, hierarchical authority) "to assimilate, to fill, to exalt, to win to God and to join together in him every man and all men, as well as every value of humanity."[6] Particularly significant for ecumenism is the fact that all of mankind's religious experiences must be assimilated into the church for their divinely-intended fulfillment. The Catholic Church already approximates that inclusiveness by the presence of a rich diversity of saints, rites, and theological systems. She respects the legitimate diversity of non-Catholic religious expressions and does not reduce them to a common denominator as they are assimilated; she does, however, purge them of whatever may be a consequence of human sinfulness.

Congar's conception of the intimate relationship of catholicity and unity underlined the necessity of an outward Catholic thrust to all people and values lying beyond the Roman Church. His ecclesiological position allowed no distinction in principle between non-Catholic Christians and non-Christians: all were outside their divinely-appointed home and all should come inside for their fulfillment. Despite the absence of such a distinction, Congar did seek to give maximal recognition to the values of non-Catholic Christians. His sympathetic treatment of the Reformation made considerable use of recent German Catholic scholarship. He maintained that at a time when many had become blind to the sources of Christian spirituality, Luther sought "to find peace of heart and a living, warm and consoling contact with his God."[7] The German friar's quest led him to become profoundly aware of God's mercy and to acknowledge that one must trust simply in God's grace for salvation. This "animating feeling of Lutheranism" is authentically Catholic. But tragically it was subverted by Luther's subsequent course. He did not accept the "spiritual attitude" that issued from his experience as reflecting only a part of Catholic spirituality and doctrine. Instead, he made it the central principle around which an entire theological system was developed. Following the "aberrant logic" of that system, he rejected other Catholic teachings and thereby compromised the truth of his original perception.

If Luther's tragic course plunged him into heresy, it also endangered the Catholic Church. Congar explained that she can become so intent upon affirming what a heretic denies that she slights other, complementary ranges of Christian truth. An imbalance is thereby introduced into Catholic teaching. That process was regrettably precipitated by the Reformation, resulting in Catholic overstress upon the church's external, hierarchical character and upon man's role in achieving salvation. Those developments have, in turn, seemed to Protestants to justify continuing the original Reformation protest against Roman Catholicism.

Among his Protestant contemporaries Congar (like Adam and Mersch) detected fragments of the authentic Christianity preserved by the reformers. Baptism remains in most Protestant communities; where it is validly administered, it plants the seeds of faith and charity in the souls of its recipients. Those seeds are nourished by the Scriptures, which are preserved and honored by most Protestant groups. But because Protestants possess only a minimum of the "elements or principles" used by God to gather and nurture his church, and because they also possess errors generated in the sixteenth century and since, their spiritual state is constantly jeopardized.

Nevertheless, among Protestant communities that have preserved their inheritance from Catholicism, those baptized persons who hold sincerely to their religion are able to retain the grace and infused faith of baptism, and thus can be saved from damnation. The name "heretic" is inappropriate for them. Calling upon Augustine for support, Congar argued that that term should be reserved for persons who deliberately break with the faith of the true church. Since present-day Protestants only inherit the fruit of their ancestors' actions and hold in good faith to the Christianity they have received, they should be called "separated brothers" or "dissidents"—but not "heretics." Moreover, Congar averred, the separated brother has been brought by baptism into a partial membership in the Roman Church. At present his membership is incomplete, imperfect, and invisible. But because the grace planted in him at baptism seeks fulfillment in the Catholic Church, the separated brother moves, albeit unknowingly, toward full and visible membership.

Congar's position allowed him to agree with the view then current in the ecumenical movement that Christians in churches other than one's own are saved not in spite of their churches, but in and through them. He added, however, that the Catholic must interpret that admission according to his belief that what the dissident churches retain of authentic Christianity is not properly their own possession, but has its true locus in the Roman Catholic Church.

Other Catholics had earlier admitted the presence of virtues and values among individual Protestants. A few had admitted a degree of legitimacy in their corporate existence, but none had attempted systematically to define its exact theological character. Congar did so by developing a single perspective from which to evaluate the entire range of non-Catholic Christian communities. The young theologian took Catholic ecumenism a giant step by his claim that those communities have a derivative and determinable degree of churchly status. They are "elements" of the true church: "elements, that is to say, to the extent that they have preserved in their very constitution as a religious body elements or principles by which the one Church is realized. These principles are the realities whereby God gathers to Himself from the midst of mankind a People which He destines to be His heirs, and which He incorporates into His Christ."[8] The "plenitude" of the "elements or principles" is found solely within the Catholic Church. Outside, because of the varied character of past schisms, they exist in disparate degrees. Within Orthodox churches they are more numerous than within Protestant communities; the former thus have a more valid theological claim to the term "church" than the latter. And some Protestant communities have more elements than others.

The central objective of Catholic ecumenism is the "reincorporation of all authentically Christian values" into the Roman Catholic Church.[9] To the non-Catholic Christian such reincorporation will bring a fulfillment of his incomplete faith. To the Roman Church it will bring a fuller actualization of her catholicity—the inclusion of expressions of the Christian life of which she now is deprived. Congar acknowledged that Catholics would be edified by reunion, and that from it would result a "whole richer than any Christian body now existing, including the Catholic Church."[10]

Although his treatment of this delicate point was sketchy, Congar wished to indicate that a future realization of unity will bring beneficial change to the Roman Church. Like Mersch (who had adapted a scholastic distinction), Congar interpreted that change as an actualization of what the Roman Church already substantially possesses. Since she is permanently endowed by Christ (with the substance of unity and catholicity), the Roman Church can receive nothing fundamental from union that she previously lacked; she can be beneficially changed but not fundamentally changed.

To facilitate reunion, the Catholic must learn to respect his separated brothers and to demonstrate by the vitality and richness of the Catholic Church's life that she is the true church intended by Christ for humanity in all its diversity and complexity. Ecumenism requires of Catholics less a program of "interdenominational activity" than a rediscovery of the well-springs of Catholicism and a more authentic living of their faith. It summons them to an intense spiritual and theological renewal through which they will make the Catholic Church "manifested as she really is."[11]

Chrétiens désunis precipitated an immediate and varied reaction among Catholics. Most scholarly responses to the book were laudatory, and many persons subsequently testified to its positive impact upon their understanding both of the church and of ecumenism.[12] An important criticism was made in an otherwise appreciative review by fellow Thomist and ecclesiological specialist Charles Journet. He argued that Luther's teaching on justification was heretical not because a truth he had grasped was subverted, but because Luther never correctly understood the church's teaching. Journet admitted, however, that authentic Christian insights and values exist alongside the fundamental Lutheran error and that reunion will occur when they triumph in the lives of Luther's spiritual descendants. The Swiss theologian claimed that his disagreement with Congar was minimal, but at stake was a critical aspect of the Catholic ecumenical problematic: might the Catholic claim, as Congar did, that Protestantism's reunion with the Roman Church would mean fulfillment of the reformer's central religious perception? Is that reunion essentially continuous with the basic religious claim of the Reformation or essentially discontinuous? Journet's assertion that Luther's perception was erroneous stressed the discontinuity. Appropriately, the key word Journet employed to indicate the process he believed necessary for the Protestant's reconciliation with Rome was "purification," not "fulfillment."[13]

Some of Congar's Catholic critics were considerably more severe. An article appearing in *Osservatore Romano* referred implicitly to *Chrétiens désunis*. Its author, a Vatican official, rejected the assertions of an unidentified Catholic that the Roman Church lacks something she can receive from dissident Christians, that certain of the religious sentiments inspiring the Protestant reformers were commendable, and that the Roman Church needs to return to the sources of her faith.[14]

Dissatisfaction in Rome stopped short of official condemnation of the book or of its removal from circulation. Congar had marshaled numerous approved sources (especially Thomas Aquinas) in support of his positions, and he had maintained a constructive, irenic tone throughout the book. Nevertheless, in the decade following World War II, as Catholics attempting to develop new patterns of theology and action for their church repeatedly met opposition from Rome, Congar was denied permission to publish a new edition of *Chrétiens désunis*, and in 1954, after a series of humiliating rebuffs, he was removed from his teaching position at Le Saulchoir.[15]

Most Protestant commentators welcomed the ecumenical intention of *Chrétiens désunis*, and some acknowledged that its arguments happily were more congruent with Scripture and more sensitive to current ecumenical questions than most Catholic theological writing. Some also observed disappointedly that Congar's "principles of a Catholic ecumenism" maintained the Roman Church's identification of herself as the true church of Christ.[16] Especially pertinent was the observation of Willem A. Visser 't Hooft, the Dutch theologian who later became chief executive officer of the World Council of Churches, that Congar had cut through trivialities and caricatures in attempting to treat the fundamental religious questions at issue between Catholicism and Protestantism. Visser 't Hooft regretted that the Frenchman's portrait of Protestantism, though not a typical misrepresentation, failed to reveal "Protestantism in its plenitude and its truth." Primarily responsible for that failure was Congar's attempt to understand Protestantism from a "psychological and subjective" point of view rather than from a "theological and objective" one. His analyses of the Reformation on the basis of Luther's religious feel-ings and of Protestantism on the basis of its values overlooked the fact that for Protestants, God—not man—is primary in the divine-human relationship. Visser 't Hooft also argued that Congar had been unconvincing in his claim that acceptance of Catholic whole-ness spells Protestantism's fulfillment. For Protestants to embrace Catholicism would in fact entail an "impoverishment and in many ways a denial of the faith that our church has received and does re-ceive in listening to the Bible."[17]

From Congar's epochal work Catholics received a new mea-sure of respect for Protestantism and a durable conceptual frame-work to guide them in their ecumenical task. That task had been shown to spring from the intrinsic nature of the church and, more fundamentally, from God's gracious purpose for his entire cre-ation: the uniting of Christians was a step on the way to the unit-ing of the whole human family. Congar's interpretation of that awesome design exposed the spiritual roots and demands of ecu-menism with a theological force rarely matched. Significantly, too, his ecclesiological and ecumenical statement had been prompted by the desire to come to terms with questions posed by the quest for unity among non-Roman churches. *Chrétiens désunis* was evi-dence that the Roman Church's absence from ecumenical organi-zations and conferences did not bespeak Catholic indifference to the issues they raised.

Congar's Protestant critics made evident a serious and (given the early hour of the ecumenical awakening on both sides) un-avoidable limitation of *Chrétiens désunis:* it did not provide a com-mon theological platform acceptable to Protestants and Catholics engaged in the pursuit of unity. Key features of his position reflect-ed an orientation alien to the theological bases of ecumenism then developing among the non-Roman churches. These truly were principles of *Catholic* (perhaps more accurately, of a particular va-riety of *Thomistic*) ecumenism.

But if *Chrétiens désunis* and its aftermath revealed the dis-tance separating even the ecumenically-oriented Catholic from the consensus arising among ecumenically-oriented Protestants, never-theless one can see retrospectively that similar insights and similar gropings for a wider unity of Christians were arising on both sides. The same year that *Chrétiens désunis* was published, Anglican

Archbishop William Temple told the Edinburgh World Conference on Faith and Order that because the church's unity is grounded in the unity of the triune God, the ecumenical task is not to create unity but gratefully to receive and appropriately to express it. Until a proper expression of unity is found, each of the divided churches is deprived of "spiritual treasure" given by God and preserved by others.[18] Included with those themes in the conference report were others that also unknowingly echoed Congar and his predecessors. The report contended, for example, that the unity sought by most Christians is some form of visible "corporate union" embracing all the diverse spiritual gifts given by God in the past. Movement toward that distant goal is hindered by "barriers of nationality, race, class, general culture, and more particularly by slothful self-content and self-sufficiency." Essential to the overcoming of both doctrinal and non-doctrinal barriers is a greater measure of mutual love, understanding, and respect; without an underlying "spiritual unity" the quest for visible institutional union will be futile.[19]

Contributing decisively to the future convergence of Catholics and Protestants was the linkage made on both sides in the late 1930s between the need for renewal and the quest for unity. In his book Congar had urged that the Catholic Church be so "reformed" that she becomes "manifested as she really is." At the 1937 Oxford Conference on Life and Work a slogan was coined that captured a conviction growing throughout the ecumenical organizations: "Let the church be the church." In spite of the different understandings associated with the two sets of words, here was common recognition that Christians must seek to make the church conform more faithfully to what God intends for her; only so will she effectively serve his reconciling purpose among Christians and among all men. To the degree that Catholic and Protestant perceptions of God's will for the renewal of the church converged, transformation begun on both sides would cause their renewing communities increasingly to resemble one another, and the discovery of kinship increasingly to occur.

Paul Couturier (1881-1953)

At the same time that Congar was constructing a theological

basis for Catholic ecumenism, the Abbé Paul Couturier was developing a pattern of prayer that directly engaged clergy and laity, Catholics and Protestants, in the pursuit of Christian unity.

Couturier lived his entire life in Lyons, France, the city of his birth.[20] Because of interest and training in the physical sciences, his first assignment as a priest was to teach mathematics, physics, and chemistry in a high school. So suited was he to that work that it occupied him for more than forty years.

In 1920 Couturier met two men who influenced him greatly. Victor Carlhian, a wealthy industrialist, helped the conservative priest overcome his suspicion of the liberal political and social movements within French Catholicism. Albert Valensin, a Jesuit professor, invited Couturier to join a group that met regularly for spiritual retreats under his direction. Three years later Valensin introduced Couturier to members of the large Russian émigré community living in the Lyons area. Moved by their poverty and suffering, Couturier sought ways to help the Russians, and soon he had won their friendship and admiration. His ministry of compassion led the Lyons priest to an interest in the relation of the Orthodox churches to his own, and by 1932 that interest had become so intense that he visited the monastery of the Benedictine Monks of Union. During a month-long stay at Amay, Couturier became thoroughly acquainted with the spirit and work of the exiled Beauduin and his disciples. He also met Congar, twenty-three years his junior, who had come to Amay to equip himself for his ecumenical vocation.[21] Couturier was so intrigued by what he learned of the Benedictines that he decided to become an oblate of their order, and he was so inspired by their ecumenical vision that he determined to bring the movement for unity to his diocese.

A deeply reverent man, Couturier made prayer the principal sphere of his labor for Christian unity. Upon returning to Lyons he took steps to introduce the Octave of Prayer for Church Unity, established earlier by Fr. Paul Wattson. Observance of the Octave began modestly among Lyons Catholics in 1933 and was repeated in 1934. The following year Orthodox churchmen also participated. Experience gained in the three successive years convinced Couturier that the Octave must be reconceived, and in articles published in 1935 and 1937, he proposed an alternative Catholic approach to prayer for unity.[22]

Such prayer, Couturier wrote, should arise from contrite acknowledgment that Christian disunity trespasses against the divine will and that every Christian community bears responsibility for it. Contrary to the assumption underlying the Octave, the Catholic Church is implicated in the scandal of disunity. Hence the Catholic too must pray humbly and penitently for forgiveness and for restoration of the visible unity of Christians.

Couturier thought it essential that prayer for unity be offered within all segments of Christendom. Divided Christians need not pray together in the same place, but they should offer the same prayer in their respective places of worship. By their converging prayers they will be lifted into the divine presence and joined together in the "heart of Christ." Even as they pray for unity, bonds of love will begin to be forged among them. As their mutual love receives tangible expression, the divided world will be given an appealing sign of the source of its own eventual peace and unity.

Couturier noted that as currently conceived and formulated the Octave could not serve as an instrument of common prayer, for it would require non-Catholic Christians to pray for their submission to Rome and thus to commit an intolerable act of disloyalty against the churches in which they had come to know and love Christ. Prayer for unity, Couturier insisted, must be offered by divided Christians—Protestants, Orthodox, and Catholics—in complete fidelity to their respective churches. He did not hide the fact that as a loyal Catholic he believed the pope was "the one and only visible center of unity." Other Christians, he knew, did not share that position. With Christians divided in their understanding of unity, how could they possibly pray the same prayer for unity?

Couturier sought to resolve the difficulty by proposing that all Christians pray for the "realization of unity such as it is willed and demanded by our Lord Jesus Christ." Although Christians do not yet agree on the exact form of their eventual unity, all do desire that it conform to Christ's will and that it come whenever he intends. On the basis of that shared conviction they can offer the same prayer. They thereby join their prayer for unity to the prayer uttered by Christ—"that all may be one"—first on the eve of his crucifixion and now eternally.

Christians who pray for unity cannot know when God will grant it; but, Couturier affirmed, they can be confident that it will come. Nor can they know the exact lineaments of the final unity willed by Christ; but, Couturier stated, it will require some change for each ecclesiastical body, it will embrace the spiritual treasures now found in each, and it will result in unmatched splendor for Christ's church.

Here was a call for venturesome innovation of the Wattson-inspired approach to prayer for unity and of the conception upon which it was based. So daring for its time was it that Couturier had had difficulty finding an editor willing to publish the articles. Some Catholics were appalled by what they read. An English Catholic journalist editorialized that among Couturier's misguided notions was a preference for corporate reunion over individual conversion as the way to unity. The writer urged other Catholics to avoid the Frenchman's mistake. Any sincere non-Catholic Christian would welcome their efforts to bring him into the Roman fold: "Why would a traveler, seated in the wrong train, be anything but grateful for being told his mistake?"[23]

Despite criticism from fellow Catholics, in the next several years Couturier incorporated his ideas into an expanding program. With the approbation of Cardinal Archbishop Gerlier of Lyons, he invited outstanding speakers—Catholic, Anglican, Reformed, and Orthodox—to participate in the Lyons observance of an amended Octave. To carry their words to as large an audience as possible, Couturier arranged for radio and newspaper coverage of some of the addresses. He also prepared annual tracts on Christian unity for use during the Octave.

Since 1920 the World Conference on Faith and Order had encouraged a similar pattern of prayer for unity, and some prominent non-Catholics active in ecumenical circles noted approvingly the Lyons development.[24] In the late 1930s Orthodox and Protestant churchmen in several additional French communities participated in the Couturier-sponsored period of ecumenical prayer. By 1939 the older name "Octave" had been replaced by "The Week of Universal Prayer of Christians for Christian Unity" (soon more simply "The Week of Prayer for Christian Unity"), and the older formulations of prayer intentions by new ones that better expressed Couturier's ideas.

In July 1937 Couturier helped initiate another ecumenical

venture. Annual theological discussions were begun among a small group of French Catholic priests and German-Swiss Reformed pastors. After three meetings Couturier realized that although the sessions had been useful, they would be more fruitful among a more homogeneous group. With the aid of a Genevan Reformed pastor, Jean de Saussure, he organized a second "inter-confessional cell," all of whose members were French-speaking and theologically adept. World War II curtailed the group's activities, but following the war they were resumed and intensified.

Like Congar, Couturier both harvested the insight of forerunners and sowed seeds for the future. Other Catholics had seen that unity is a gift from God which must be prayed for by all Christians and which must take hold in every person's soul. But none had given that perception Couturier's effective expression and implementation. A few, too, had realized that full visible unity lies in an indeterminate future and defies precise description by those still far from its realization.[25] But none had given that view Couturier's consistent and eloquent expression.

The Week of Prayer was an extension of Couturier's own ecumenical experience. The French priest had religious (some said "saintly") qualities that enabled non-Catholics to know him to be a profoundly Christian man. His unwavering loyalty to the teaching and authority of his church made equally evident that he was a Roman Catholic Christian.[26] By calling Catholics to seek and accept the will of their Lord for unity, the Week of Prayer involved them in an act that other Christians knew to be genuinely Christian. And yet non-Catholics could recognize, too, that Catholics brought to their prayers for unity a loyalty that they did not share and convictions with which they did not agree.

As Protestants came increasingly to participate in the Lyons pattern of prayer, they not only saw Catholics in a new light but also enabled Catholics to view them in a like manner. The Protestant, too, opened himself to Christ's will, thus attesting the quality of his faith. And he also brought to the prayer beliefs and commitments that the Catholic did not share.

Thus the Week of Prayer for Christian Unity allowed divided Christians to know each other unmistakably as *Christians*, but without denying that they were *Protestant* Christians and *Roman*

Catholic Christians. They thereby met poignantly the ecumenical tension that growing numbers of twentieth-century Christians were to experience—the tension rising from the presence of both newly-discovered agreement and continuing disagreement. Each side, they discovered, was committed to the preservation and celebration of some of the same basic Christian realities. The shared commitment bound them permanently as brothers in Christ. But their fraternity was limited by an equally patent fact: they did not yet share certain other commitments to what each also considered basic Christian realities. The co-existence of the two facts proved vexing but creative. By the one, divided Christians were given an anticipatory taste of their unity in Christ. By the other, they were prompted to submit barriers to full unity to re-examination and dialogue.

Max Josef Metzger (1887-1944)

Germany, the land of Fr. Metzger's birth and death, was convulsed in the first half of the twentieth century by social, political, and military struggles of an intensity rarely experienced by nations. The sensitive priest felt the pain of his people and sought to bring healing throughout the social order. For him the reunion of Christians was an essential ingredient in the wider recuperative process. But his mission of peace clashed with what the Nazi regime believed to be the mission of Germany, and because it did Metzger was martyred.

The pattern of Metzger's response to what a British historian has termed "the era of violence" was evident by 1920.[27] While serving as an army chaplain during World War I, Metzger and two colleagues were so moved by what they saw of human misery that they decided to organize Catholics in an effort to seek and preserve peace, and by 1916 they had founded the World Peace League of the White Cross. Following the war Metzger helped establish and direct the Society of Christ the King, which sought to introduce clergy and laity to the fruit of the nascent Catholic liturgical and biblical movements, and to contribute to the reconstruction of German society by caring for the orphaned, the alcoholic, and the aged.

The lively social consciousness of Metzger was directed principally to the need for international understanding. Frequent trips were undertaken on its behalf, including one that brought him the distinction of being the first German to speak in Paris following the Armistice. In 1919 he helped organize the International Fellowship of Reconciliation; Metzger's activity in that ecumenical body led its official historian later to acclaim him as "perhaps the noblest and holiest leader which the Fellowship has been privileged to enroll."[28] His persistent labors in pursuit of world peace were guided by a conviction voiced in 1928: "We need to organize peace as men have organized war . . . Men of all peoples and nations, unite against this inhuman thing and declare that you will have no part in it."[29]

Metzger's work for peace was linked intimately with his work for Christian unity. In the International Fellowship of Reconciliation he collaborated regularly with non-Catholic Christians. Interest in the ecumenical movement led him to attend the 1927 Faith and Order conference at Lausanne. During the 1930s he was in touch with the increasing numbers of German Christians who crossed confessional boundaries to discuss their common faith and its implications for their struggle against nazism.

In 1938 Metzger began to gather the scattered associations that had arisen between German Catholics and Protestants into a loose federation he called the Una Sancta Brotherhood. Other groups were established by the peripatetic Metzger and brought into the Brotherhood. Persons participating in Una Sancta circles were urged to pray for unity and to seek its realization through every possible means. Metzger encouraged each circle to find the form of meeting best suited to its circumstances. He suggested that sessions be opened and closed with either a prayer said by all or a reading of Scripture. Should the Lord's Prayer be used, Catholics ought not to hesitate saying the ancient ending normally used only by Protestants.

Like ecumenical pioneers before him, Metzger believed that temperate discussion would uncover hidden realms of theological agreement. When one side seeks to present its positions to the other in the latter's idiom, "it often turns out that the one side's thinking on fundamentals is not essentially different from the other side's." Moreover, even positions that appear hopelessly to conflict can be reconciled when partners in dialogue discover that truths contained in both positions have been overstated and can, with proper restatement, be harmonized "in a higher unity."[30]

In 1939 Metzger called a conference of the Una Sancta Brotherhood at Meitingen, Germany. Sixty Catholics and Protestants attended. A second conference was organized by Metzger the following year. Already he had been imprisoned three times by Nazi officials suspicious of his activities, and continued surveillance led to the presence of two Gestapo agents at the 1940 conference (one of them disguised as a priest). In June 1943 Metzger was arrested a final time. He had been betrayed by a woman he had asked to deliver a secret memorandum to the Lutheran Archbishop of Uppsala for transmittal to Allied leaders. In it Metzger had sketched his hope for the moral reconstruction of Germany following Hitler's inevitable defeat. The Allies, he had pled, must impose the moderate peace terms on his country that will facilitate her return to a respected place in the family of nations. For that treasonable act the People's Court of Berlin condemned him to death. A few moments after sentence was pronounced, Father Metzger told three friends, "I have offered my life to God for the peace of the world and the unity of the church."[31] Six months later, on 17 April 1944, he was beheaded.

In letters written from the several prisons in which he was placed by Nazi justice, Metzger's dream of the peace and unity for which he gave his life was eloquently communicated.[32] A letter intended for Pope Pius XII near the end of 1939 (but apparently never delivered) is the most complete statement of Metzger's ecumenical hope. A major reason that the nations seek one another's destruction, he wrote, is that the churches have no role in world affairs. They are without influence because they are divided. The gravity of the historical moment "imperatively demands the utmost effort to heal the dismemberment of the Christian Church, to make Christ's kingdom of peace effectual throughout the world."[33]

Metzger wrote Pius of his conviction that psychological factors weigh more heavily than doctrinal ones in the continuation of Catholic-Protestant division. The Protestant too often finds attitudes of self-righteousness and pride in the Catholic Church that undercut her claim to be the church indwelt by God's Spirit. Catholic leaders must take Protestant criticisms to heart and show the genuineness of their humility and love by a readiness "to listen to the Holy Spirit even when he speaks through a brother in Christ who differs from them in belief."[34]

From his prison cell Metzger encouraged the pope to appoint a commission of twelve respected Catholics to meet with a like group of non-Catholic Christians for confidential discussion of differences and of possibilities for reconciliation. After their work was completed, a pontifical commission should study the findings of the mixed group and take steps to effect reunion. The consummation of this effort should be "the calling of a General Council to give the reunited Church a new vision."[35]

Metzger knew that his proposal was daring, but he was convinced that only bold steps could redirect the foreboding flow of events. Large numbers of people were eager for a "great effort to save the human race."[36] Metzger's reunion proposal was typical of the imagination and determination that marked his career. His death took from the Catholic Church one who following the war doubtless would have become a key ecumenical leader. But his death as a martyr ensured the remembrance of his dream and example.

Josef Lortz (b. 1887)

Pictures of the Reformation that had been drawn by Denifle and his followers (as well as those drawn by their Protestant counterparts) offered no aid to persons seeking Catholic-Protestant rapprochement; there one side's heroes were the other's villains. In the 1920s and '30s revisionist Catholic historians repudiated such polemical historiography and produced alternative, more irenic interpretations of the Reformation. Their work was crowned by the writing of Josef Lortz, who, more than any other person, is responsible for the flowering of a positive Catholic assessment of the Reformation.

Fr. Lortz, born in Grevenmacher, Luxemburg, spent most of his scholarly career in Germany. After earlier academic appointments at Bonn and Braunsberg, in 1935 he became a University Professor in the theological faculty at Münster-in-Westphalia. During the early 1930s Lortz (along with many other German

Catholics) believed that the rise of Hitler's National Socialism was a boon for Germany and for Catholicism. Nazism and Catholicism alike, he wrote, were opposed to the rampant evils of relativism, bolshevism, atheism, and liberalism. Two months before conclusion of the 1933 concordat between Hitler and Pius XI, he joined the National Socialist Party. But by 1936 his enthusiasm for nazism had waned and he withdrew from the Party.[37] In the tumultuous 1930s Lortz also became convinced of the desirability of an alliance between Catholicism and Protestantism, and that theme became a prominent and lasting one in his scholarship.

The novelty of his approach to the Reformation was evident in a single-volume history of Catholicism first published in 1932. Lortz argued that a proper understanding of divine providence will lead the Catholic to expect God to make every major historical occurrence serve the divine purpose. Not even the "fatal act of the reformers" is without positive significance. Invoking Newman's teaching, he urged his readers to acknowledge ungrudgingly that enduring non-Catholic religious movements possess genuine Christian values. In Protestantism the Catholic will find "a central point of Christianity, the trustful placing oneself in the hands of the Father in heaven."[38]

These motifs were developed in great detail in Lortz's epochal *Die Reformation in Deutschland*, a two-volume work published in 1939 and 1940.[39] Here Luther was the central figure, and the German reformer's personality and ideas received close, sympathetic scrutiny. Since for Lortz the German Reformation was a vaster phenomenon than the reformer, considerable attention also was given the web of religio-social developments preceding and following Luther. Properly to understand sixteenth-century Catholicism, Lortz argued, is to recognize that reform was long overdue and urgently needed. Medieval Christian civilization was shattered, and disintegration reached into every sphere of life. The late Middle Ages were not completely devoid of religious vitality or reforming efforts, but never were the reforms sufficiently potent to rid the church of her blemishes. Rome's spiritual authority was severely undermined by the Avignon papacy, by the western schism, by the conciliar movement, and by the blatant worldliness of the Renaissance papacy. Corruption in Rome (especially greed for political power and material comfort) bred corruption in monasteries and among the clergy. A coarse, individualistic, and moralistic piety became widespread. More disastrously the teachings of Occam the nominalist and Erasmus the humanist created theological confusion in the church. Especially because of the erosive influence of relativistic humanism, the church's dogmatic tradition was rarely understood. With the church's health severely impaired, her critics grew in number and in the radicalness of their demands for change.

Religious dissolution was accompanied by political and social instability. Individual rulers egotistically guarded their political authority, thus abetting the sway of centrifugal forces over German society. The shift from a rural economy to an urban one improved the lot of some (merchants and artists) but worsened the lot of others (knights and peasants). The latter were ready to give themselves to any cause that might overthrow the order they found oppressive. In church and society the stage was set for Luther.

Lortz's Catholic Luther was a man of keen religious sensitivity and insight. As a young friar, intense religious struggles led him to an authentically Christian understanding of God being incarnate and crucified for man's salvation. Armed with that conviction, with unfailing courage, and with extraordinary creative powers he fought to end corruption in the church. His battle was launched, Lortz insisted, to recapture what Luther believed to be "the authentic form of Christianity."[40]

Luther and his followers received the evangelical elements of Reformation religion from a church that, however imperfectly, had continued to transmit the gospel. But as children of a disintegrating Christendom, they unfortunately also received attitudes and understandings that were antithetical to the gospel. Occam's teaching had implanted in young Luther the erroneous beliefs that a virtuous man might win God's favor and that the capricious God could arbitrarily predestine even a good man to hell. Luther's study of the Bible fortunately led him to reject those unorthodox notions in favor of a newfound conviction of justification through faith in the unfailing mercy of God. But he mistakenly believed that the theory and practice of "works righteousness" he rejected was the authentic teaching of the Roman Church, and he failed to realize that the gospel treasure he "discovered" actually was her traditional (albeit obscured) teaching. Tragically that treasure was soon compromised by Luther, for he had been stamped by the age's encouragement of the individual to think and act independently of the objective realities given by God. That subjectivism, accentuated in Luther by unusual creativity, led him to heed only the passages of Scripture that conformed to his own experience of God's redeeming grace and man's utter sinfulness; to reject the papal church that attempted to bring him to a more balanced, Scriptural affirmation of divine-human cooperation in the achievement of salvation; and to construct a new church on the basis of his own, onesided view of the gospel.

Luther had been led to heresy by attempting to recover the gospel, he had strayed outside the church by attempting to reform her. If a tragic nobility characterized Lortz's portrait of the young Luther, the older Luther was presented as a man driven by pride, hatred, and destructiveness. The churches that issued from Luther's revolution were built upon the same subjectivistic impulses that led him deeper into heresy. Soon the immorality that had flawed pre-Reformation Catholicism was rampant in Lutheranism. With each group following its own lights, Protestant churches were inevitably divided. Forsaking the revelation that Luther had wished to serve, they fell prey to the rationalistic currents of the time. By the twentieth century little remained in them of the gospel Luther had fought to preserve and of the Catholic heritage he had retained in the early Lutheran communities.

Lortz acknowledged that initially the Catholic Church's response to Luther had been lamentably weak. Political preoccupations and theological confusion prevented swift, decisive facing of the serious issues raised by the Wittenberg reformer. Finally, however, a reform movement within the Roman Church found able champions, and fresh spiritual life spread throughout Catholicism.

The post-Reformation record of Protestant decline and Catholic rebirth, Lortz contended, gave added justification to the Roman Church's rejection of the Lutheran movement. So far has that double development proceeded, he concluded, that the real heir of Luther's valid evangelical perception is not Wittenberg but Rome: "Today the Catholic Church may justly claim to have taken care of important concerns of the reformers better than they have done themselves."[41] On the basis of that judgment Lortz seconded the claim made by Congar three years earlier in *Chrétiens désunis* that Protestants would find in the Roman Church the fulfillment of their authentic religious values inherited from the Reformation.

During the dark years of World War II the relatively few German Catholics and Protestants who read Lortz's study welcomed its construction of what they considered a promising bridge between the confessions.[42] It had confounded the simplistic and absolutist evaluations that each side customarily made of the Reformation. Especially were Catholics pressed to acknowledge that their forebears shared responsibility for the eruption of the Reformation and that however serious Luther's faults, he was a brilliant, well-intentioned son of the Roman Church. If he must not be too uncritically venerated by Protestants, neither must he be too hastily chastized by Catholics. Following the war Catholic and Protestant critics of Lortz's study became more vocal. A German Catholic scholar, Johannes Hessen, rejected Lortz's contention that Luther's error resulted chiefly from subjectivism.[43] A German Lutheran theologian, Walther von Loewenich, charged that Lortz's commitment to the Roman Church had precluded both real understanding of Luther's refusal to submit to Rome and genuine admission of Catholic guilt for the Reformation.[44] He and most other critics agreed, however, that Lortz's study had helped Protestants and Catholics move beyond the making and breaking of emotion-laden caricatures and nearer the central theological questions at issue between them. The possibility of substantive dialogue had been greatly enhanced.

*   *   *

Twentieth-century Catholic pioneers of ecumenism found it extraordinarily difficult to win acceptance for a new stance toward Protestantism. Many in authority sought to pressure the pioneers into conformity with the past. Vatican harassment of Congar led him later to state candidly that "from the beginning of 1947 to the end of 1956 I knew nothing from that quarter but an uninterrupted series of denunciations, warnings, restrictive or discriminatory measures and mistrustful interventions."[45] Rome's reluctance to depart from her habitual method of seeking unity gave a distinct cast to the work of the pioneers. In the late 1930s and throughout the middle decades of the twentieth century —they were forced to penetrate to the Roman Church's foundational convictions and to formulate their ecumenical vision at that level of religious depth. In no other way could they demonstrate that the ecumenical course they advocated was (as Congar later wrote) "profoundly serious and based on tradition."[46] Only then could they begin to persuade other Catholics to re-examine and re-shape firmly entrenched ideas, attitudes, and behavior. Nothing less than an *ecumenism-in-depth* could win the Roman Church to a fresh conception of her unitive responsibility.

The careers of Congar, Couturier, Metzger, and Lortz also demonstrated the breadth of the frontier on which ecumenism was pioneered. The four priests brought different talents and temperaments to key problems in distinct realms—theological, spiritual, social, and historical—where patterns of disunity had been securely lodged. Because the chief thrusts of their respective labors were distinct, they tended to reach different audiences on behalf of the ecumenical cause. And because their contributions were also complementary, they helped to ensure that should this cause be accepted within the Roman Church, its impact would be comprehensive and far-reaching.

The pioneers performed their task well, for the ecumenical outlook that eventually emerged from their labors possessed a profundity and breadth that gained it the Roman Church's official endorsement at the Second Vatican Council. And because its roots went deeply into both the common Christian tradition and the Roman tradition, it became a potential rich resource for the entire ecumenical movement.

The pioneers' victory, however, was won at a high price. Hans Küng's account of the suffering inflicted upon pre-Vatican II advocates of Catholic renewal applies to the early ecumenists: "They were often suspected by fellow Christians and by some church leaders, hindered in their work, disavowed, accused of heresy, persecuted. They were considered dangerous, extremist, radical, even revolutionary . . . Often they stood in the foremost line of fire without any human protection, with only the gospel of Jesus behind them."[47] Remarkably such opposition neither deterred the ecumenical pioneers from their labors nor filled them with enervating bitterness. Congar's retrospective reflection upon the meaning of his own suffering points to a strength that emerged from adversity: "The cross is a condition of every holy work. God himself is at work in what is a cross for us. Only through it do we reach a certain authenticity and profundity of existence . . . Only he who has suffered for his convictions attains in them a certain force, a certain quality of the irrevocable, and also the right to be heard and respected."[48]

The opponents of the ecumenical innovators should not be faulted too hastily. They believed themselves to be preserving the "gospel of Jesus" and especially the unity that he had given his church. Forebears had taught them to understand this unity principally as hierarchically enjoined unanimity and uniformity. They consequently were ill prepared to grasp the view of unity then developing in the ecumenical movement that stressed the *agapeic*, pluralistic quality of Christians' life in community. The Catholic ecumenists had deep sympathy for the newer view and could argue its compatibility with earlier ranges of Catholic tradition (as well as with selected teachings of recent popes). But until it received more widespread acceptance and became operative in their church, they would endure the fate of unwelcome innovators and the Roman Catholic Church would bear the burden of championing an archaic form of unity in an age eager for a fresh vision of unity.

NOTES

1. The title was bestowed in an unsigned editorial comment prefacing an article by Congar in *The Ecumenist* 4 (1966): 57. More recently, W. A. Visser 't Hooft has called Congar "the father of Roman Catholic ecumenism" (*Memoirs*, p. 319).

2. Congar, *Dialogue Between Christians*, p. 4. This volume contains a highly informative autobiographical essay. Useful information about Congar and his work also is contained in Jean-Pierre Jossua, *Yves Congar: Theology in the Service of God's People* (Chicago: Priory Press, 1968). The variety of first names used by Fr. Congar has caused some

confusion. It may be helpful to explain that the name given him at birth was Yves; when received into the Dominican order he took the religious name Marie-Joseph. In recent years he has resumed use of his original first name, and at times has used them both.

3. *Chrétiens désunis*, p. 72.

4. Stanislas Jaki, *Les tendances nouvelles de l'ecclésiologie*, p. 221.

5. *Chrétiens désunis*, pp. 78, 98, 108.

6. Ibid., p. 117. Congar's discussion of catholicity reflected views developed in the first two decades of the twentieth century by another French Dominican, Ambroise de Poulpiquet; see Gustave Thils, *Les notes de l'église dans l'apologétique catholique depuis la Réforme* (Paris: Desclée, de Brouwer, 1937), pp. 250-53. Congar's position also resembled what we have seen in the writing of Karl Adam and Emile Mersch; that he had been influenced by the former was indicated by his appreciative remarks concerning the French translation of *Das Wesen das Katholizismus* in 1932; see *La vie intellectuelle* 15: 25.

7. *Chrétiens désunis*, p. 23.

8. Ibid., p. 302. Earlier stages of Christian thought on this issue are discussed in S. L. Greenslade, *Schism in the Early Church* 2nd ed., (London: SCM Press, 1964); for a suggestion of Congar's indebtedness to St. Thomas see p. 182.

9. *Chrétiens désunis*, p. 56.

10. Ibid., p. 321.

11. Ibid., p. 341. Congar's dedication to the theological aspects of renewal was evidenced by the fact that *Chrétiens désunis* was the first volume in a significant series of ecclesiological studies (bearing the title "Unam Sanctam") that he founded, directed, and to which he made substantial contributions as an author. Of the ecumenical significance of such theological labor Congar has said: "It seemed to me . . . that each individual's ecumenical task lay in the first place at home among his own people. Our business was to rotate the Catholic Church through a few degrees on its own axis in the direction of convergence towards others and a possible unanimity with them, in accordance with a deeper and closer fidelity to our unique source or our common sources." *Dialogue*, p. 21.

12. Henri de Lubac, *Etudes* 233 (1937): 507-11; Claeys Bouaert, *Nouvelle revue théologique* 65 (1938): 347-51; C. Lialine, *Irénikon* 15 (1938): 279-81; Ludwig Lambinet, *Catholica* 8 (1939): 150-64. Evidence of its further impact is found in Congar, *Dialogue*, p. 25; *La vie intellectuelle* 61: 16, 33-4; Luis V. Romeu, ed., *Ecumenical Experiences*, trans. and ed. Lancelot C. Sheppard (London: Burns and Oates, 1965), p. 7; A. M. Allchin et al., *Semences d'unité* (Casterman, 1965), p. 157.

13. *Nova et vetera* 13 (1938): 346-7. *Chrétiens désunis* also received a mixture of praise and criticism from the more conservative Thomistic perspective of M. J. Nicholas in *Revue thomiste* 44 (1938): 381-90.

14. 22 March 1940. See also Congar, *Dialogue*, p. 29.

15. Ibid., pp. 29-43.

16. A. Jundt, *Revue d' histoire et de philosophie religieuse* 18 (1938):

274; F. Leenhardt, *L'église et le royaume de Dieu* (Geneva: Editions Labor, 1942), pp. 39-43.

17. *Foi et vie* (1938), p. 307.

18. Skoglund and Nelson, eds., *Faith and Order*, pp. 18, 73.

19. Lukas Vischer, ed., *A Documentary History of the Faith and Order Movement: 1927-1963* (St. Louis: Bethany Press, 1953), pp. 61, 63, 69.

20. The principal Couturier biographies written thus far are Maurice Villain, *L'Abbé Paul Couturier* (Casterman: Tournai, 1957) and Geoffrey Curtis, *Paul Couturier and Unity in Christ* (London: SCM Press, 1964).

21. In 1964 Congar wrote of his esteem for Couturier (*Dialogue*, pp. 17-22), and indicated that his deep appreciation of the Lyons priest's ecumenical contribution had not been reciprocated. According to a friend of both men, that statement probably reflects the fact that earlier Congar and like-minded Catholics in the Paris area had tended to view Couturier and his disciples as too sentimental in their approach to ecumenism, whereas the latter group had tended to view the former as too intellectualist. This difference was one more of personality and method than of fundamental outlook. It lessened with time (though apparently had not been overcome by 1953 when Couturier died) and never assumed sufficiently large proportions to skew the essential complementarity of the Congar and Couturier approaches. Interview with Fr. René Beaupère, May 1969.

22. "Pour l'unité des chrétiens: psychologie de l'Octave de prières du 18 au 25 janvier," *Revue apologétique* 61 (1935): 684-703; "L'Universelle prière des chrétiens pour l'unité chrétienne," 65 (1937): 411-27, 562-78. Both articles (the second one published in two installments) have been reproduced in M. Villain, ed., *Oecuménisme spirituel* (Casterman: Tournai, 1963), pp. 46-89.

23. Reprinted from *Month* in *Catholic Mind* 34 (1936): 124.

24. Especially significant was a 1936 resolution of support by the National Synod of the French Reformed Church. Curtis, *Couturier*, p. 123.

25. Couturier's assertions of this point are reminiscent of Portal's words to Anglican friends in 1896; see p. 38 above. It is likely that Couturier had read Portal's statement in the library of the Monks of Union during his visit to Amay in 1932.

26. Both points recur in a collection of tributes to Couturier: Villain et al., *Paul Couturier: apôtre de l'unité chrétienne, Témoignages*, Ronds points, 6 (Lyons: E. Vitte, 1954).

27. David Thomson, ed., *The Era of Violence*, The New Cambridge Modern History, Vol. 12 (Cambridge: The University Press, 1960). The most complete studies of Metzger's life and work are Lillian Stevenson, *Max Josef Metzger, Priest and Martyr, 1887-1944* (London: SPCK, 1952); Leonard J. Swidler, *Ecumenical Vanguard;* and Marianne Mohring, *Täter des Wortes, Max Josef Metzger, Leben und Wirken* (Freising, 1966).

28. Vera Brittain, *The Rebel Passion*, p. 130.

29. Stevenson, *Metzger*, p. 11.

30. Swidler, *Ecumenical Vanguard*, p. 152.

31. Ibid., p. 164.

32. Metzger's gifts of expression also led to the composition of poetry, some of which he set to music. Many of his writings have been collected in Matthias Laros, ed., *Gefangenschaftsbriefe*, (Meitingen, 1948). A small portion of Metzger's letters and poetry has been translated and published in Stevenson, *Metzger*.

33. Stevenson, *Metzger*. p. 47.

34. Ibid., p. 52.

35. Ibid., p. 54.

36. Ibid., p. 52.

37. Lewy, *Catholic Church*, pp. 107-8. Lewy reports (p. 365) that he has not found a record at the Berlin Document Center confirming Lortz's claim that he withdrew in 1936. But it would seem that absence of such a record (lost, destroyed, never entered?) weighs less heavily than Lortz's own testimony. Unfortunately we do not yet have biographical or autobiographical studies of Lortz.

38. *History of the Church*, adapted from the 5th and 6th German eds. by Edward G. Kaiser, 2nd Engl. ed. (Milwaukee: Bruce Publishing Co., 1939), pp. 348, 349.

39. Vol. 1: *Voraussetzungen: Aufbruch; Erste Entscheidung*, 1939. Vol. 2: *Aus bau der Fronten: Unionsversuche; Ergebnis*, 1940. From the third edition (1949) an English translation has been made: *The Reformation in Germany*, trans. Ronald Wells (London: Darton, Longman and Todd; New York: Herder and Herder, 1968). A fourth German edition was published in 1962.

40. *The Reformation in Germany* 1:14.

41. Ibid., 2: 342.

42. The critical response is discussed in Swidler, *Ecumenical Vanguard*, pp. 25-32; Stauffer, *Luther*, pp. 42, 55-8; and von Loewenich, *Modern Catholicism*, pp. 282, 288-9. See also Rudolf Goethe, "The Open Door," in Karl Hardt, ed., *We Are Now Catholics* (Westminster, Maryland: Newman Press, 1959), p. 37.

43. Stauffer, *Luther*, p. 44. In a later chapter we shall return to the postwar Catholic assessment of Luther.

44. Von Loewenich, *Modern Catholicism*, pp. 288-9.

45. *Dialogue*, p. 34.

46. Ibid., p. 10.

47. Swidler, *Ecumenical Vanguard*, p. ix.

48. Cited in Jossua, *Congar*, p. 56.

VI
A Time for Sowing

During the late 1930s emergent Catholic ecumenism was confined to a small circle of European priests. Despite the profundity of the pioneers' intellectual and spiritual travail, there was no assurance that a harvest would issue from the seeds they had planted. But, fatefully, conditions within the world and among the churches during the next two decades became extraordinarily congenial to the dissemination and germination of those seeds.

The soil of Europe was especially well prepared for sowers of an ecumenical vision. Generations of prior growth were felled by powerful storms: "Not since the downfall of the Roman Empire and the centuries of the barbarian invasions," wrote American historian Kenneth Scott Latourette, "had so much of Europe been so profoundly disrupted."[1] As old institutional and intellectual patterns tottered or collapsed, new ones rushed to take their places. The churches did not escape the turbulence. Strong winds of change blew among Catholics, undermining old ways and bringing fresh patterns of thought and action that frequently abetted the movement already underway toward rapprochement with Protestants. As before, the centripetal pressures were exerted most forcibly in several western European lands. But increasingly the same winds of change spread globally, and wherever they reached, they augured advances toward Catholic-Protestant solidarity.

The next three chapters will examine the progressive maturation of the irenic Catholic stance toward Protestantism in the years between World War II and Vatican II. The present chapter will focus upon factors in the secular and religious environment which favored that maturation; Chapter VII the major instances of Catholic-Protestant rapprochement; and Chapter VIII the chief developments in Catholic ecumenical thought.

World War II

Only two decades after the end of World War I, mankind plunged into an even more devastating conflict. Before the war's termination in 1945, fifty-six nations had become belligerents. Massive technological and psychological support was harnessed for military objectives, and enormous destructive power was unleashed. Over fifteen million military personnel were killed. Untold numbers of civilians perished, including the six million Jewish victims of Nazi barbarism. Incalculable suffering was endured around the world.

Pope Pius XII (1876-1958) began his pontificate on the eve of war. As Vatican Secretary of State he had worked with Pius XI in a futile effort to avert the looming conflict. Repeatedly during the early 1940s Pius XII pled for men to acknowledge the God-given unity of the human family so disastrously denied by global warfare. He urged Catholics to labor with other Christians and men of good will for a world order built upon the proven wisdom of the ages.[2] During the dark years of war collaboration between Catholics and Protestants ensued widely, producing ties that persisted in several lands after 1945.

Especially in Germany the war occasioned new solidarity. Christians there took contrasting positions toward Hitler's policies. Some welcomed them. Most acquiesced in them, though some of that number regretted and occasionally even protested flagrant Nazi excesses. In totalitarian Germany no opposition to Nazi policy was brooked; hence active protest normally brought imprisonment, and it could mean death. Knowing that, a third group, a small minority among Protestants and Catholics, nevertheless deliberately sought Hitler's downfall.

It was among German Christians who became suffering victims of Nazi terror that the deepest bonds were forged. In 1942 a small anti-Nazi band, the "Kreisau Circle," was formed to plan a Christian social order for the Germany they hoped would emerge after Hitler's defeat. Two years later, most of the group, including Count Helmuth von Moltke, a prominent Protestant layman, and Fr. Alfred Delp, a prominent Jesuit priest, were arrested and executed. Other German Christian leaders, notably Fr. Metzger and Dietrich Bonhoeffer, a Protestant theologian, actively opposed the

Hitler regime and were executed.[3] But Nazi persecution of Christians extended beyond those active in the German opposition to Hitler. "We shall not rest," said the Führer, "until we have rooted out Christianity."[4] Thousands of church leaders from Germany and lands conquered by German armies were arrested for fear that they would make the churches a bastion of resistance against complete Nazi domination of life. Many Protestant pastors and Catholic priests were incarcerated at Dachau, where normally they were quartered in the same barrack.[5] For most this was the first opportunity for direct and sustained contact with "separated brothers." Long-held caricatures were broken, as when a German Lutheran pastor's conversation with a priest was punctuated by the latter's surprised and relieved comment, "So you do believe in Jesus as the Son of God!" Protestant and Catholic clergy viewed one another's separate Sunday services and discovered the similarity of their liturgies and beliefs. Near the end of the war patterns of common worship were developed. A passage of Scripture, chosen in advance by a representative committee, was read; the men meditated silently upon it; then together they recited the Lord's Prayer. Worship was shared on Thursdays, the day Christians have traditionally associated with Jesus' prayer for the unity of his followers.[6]

In some German concentration camps Couturier's Week of Prayer for Christian Unity was observed. Occasionally Catholic and Protestant prisoners met under the joint direction of a priest and a pastor to discuss their common faith and to pray together. Fr. Congar, imprisoned for five years in four different camps, became a roving ambassador for Christian unity among fellow prisoners.[7]

New ties also were established within Hitler's armies, especially among German pastors, priests, and seminarians who had been drafted into military service.[8]

Christians in several European lands occupied by German armies made comparable discoveries of their solidarity. Clergy and laity from both groups occasionally collaborated to aid Jews attempting to escape their Nazi tormentors. In Holland joint protests against Nazi persecution of Jews were made by Protestant and Catholic leaders, and the Interchurch Council was established as an instrument of Protestant-Catholic wartime cooperation.[9]

Protestants and Catholics active in the resistance against Nazi occupation forces, especially in France and Holland, entered into unaccustomedly close contact. In France a team of Catholic priests published an underground paper, *Cahiers du témoignage chrétien*, which reported Protestant and Catholic opposition to nazism and articulated a religious foundation for it. Approximately 44,000 copies of each issue were secretly written, printed, and distributed with Protestant assistance. Religiously-oriented papers clandestinely published in Holland and Denmark similarly contributed to the shaping of a common Christian front against the Third Reich.[10]

In Allied lands not overrun by German armies the enemy's threat provoked unprecedented acts of rapprochement among Christians. Early in the war many Catholics in England rallied to a new organization, The Sword of the Spirit, which was headed by Catholic Archbishop Arthur Hinsley and dedicated to "the restoration in Europe of a Christian basis for both public and private life, by a return to the principles of international order and Christian freedom."[11] A like interest emerged among Anglicans and Free Churchmen, and the three groups of English Christians soon explored possibilities of ideological agreement and cooperative action.

The first public expression of their common cause was a letter published in the 21 December 1940 edition of the London *Times*. Signed by the two Anglican archbishops, by Cardinal Hinsley, and by the moderator of the Free Church Federal Council, the letter affirmed ten principles necessary for permanent peace in Europe. Five of them had been enunciated by Pius XII and the other five had emanated from the 1937 Oxford conference of the Universal Christian Council for Life and Work.[12] The *Times* letter stimulated wide discussion across traditional ecclesiastical barriers. On 10 and 11 May 1941, during a period of heavy German bombardment, Catholics, Anglicans, and Free Churchmen filled London's spacious Stoll Theater. They were addressed by the ranking ecclesiastical leaders of the land. Cardinal Hinsley's words voiced the hope of many: "Our unity must not be in sentiment and in word only, it must be carried into practical measures. Let us have a regular system of consultation and collaboration from now onwards

. . . to agree on a plan of action which shall win the peace when the din of battle is ended." At the close of the meeting the cardinal departed from an established English Catholic tradition by publicly praying the Lord's Prayer with non-Catholic Christians.[13]

Many thought that the rising commitment to a common Christian mission would be best served by including all interested persons within The Sword of the Spirit. However, on 9 August 1941 Cardinal Hinsley explained that that organization was under the Catholic hierarchy's control and could accept only Catholics into voting membership. Steps then were initiated by Roman and non-Roman leaders to develop an acceptable pattern of collaboration. On 20 May 1942 they announced that a Joint Committee would be formed to guide and extend cooperation among English Christians. The Sword of the Spirit would continue to group concerned Catholics, and a comparable organization, Religion and Life, would link similarly-minded Christians of other churches. On religious matters the two organizations would go separate but parallel ways; "in the social and international field" they would work jointly. For the next two years cooperative efforts spread across England. "Joint Weeks" were held in nearly thirty localities in 1943; Roman Catholics joined Anglicans and Free Churchmen in the "local Christian council" organized in many communities; and several common pronouncements were made by Roman Catholic and non-Roman national leaders.

But the attempt to avoid long-controverted religious questions only partially succeeded, and polite disputes over them recurred. Catholics could not accede to the wish of their non-Catholic partners to include the word "churches" in the title of the councils that had been created. Nor could many of them conscientiously follow Cardinal Hinsley's example of praying with Anglicans and Free Churchmen. Some English Catholic bishops did not share Hinsley's commitment to Christian cooperation, and following his death, as the tide of battle turned in the Allies' favor, Catholic involvement in cooperative projects waned.[14]

The need for Protestant-Catholic collaboration was recognized elsewhere in the world, though not as intensely as in the European lands hardest hit by the war. Joint wartime statements were issued by Protestant and Catholic leaders in Canada, Australia, and (with Jewish co-signers) in South Africa. A discussion and public lecture program on "Christianity and World Order" was developed in Cairo in 1941 by Roman Catholic, Orthodox, and Protestant leaders; in 1944 they formed the Committee of Liaison Between the Communities to defend the religious liberty of non-Muslim groups in Egypt. In areas of China invaded by Japanese armies, Protestant and Catholic missionaries helped care for one another's personnel and property. In Japan, the Roman Catholic Church joined the Christian Commission on Cooperation, which was established under government pressure as a liaison body between the churches and the state. Catholic Archbishop Doi of Tokyo became its first chairman.[15]

The United States' entry into the war in late 1941 brought large numbers of American Protestant and Catholic clergymen into the military chaplaincy. In bases and in battle the chaplains frequently came to know one another well and to recognize the professional and religious bonds existing between them. Jewish rabbis often shared that fellowship. One tangible fruit was the *Soldiers and Sailors Prayer Book*, prepared for servicemen of the three religious groups. More poignant expression of the bonds linking Protestants, Catholics, and Jews was provided by a widely-publicized event that occurred in February 1943. An American troopship was torpedoed on the frigid North Atlantic, and as she sank, it became evident that some men waiting to abandon ship did not have life preservers. Four military chaplains—two Protestants, one Jew and one Catholic—quickly gave their own to four persons without them. Then, praying, they locked arms as the sinking vessel carried them to their deaths.[16]

Instances of Protestant-Catholic collaboration among the American civilian population were rare, but Catholic theologians were prompted to consider its feasibility. Some feared that contact with Protestants established because of a supposed commonality of religion would menace Catholics' faith. Several Jesuit scholars, however, argued in the pages of their new journal *Theological Studies* for common labor with other Christians. John Courtney Murray (1904-1967), editor of the publication and theology professor at Woodstock College in Maryland, contended that a firm basis for cooperation had been developed in recent papal teaching.

He applauded the cooperative action taken by English Catholics and regretted that in the United States there was not yet sufficient awareness of the spiritual crisis of the time to push American Catholics and Protestants to comparable steps.[17]

Among some Protestants and Catholics the friendship and respect developed during the harrowing war years would prove fleeting; with the return of more normal circumstances the grip of well-known patterns of isolation and estrangement would again tighten.[18] But for others, the knowledge gained of brother Christians' faith and courage would not be forgotten. Early in the war Emile Mersch (who was killed in a strafing attack while helping refugees near a Belgian village) expressed a conviction that spread among Catholics and lingered beyond the war's end:

> More deeply than human lack of understanding, Christ with his unity lives in all His followers who have not sinned against the light and against charity; and such followers are numerous, and Christ's life is in them. As we write this we are thinking respectfully of the Christians of the Russian Church and of the Protestants of the German confessions who . . . remained faithful to Christ even at the cost of life.[19]

The war years, though enormously destructive, were also a time of creative dreams. Sensitive men and women looked beyond the pain and hatred of the moment to what might yet be. To some came the vision of a new Europe in which religious, political, and ideological divisions were overcome and a lasting fraternity achieved. "European unity," wrote one man at the height of the storm, "is being made by an equal distribution of suffering."[20] And to some came the audacious dream of a global commonwealth embracing even the most diverse peoples. Such hope sustained men and women in their darkest hours and proved fertile ground for apostles of Christian unity.

Return to the Sources

While war still raged across Europe, Christians there were stirred to intensify the search begun earlier for the wellsprings of their faith. A person in occupied Europe explained that "our hearts

and minds are under pressure, and we do not wish to live on anything except that which is eternal."[21] The desire to recover spiritual
fundamentals spread among Protestants and Catholics alike and
persisted into the postwar period. It both fed and was stimulated
by an expanding body of theological scholarship. Among Catholic
scholars three central sources for the nourishment of Christian life
and thought were re-examined: the Scriptures, the liturgy, and the
early Fathers of the church. Until the Second Vatican Council this
burst of theological activity centered in Germany, France, and Belgium, although by then Catholic scholars in other lands were
making notable contributions.

Each of the three intellectual currents bore important ecumenical consequences, with the most substantial ones issuing from the
biblical renewal.[22] Despite the crippling of Catholic biblical scholarship by the Modernist controversy, some daring academicians,
especially the French Dominican M. J. Lagrange and his Biblical
School at Jerusalem, had persisted in the search for patterns of interpretation cognizant both of traditional Catholic teaching and of
modern biblical criticism. Much of their achievement was endorsed
and the importance of the Bible stressed by a 1943 encyclical of
Pius XII, *Divino afflante Spiritu.* Thereafter Catholic biblical specialists produced a growing literature in which they employed previously suspect methods of historical-critical analysis and in which
they addressed the religious and theological themes of the Old and
New Testaments more than the historical and philological questions that had dominated earlier Catholic biblical scholarship. Numerous fresh translations from the original languages were a
major visible fruit of their labors.

The work of Old and New Testament specialists influenced
scholars working in related fields. Significantly, some Catholic
dogmatic theologians came to view the Scriptures as the primary
locus for the church's understanding of divine revelation. In the
writings of a growing number, central doctrines—God, man,
grace, Mary, the sacraments, the church—more directly reflected
biblical accents. Typically, the church began to be viewed in the
light of such Scriptural categories as "People of God" and "Royal
Priesthood."[23]

The prodigious wave of biblical scholarship quickly reached

Catholic parishes. Numerous Bibles were bought and read, often in conjunction with new commentaries. Groups were established for Bible study. A measure of the biblical renewal's penetration of French Catholicism was the remark of Marc Boegner, long-time head of the Protestant Federation of France: "As a pastor I am made jealous by watching the development of Bible groups in the Catholic parishes of my country!"[24]

Closely related to revived Catholic interest in the Bible was a greatly increased appreciation of the centrality of the liturgy for the church's life.[25] Building upon earlier achievements and encouraged by Pius XII's 1947 encyclical *Mediator Dei*, leaders of the postwar liturgical renewal sought to focus Catholic worship more directly on the foundational events of Christianity—especially the death and resurrection of Jesus Christ—and to facilitate active, informed participation by Catholic lay people in corporate worship. As in the biblical renewal, theological scholarship provided a substantial intellectual base for popular interest. Among the fruits of the liturgical renewal were expanded use of vernacular languages in worship, fuller incorporation of the Scriptures into the liturgy, and heightened awareness of the communal character of the Christian life.

The third "source" receiving fresh scholarly and popular attention was the patterns of Christian thought dominant in the first six centuries of the Christian era.[26] Employing historiographic tools developed in preceding decades, Catholic scholars analyzed the Greek and Latin works of the Fathers and translated many of them into modern languages. Patristic authors won popularity because Catholics found in their writings a richer harmonization of theology, liturgy, and piety as well as a more direct affirmation of the biblical message than they usually found in the writings of authors who lived in later, more analytical periods. Moreover, prescholastic theologians often attempted to understand Christianity in relation to categories of thought also important for the modern age, especially its interests in history, in earthly realities, and in the corporate dimension of human life.

The work of Catholic biblical, liturgical, and patristic specialists closely paralleled that of Protestant scholars, and soon their labors converged productively. Protestant and Catholic liturgical specialists—like their counterparts engaged in patristics research—consulted one another (and at times Eastern Orthodox colleagues) about issues of common concern, regularly kept abreast of liturgical developments in each other's churches, and manifested increasingly a single mind regarding liturgical principle and practice.[27] The emergence of a community of scholarship was even more pronounced among biblical specialists. Catholic scholars appropriated—though not uncritically—the methodology and conclusions of Protestant biblical scholars such as C. H. Dodd, Oscar Cullmann, and William J. Albright.[28] The writings of some Protestant students of the Bible (such as Suzanne de Dietrich's *Le Dessein de Dieu*) were read avidly by Catholic laymen. As the younger Catholic biblical movement matured, Protestant scholars reciprocated the appreciative interest of Catholic colleagues. Increasingly Catholic and Protestant biblical scholars considered the same issues, were helped by each other's research, agreed and disagreed without regard for ecclesiastical boundaries, and alike sought to bring the biblical message into a more prominent position in their churches.[29]

A dramatic symbol of the convergence that occurred among biblical scholars and of the enduring common ground occupied by Catholics and Protestants was the decision to collaborate in translating, publishing, and interpreting the Bible. In 1953, with the support of Bernard W. Griffin, Cardinal Archbishop of Westminster, English Catholic scholars began the task of editing and adapting the Revised Standard Version of the Bible (translated and published the previous year under American Protestant auspices); however, the death of Cardinal Griffin in 1956 delayed publication of the RSV Catholic edition until 1966.[30] On 24 October 1956 the crucial first public sign of the Bible's ecumenical role was provided by Archbishop Bernhard Alfrink of Utrecht, who granted permission for publication of a Catholic Bible translated into Frisian by Protestant scholar Ulbe van Houtan.[31] In 1959 an American Jesuit, Walter A. Abbott, publicly urged that Protestant and Catholic scholars collaboratively prepare a new English translation of the Bible.[32] The following year a project was launched under the direction of two American Protestant biblical scholars, William J. Albright and David Noel Freedman, in which Protestant, Catholic, and Jewish scholars were to produce a multi-volume translation and commentary of the entire Bible, each volume of the "Anchor Bible" being the product of a single scholar's labor.[33] During the Second Vatican Council French Catholic, Protestant, and Orthodox scholars began a joint translation of the entire Bible. By 1965, with encouragement from the Council, similar projects had been launched in eleven other lands.[34]

Catholic "return to the sources" fostered rapprochement in other realms as well. Heightened appreciation of Scripture moved some Catholic theologians nearer Protestantism's traditional emphasis upon the primacy of Scripture for the church's understanding of revelation. Where Catholic teaching manifestly reflected biblical perspectives, Protestants (especially those who also were undergoing a biblical renewal) judged it more faithful to the gospel than earlier Catholic doctrinal formulation and thus a more promising base for dialogue. Catholic theologians who utilized language and methodology akin to those of Protestants at times showed undisguised respect for certain insights of Protestant theologians. The possibility of fruitful theological exchange on issues of common interest was measurably heightened, and by the late 1950s instances of dialogue multiplied.[35]

The Catholic movements of renewal converged in many parishes to produce a more evangelical sense of Catholics' self-identity as Christians—in fact some spoke openly of an "evangelical Catholicism." Because their spirituality was strikingly similar to that simultaneously evolving among some Protestants, its ecumenical consequences were substantial. Catholics seemed to be becoming more like Protestants and Protestants more like Catholics. In 1960 the Swiss Catholic theologian Hans Küng described the discovery made by a growing number:

We are constantly able to affirm the similarity that has developed between the spirituality of leading Catholics and leading Protestants; and spirituality is more important than any number of divisive externals. Over and over again, Catholics and Protestants who get to know each other better realize with astonishment how alike—despite their remaining differences—they have become. It is a likeness founded ultimate-

ly upon our faith in one Father through one Jesus Christ in
one Holy Spirit, in our praying of the same Lord's Prayer and
the same psalms, our meditation and study of the same Holy
Scriptures, our life nourished by the same baptism, the same
Spirit and the same—still too little realized—great common
Christian tradition.[36]

Wherever that "likeness" was recognized, warm relationships between Christian brothers would flourish.

By the eve of Vatican II the renewing currents that first
emerged in the nineteenth century exerted their widest influence
yet, but they did not reach far beyond an elite of Catholic laity and
clergy in western Europe. They had sufficiently demonstrated their
potency, however, to indicate that given free rein they likely would
effect a far-reaching transformation of Catholic thought and practice. Some feared that change and actively sought to prevent it.
Others welcomed the change and sought to maximize its construc-
tiveness. As early as 1950 Congar again had led the way (in *Vraie
et fausse réforme dans l'église*) by calling upon Catholics penitently to admit their church's inadequacies and wrongs, and to foster
her continuing reform built upon fresh penetration to the sources
of Catholic faith and upon re-expression of that faith in forms appropriate to the time. Theologians Karl Rahner, Edward Schillebeeckx, and others argued for recognition that God's self-revela-
tion in history prompts necessarily limited and shifting
formulations of the content of revelation. To the degree that Congar and his allies were persuasive, the prospect for an intensification of the Catholic renewing currents (and of their ecumenical
consequences) was bright. To that degree, too, Catholics would
move toward the *ecclesia semper reformanda* principle originally
championed by the Reformation and currently undergoing refur-
bishment among Protestant churches within the World Council of
Churches.[37]

Encounter with the Postwar World

Following World War II, the Catholic Church entered into
spirited encounter with the non-Catholic world. Catholics both assimilated orientations characteristic of twentieth-century life and

sought to influence the minds and acts of their contemporaries by the gospel. Catholic ecumenism was affected by both aspects of the reciprocal movement between church and world.

As had been true earlier, Catholics felt the impact of the centripetal forces of the time. Accelerated technological advance and heightened economic prosperity made radio, cinema, television, magazines, newspapers, and books widely available. Travel became quicker and more accessible. Industrialization and urbanization created new possibilities for wealth, education, and leisure. Expanded mobility regularly exposed persons to ideas and milieus from which they had been isolated. Lingering Catholic ghettoes (and traditional ghettoes of every kind) were progressively undermined by the pace and style of modern life. It was, as an American scholar observed, an "age of communication. . . . All communication, all dialogue has this effect: it unites, and this despite the greatest difference."[38]

The vastness and complexity of modern society encouraged an intensified grouping of persons and organizations for the pursuit of shared objectives. That "socialization" of life[39] was manifested on an international scale by ventures such as the European Common Market, and among the masses it was experienced more and more commonly in such diverse sectors of society as industry, medicine, and athletics. But groups now could also organize more easily against one another, and the interplay of the powerful centrifugal and centripetal forces operative in the postwar years was manifested conspicuously by the forms of collaboration designed by each side in the Cold War to counter the other's ideological and military might. Among Catholics the threat of "atheistic communism" (like that of nazism earlier) spurred a search for allies among other Christians, and the mood of the time readily encouraged the minimizing of differences for the sake of that alliance.[40]

In the postwar world, too, the nervous recognition spread that the enormous technological power amassed in the West and thence spread globally could be employed for mankind's gradual dehumanization or sudden annihilation. As never before the fate of the entire human race was at stake. For it to endure, peace must be built upon commitments that would, as an international team of historians wrote, "sustain human compassion and respect for the essential dignity of every man."[41] The urgent need to "live and let live" helped spawn a mentality extolling tolerance toward outsiders. For many the United Nations best symbolized the hope that nations, classes, races, and religions would turn their swords into plowshares and pursue the tasks of peace. But though men possessed the technical means for making the earth a garden, the clamor of continuing East-West tensions and of additional fresh hostilities bespoke an unwillingness to abandon the self-aggrandizing ways that threatened to turn it into a desert.

Roman Catholic voices were added to the chorus affirming universal human dignity and interdependence. The esteemed philosopher Jacques Maritain urged insistently that "the deepest value of the human person's dignity consists in his property of resembling God."[42] A Belgian Dominican theologian, Augustin Léonard, wrote that the Creator God has given the human race a single nature and destiny, and that because divine grace operates among Christians and non-Christians alike, all may contribute toward the building of a regenerated humanity. In fact, claimed Léonard, through their pursuit of justice, universal brotherhood, and world peace some "infidels" do more than some Christians for the construction of God's kingdom.[43]

Several influential European Catholics similarly argued that not only must Catholics respect the non-Catholic for his God-given dignity, but, more than that, they must value him as one by whom their own pursuit of truth and virtue can be aided. A Louvain philosopher, Albert Dondeyne, maintained that "we all have need of each other, all having to receive from others and to give to others. . . . Buddhism, Hinduism, Protestantism, the old African cultures, and Marxism have something to teach us and we admit it."[44] This theme, partly a fruit of the neo-Thomism that had emerged a half century earlier, also reflected accents of contemporary philosophy. Congar wrote appreciatively of philosophers who teach that the mind is fashioned for dialogue with persons different from oneself. He agreed that dialogue is essential for personal growth: "Monologue runs the risk of sterility . . . Man realizes himself only in dialogue with the world and with men."[45] Human interdependence was affirmed in the privately-circulated writings of the provocative and controversial French Jesuit paleontologist, Pierre Teilhard de Chardin. According to Teilhard the entire created order evolves toward unity. The place of man and his history within that movement was summarized simply: "Life moves toward unification. Our hope can only be realized if it finds its expression in greater cohesion and greater human solidarity."[46] Teilhard's reading of a divine intent operative in evolution was reinforced by the conviction spreading among some Catholic intellectuals that the movement of history has revelatory significance. The Flemish Dominican theologian Edward Schillebeeckx wrote that "however vaguely, life itself becomes a truly supernatural and external revelation, in which creation begins to speak to us the language of salvation, in which creation becomes a sign of higher realities."[47]

These confluent currents profoundly affected Catholic attitudes to all outsiders inhabiting the modern world. Three consequences for Catholic ecumenism can be observed.

Among an expanding body of Catholics (especially those attuned to recent intellectual developments), the importance of dialogue with other Christians became apparent. The Catholic, they believed, must be open to the other Christian, both to his valid apprehensions of truth, which can be assimilated, and to his incomplete truths and errors, which can stimulate the Catholic to rethink and thereby deepen his own faith.

In the late 1940s Catholic scholars (ecumenists prominent among them) began to articulate an understanding of religious liberty in which the right of free religious choice and action for every person was upheld. During the pontificate of John XXIII this position won numerous allies—including the pope. In the United States, where considerable friction had risen over alleged Catholic denial of religious liberty, the progressive position was endorsed by John F. Kennedy, the first Catholic President. The edge thus was removed from a major traditional source of ideological and social conflict between Protestants and Catholics.[48]

Some Catholics began to perceive how directly ecumenism accorded with the grain of history. Especially as viewed through a Teilhardian lens, modern life seemed to move toward increased unity and to confirm the relevance of biblical and theological speculation about an eventual consummation of the historical process in which "all things are recapitulated in Christ" (Ephesians 1:10). In that awesome perspective unity among Christians was seen as a task to be accomplished in order that men might be given a winsome sign of the direction toward which all history moves. At the Second Vatican Council that theme was to become a key strand in the emerging Catholic perception of the church's responsibility in the world.[49]

In the years between World War II and Vatican II a creative burst of Catholic missionary effort sought fresh ways to relate the gospel to the world. "The greatest error of the Christians of the twentieth century," wrote Cardinal Emmanuel Suhard of Paris, "would be to let the world take shape and unite without them, without God—or against Him."[50] The Catholic attempt to shape the postwar world was innovative, varied, and far-flung. Persons skilled in sociological analysis gathered data and reached provocative conclusions about the erosion of the traditional alliance between Christianity and western society. The church's apostolate in the modern world was seen to require the dedicated action of every Catholic; articulate voices urged that without a more deliberate participation by the laity the church's mission would be gravely handicapped. Imaginative laymen and priests undertook to establish a Catholic presence among segments of society estranged from the church, some priests in France dramatically doing so by assuming the life-style of factory workers, others in India the life-style of Hindu holy men. Catholics committed to an intellectual apostolate addressed modern philosophies such as existentialism and attempted to incorporate their insights into a Christian understanding of reality.[51] Guiding much of this ferment was a conception of the mutual dependence of church and world that had been stated succinctly in Cardinal Suhard's widely-read 1947 pastoral letter: "The world needs the Church for its life; the Church needs the world for its growth and fulfillment."[52] A new world order could be built and preserved only if its soul were nurtured by the church; the church could grow to its divinely-appointed dimensions only if she embraced and cleansed the entire life of mankind.

In several respects the Catholic missionary revival quickened interest in a fresh approach to Protestantism. Earlier, Protestant missionaries and native churchmen in Asia, Africa, and Latin America had been among the first to insist that ecclesiastical divisions must be overcome so that they no longer undercut the churches' evangelistic program. Catholics in those lands made no comparable contribution to the formation of a Catholic ecumenical perspective. But some European Catholics sensitive to their church's worldwide mission saw that it was impeded by the divisions of Christians, and they sought to make that regrettable consequence of disunity evident to other Catholics.[53]

The Catholic missionary enterprise was influenced by most of the same pressures and dealt with many of the same problems that confronted the parallel Protestant endeavor. Increasingly Catholic and Protestant views about particular missiological issues and about the fundamental missionary nature of the church converged. Occasionally the two groups considered each other's thought and activity, but not until the early 1960s did the possible fruitfulness of that convergence begin to become a major consideration for either.[54]

With the Catholic laity encouraged to take more initiative in many realms of their church's life, lay men and women increasingly played important roles establishing new relations with Protestants in their communities.[55]

The resemblance noted earlier between the more appreciative approach to non-Christians and the emerging irenic Catholic approach to other Christians continued in the two decades prior to Vatican II. "Openness," "dialogue," and "fulfillment" were central categories in dealing with both groups. An important difference was recognized between them: one was Christian and the other not. Nevertheless, toward the two groups Catholics were encouraged to maintain a single posture, for the work of "mission" and the work of "ecumenism" were conceived as distinguishable but continuous expressions of the same fundamental purpose—to "bring the dispersed children of God to unity."[56] Inclusion of those "children," Christian and non-Christian, within the unity intended for them by God would mean fulfillment of both their destiny and that of the Roman Catholic Church. Among many persons marked by the missionary consciousness that spread widely by the time of the Council there also was a predisposition to ecumenical dialogue.

Postwar Protestantism

Following World War II the theological, liturgical, and ecumenical currents among Protestants that earlier had attracted sympathetic Catholic attention grew more prominent. The Protestants most affected by them proved of greater interest to Catholics than did their more traditionalist brothers (who usually were less interested in rapprochement with Catholics than the former).

The writings of such theological giants as Karl Barth, Paul Tillich, and Rudolf Bultmann dominated postwar Protestant theology and often dealt with subjects of considerable interest to Catholic scholars. Though disagreeing sharply at some points these Protestant theologians sought to interpret the gospel (especially as presented in Pauline and Reformation sources) in an idiom cognizant of the questions and orientations of the modern mind. The issues pondered by a growing number of Protestant and Catholic theologians, the methodologies employed, and the insights reached were sufficiently similar to create a community of scholarship approximating that formed among biblical scholars. Even when the Catholic theologian disagreed with his Protestant counterpart, he frequently found that the profundity of the latter's thought required him to re-examine his position and to restate it at a deeper level. The enrichment of Catholic theology through encounter with Protestant thought was judged by a Catholic analyst to be the most significant development within Catholic theology in the second decade following World War II.[57]

In the postwar years the Protestant liturgical renewal also enjoyed a widening impact. New hymnals and worship books adapted liturgies of the early church and of the Reformation period for contemporary usage. A greater prominence for the eucharist was a characteristic feature of the new liturgies. The resemblance of Protestant and Catholic worship was heightened, and the field of common action by Protestant and Catholic liturgical specialists expanded.

Some Protestants took more radical "catholicizing" steps. The Community of Taizé, a monastic group of Protestant clergymen and laymen based in eastern France, attracted wide attention by its imaginative effort to bridge the liturgical, theological, and spiritual gaps between Protestantism and Catholicism.[58] In the mid-1950s a group of German Lutheran pastors and laymen formed an organization called the Gathering (die Sammlung), which deliberately emphasized the most Catholic-like features of Protestantism. Their views aroused the ire of numerous German Lutherans who judged that the group's catholicizing tendencies had led them to compromise essential Protestant positions. In 1960 Pastor Max Lackmann, a leader of the Gathering, founded the League for Evangelical-Catholic Reunion. Like German predecessors in the 1930s, Lackmann favored a union of Protestant groups with Rome that would allow them to retain aspects of traditional Lutheran doctrine, polity, liturgy, and piety in "fundamental agreement" with Roman Catholic counterparts.[59] The League attracted a small following in Europe and North America, but as in the 1930s this model of unity proved unappealing to the vast majority of Protestants.

The ecumenical movement's impact upon Protestantism mounted. By 1961, 198 Protestant and Orthodox churches in 70 countries were affiliated with the World Council of Churches. Between 1945 and 1962, 50 Protestant denominations merged to form 18 united churches. Numerous ecumenical agencies stimulated common activity and thought among Christians. Large pockets of resistance and indifference remained, but with increasing justification some spoke of the period as an "ecumenical age."

Although the Roman Church abstained conspicuously from membership in interchurch organizations, the profusion of ecumenical activities among other Christians forced consideration of her relationship to the quest for unity and to individual churches engaged in it. Some Catholics evidenced, as W. A. Visser 't Hooft observed in 1949, a disdainful air toward non-Roman Christians who "have such difficulty in finding what the Roman Catholics have always possessed."[60] In the next decade that attitude gave way to growing appreciation for the achievements of the ecumenical movement. Nevertheless, increased appreciation often appeared to be based upon a deeply-ingrained conviction that the best accomplishments of churches participating in the ecumenical movement were bringing them nearer positions held already by the

Roman Church. Following the 1957 Oberlin Faith and Order conference, traces of that stance could be detected in an appraisal by the American Jesuit ecumenist Gustave Weigel:

> Where is the Ecumenical Movement after Oberlin? First, there is an eager recognition that the Church of Christ is visible and something ontologically prior to its members. Second, it is not a matter of indifference that Christians are disunited. Christ wants the greatest visible union of all, for He has made the ontological Church one. Third, the sacraments of the Church are a cause and sign of unity. They are more than dramatic professions of individual faith. Fourth, tradition conceived of as the doctrines of the historical churches is somehow directive of belief; the Fathers, the Councils and the Confessions cannot be ignored. Even the Bible itself cannot be taught without reference to this tradition. . . . For a Catholic these are consoling developments. These positions are closer to his own than those of nineteenth-century Protestantism. The Catholic cannot but look on these achievements as gains.[61]

The growth of Catholic interest in the ecumenical movement can be measured partly by the spate of informative and analytical literature produced. Catholic scholars published monographs on varied facets of the ecumenical movement and numerous articles in the Catholic ecumenical journals *Istina, Irénikon, Unitas, Vers l'unité chrétienne, Catholica*, and *Eastern Churches Quarterly*. Increasingly, too, other Catholic publications treated ecumenical topics, especially conferences sponsored by the World Council of Churches.[62] The quality and influence of Catholic analyses has been attested by a leader of the World Council of Churches: "It has often been said that the findings of the World Council were far more carefully studied, analysed, and interpreted on the Roman Catholic side than they were in many member churches. The work of interpretation did not pass unheeded in the World Council and it is no exaggeration to say that in this quiet and unobtrusive way Roman Catholic theology was a continuing partner in the discussions in the World Council. Except for the Roman Catholic contribution many questions would have been posed differently."[63]

Quickened Catholic interest in the ecumenical movement led some to seek the Roman Church's direct involvement in major ecumenical conferences. Ten Catholic "unofficial observers" were invited to the founding Assembly of the World Council at Amsterdam in 1948, but the Holy Office forbade their attendance. Four years later the official Catholic policy of abstention from all World Council gatherings was altered when the Vicar Apostolic in Sweden appointed four "accredited visitors" to attend the Lund Faith and Order conference. Catholic attendance at the 1954 Evanston Assembly was proscribed by the cardinal archbishop of Chicago. Some Catholic lay persons were present, nevertheless, as journalists, and the European priests who had come privately to observe the Assembly followed proceedings from an adjoining town. An organization of European Catholic ecumenists prepared a paper on the Evanston theme for World Council consideration. In 1957 two American Catholic theologians were allowed to attend the North American Faith and Order Conference at Oberlin, Ohio, as "unofficial observers." In 1960 three "official observers" were appointed by the Vatican to attend the Faith and Order Commission and Central Committee meetings at St. Andrews, Scotland. The peak of evolving Catholic participation in ecumenical conferences in the pre-Vatican II period was reached with appointment of five "official observers" to the 1961 New Delhi Assembly of the World Council.[64]

Immediately before the 1961 World Council Assembly, M.J. LeGuillou, a French Dominican theologian who served as a Catholic observer at New Delhi, explained that his church had come to believe that she should be actively represented at major meetings of the World Council and should collaborate in certain of its projects. In this way she could contribute to the Council's quest for unity without becoming a member. Although membership would not require the Roman Church to compromise her self-understanding (because of the ecclesiological implications of membership stated by the World Council in 1950), such a step would appear as a surrendering of her claim to be the true church and the unique locus of Christian unity. To allow a misunderstanding of such magnitude to rise would have an intolerable effect upon her mission. LeGuillou added that in the future, however, the Roman Church may judge conditions to have changed sufficiently to permit entrance into the Council without attendant appearance of compromise.[65]

Some Protestants were appalled by the prospect of steps leading to closer Roman ties with Protestantism in the ecumenical organizations or elsewhere. Their reaction reflected an intensification of long-standing criticisms of Catholicism that occurred in the postwar period. Protestant objections were loudly voiced following Pope Pius XII's infallible declaration of the Virgin Mary's bodily assumption. Also galling were the restrictions placed upon Protestant religious activity in Catholic-dominated lands such as Spain and Colombia. Many Protestants concluded that the Roman Church was hopelessly oppressive and retrogressive, and a bellicose handful did not hesitate to declare her an "unmistakable offshoot of the ancient pagan religions."[66] Among some, aggressive denunciations of Catholicism perhaps betrayed resentment and even envy of the Roman Church's increased religious vitality and social impact.

More determinatively another minority of Protestants stimulated a profound re-evaluation of Roman Catholicism. The role of Lutherans was pivotal. A Danish Lutheran theologian, Kristen E. Skydsgaard, informed the 1948 World Council Assembly that renewing currents were rising within the Roman Church and creating undreamed-of possibilities for ecumenical dialogue and cooperation. "Everything is still in its beginning. . . . That which today takes place quietly *may* some day break through and be of an importance at which we at this moment cannot guess."[67] In 1953 Skydsgaard delivered a series of perceptive lectures in Copenhagen on the current status of theological issues traditionally debated by Protestants and Catholics. Each party, he urged, should seek afresh to discover at what points it must direct its "Yes" and its "No" to the other, guided in that endeavor by a "third party . . . the truth itself." Their sensitivity to the demands of truth must be accompanied by a sensitivity to the demands of love, for love alone will sustain Protestants and Catholics in the search for mutual understanding.[68]

In 1955 a German Lutheran theologian, Ernst Kinder, argued

in the *Ecumenical Review* (published by the World Council of Churches) for increased Protestant initiative in the encounter with Roman Catholicism: "Any ecumenical thought and action, which definitely excluded the Roman Catholic Church because of the difficulties involved, would no longer be truly ecumenical. . . . On both sides many far-reaching changes must be carried out and many accretions removed, so that that which is truly Christian (which is there and for which we need one another's help) can develop more freely and truly."[69] In 1957, at the urging of German Lutherans, the Lutheran World Federation took the first steps toward establishment of an international Lutheran study commission focused principally on Roman Catholicism and directed by Skydsgaard. In 1961, on the eve of the Second Vatican Council, the commission sponsored a probing evaluation of the Council's prospects by seven Lutheran scholars.[70]

By the time of Vatican II a small corps of Protestant theologians was aware of the profound shifts occurring in Roman Catholicism and had begun to awaken fellow Protestants to the need for updating their traditional responses to the Roman Church.[71] The message of the watchmen moved few, however, for the great majority of Protestants were surprised and many incredulous at what the Council revealed of the evangelical and ecumenical ferment within Roman Catholicism. Nevertheless, during the 1950s, because a handful of Protestant scholars brought to their Catholic partners in dialogue an appreciative knowledge of current Catholic life and thought, their discussion moved beyond the correcting of caricatures to a grappling with substantive issues. Because these Protestant theologians also brought an informed (though not uncritical) commitment to Reformation understandings of the gospel, they confronted their Catholic colleagues with the historic core of Protestantism. And because they too had been opened to new theological vistas by currents of renewal similar to those flowing through Catholic circles, they were turned in the same direction as their Catholic brothers to detect the presence of the "third party" in their midst.

The participants in dialogue discovered both that a more substantial common ground existed than had been supposed and that their fundamental differences often lay at points other than had been expected. They did not yet agree on how the fact of co-existing commonality and difference should be interpreted and resolved. The Catholic ecumenical problematic encouraged incorporation of Protestant views and values into Catholic wholeness. Protestants tended to regard continuation of the distinctive character of each of the co-equal communities as necessary for the full life of the other. Through sustained dialogical encounter each could help the other become more truly itself.[72] One of the most highly developed statements of that position was made by Swiss Professor Franz Leenhardt. There are, he wrote, two types of biblical faith and spirituality, the Abrahamic and the Mosaic; Protestantism represents the former and Catholicism the latter. Neither dare attempt to absorb or neutralize the other. "It is through a tension sustained by a dialogue in which each questions the other and allows itself to be questioned that—so it would seem —might be most usefully realized the unity of the Abrahamic and Mosaic spiritualities at the heart of the one church."[73] The difficult question of how that tension and unity should be given institutional expression was not pursued by Professor Leenhardt.

Despite unresolved differences, the dialogues of the 1950s and early 1960s were so fruitful that Pope John was inspired to bring such encounter into the Second Vatican Council, thereby introducing Roman Catholic leadership to a fundamental facet of ecumenical experience.

*   *   *

The Catholic and Protestant scholars who engaged in dialogue increasingly were rewarded both with the exhilarating discovery of unsuspected realms of shared theological ground and with the joy of new-found personal kinship in Christ. That experience tempted them—as it has tempted others working on frontiers of intra-Christian discovery—momentarily to lose sight of the wider context of ecumenism. Since the time of Leo XIII, most Catholic ecumenical pioneers had insisted (similarly to their Protestant counterparts) that Christian unity is intended by God to facilitate the wider unity of the human family. In the early 1960s some Catholics sought to remind their cohorts of the potential secular relevance of ecumenism. Their case rested upon three convictions.

First: the problems that tear mankind asunder are addressed by the gospel of Jesus Christ. Second: the churches today, more widely deployed than ever before, are uniquely situated to administer the healing peace of Christ throughout the world. Third: until the churches can demonstrate the effectual presence of that peace among themselves, they are ill-prepared for their larger mission, and the world's taunt, "physician, first heal thyself," is not undeserved.

NOTES

1. *A History of the Expansion of Christianity*, 7 vols. (New York: Harper and Bros., 1945), 7: 67.

2. Roger Aubert, "The Church of Rome," in Stephen Neill, ed., *Twentieth-Century Christianity* (Garden City, New York: Dolphin Books, 1963), pp. 58-9; Wilfrid Parsons, "Intercredal Co-operation in the Papal Documents," *Theological Studies* 4 (1943): 169-73; J. Y. Calvey and J. Perrin, *The Church and Social Justice*, trans. J. R. Kirwan (Chicago: Henry Regnery Co., 1961), 85-8, 427-32; Congar, *Christians Active in the World* (New York: Herder and Herder, 1968), pp. 142-4. It should be noted that only a few years earlier, in July 1939, the Apostolic Delegate in London had turned down an overture from Anglican Bishop George Bell seeking clearance for Roman Catholics to meet in Rome with theologians from other churches to discuss the relevance of Christian faith to burning international problems. Visser 't Hooft, *Memoirs*, pp. 106-7.

3. Thomas Merton, "Introduction," *The Prison Meditations of Father Alfred Delp* (New York: Herder and Herder, 1963), pp. viii-ix; Conway, *Nazi Persecution*, pp. 189-90. The varied shades of Christian resistance to Hitler are discussed by Eberhard Bethge, *Dietrich Bonhoeffer* (New York: Harper and Row, 1970), pp. 696-700.

4. Conway, *Nazi Persecution*, p. 299.

5. Conway states that Dachau held 2771 Catholic priests, of whom at least 1000 died because of sickness, hunger, and ill-treatment. Ibid., p. 198. Cf. Swidler, *Ecumenical Vanguard*, p. 170.

6. Max Lackmann, Lecture in Worthington, Ohio, October 11, 1968. See Robert Grosche, "La situation oecuménique en Allemagne," *Istina* 7 (1960): 12-13.

7. Jean Guitton, *Journal de captivité* (Paris: Aubier, 1943), pp. 167-80; cf. *International Christian News and Information Service*, No. 25, 1944 (hereafter cited as *ICNIS*). A Catholic layman in Lyons, France, told the author (February 1961) of Congar's introduction of ecumenism to

him while the two men were imprisoned in Germany. See also Congar, *Dialogue between Christians*, pp. 17, 28-31.

8. *ICNIS*, Nos. 28/29, 1947.

9. *ICNIS*, No. 9, 1943; Emile C. Fabre, ed., *God's Underground* trans. William and Patricia Nottingham (St. Louis, Bethany Press, 1970), pp. 11-25; *ICNIS*, No. 15, 1943; *ICNIS*, No. 7, 1944; *ICNIS*, No. 26, 1945; Guenter Lewy, *The Catholic Church and Nazi Germany* (New York: McGraw-Hill Book Co., 1964), p. 304; *La documentation catholique* 42 (1945): cols. 87-91; Henri Cadier, *Le Calvaire d'Israel et la solidarité chrétienne* (Geneva, 1945), pp. 48-52, 95; Hugh Martin et al., *Christian Counter-Attack* (London: SCM Press, 1943), pp. 97-8, 101-2; H. P. Van Dusen, "The Church Did It," *Catholic Digest*, (1944), 49-52; Johan M. Snoek, *The Grey Book: A Collection of Protests Against Anti-Semitism and the Persecution of Jews Issued by Non-Roman Catholic Churches and Church Leaders During Hitler's Rule* (New York: Humanities Press, 1970), pp. 125-6, 131, 144, 199-200, 205-6. The first Dutch Catholic-Protestant joint statement prompted the sardonic comment of a secular newspaper: "What God has been unable to achieve for centuries, the Jewish star has achieved." Ibid., p. 126.

10. Stuart R. Schram, *Protestantism and Politics in France* (Alencon: Imprimerie Corbière et Jugain, 1954), p. 122; Martin *Christian Counter-Attack*, p. 105; *ICNIS*, No. 2, 1943; *ICNIS*, No. 33, 1944; Henry P. Van Dusen, *What Is the Church Doing?* (New York: Charles Scribner's Sons, 1943), p. 25; *ICNIS*, No. 24, 1944; *ICNIS*, No. 8, 1944.

11. John C. Heenan, *Cardinal Hinsley* (London: Burns, Oates and Washbourne, 1944), p. 183.

12. The *Times* letter is reproduced in Ibid., pp. 180-1. See also Tomkins, "Catholic Church," p. 688, and Ronald C. D. Jasper, *George Bell, Bishop of Chichester* (London: Oxford University Press, 1967), pp. 245-55. Several years after publication of the letter Adolph Keller, a Swiss ecumenical leader, correctly observed that an "astounding parallelism" had developed between recent ecumenical statements and papal encyclicals regarding the "practical application of Christian principles to life." *Christian Europe Today*, p. 255.

13. Heenan, *Cardinal Hinsley*, p. 193. The words of Margaret Clitherowe, a sixteenth-century Catholic martyr, had voiced the sentiment of successive generations of English Catholics; "I will not pray with you, nor shall you pray with me; neither will I say Amen to your prayers, nor shall you to mine."

14. *ICNIS*, No. 1, 1943; *ICNIS*, No. 2, 1944; *ICNIS*, No. 35, 1944; *ICNIS*, No. 30, 1944; *ICNIS*, No. 17, 1945. An especially informative account of the entire development was provided by A. C. F. Beales, "Local Christian Councils," Sword Paper No. 14, April 1944 (Beales, Barbara Ward, and Christopher Dawson were the key lay leaders of The Sword of the Spirit). The early discussion among English Catholic theologians of the principles governing cooperation was summarized by John Courtney

Murray, "Christian Cooperation," *Theological Studies* 3 (1942): 413-31. Retrospective views are contained in Maurice Bévenot, "Relations with Non-Catholics," *Catholic Mind* 46 (1948): 728-30; and Columba Carey-Elwes, "The Problem of Reunion in England," *Unitas* 3 (1951): 75-84.

15. *ICNIS*, No. 5, 1944; *ICNIS*, No. 14, 1943; *ICNIS*, No. 12, 1943; *ICNIS*, No. 30, 1946; *ICNIS*, No. 35, 1946; S. A. Morrison, "The Ecumenical Movement in Egypt," *Ecumenical Review* 3 (1950-51): 26-8; K. S. Latourette, "Ecumenical Bearings of the Missionary Movement and the International Missionary Council," in Rouse and Neill, eds., *Ecumenical Movement*, p. 394; *ICNIS*, No. 21, 1944; Latourette, "Ecumenical Bearings," p. 388; *ICNIS*, No. 16, April 1944; *ICNIS*, No. 29, July 1944.

16. Kenneth G. Stack, "God and Guadacanal," *Catholic Digest*, April 1944, p. 55; Adrian Poletti, "Bomber Base in England," *Catholic Digest*, August 1944, p. 80; Leroy R. Priest, "This Is My Experience," *The Chaplain*, October 1960, p. 42; *ICNIS*, Nos. 13/14, March 1944; David G. Wittels, "Are the Chaplains Doing a Job?" *Catholic Digest*, February 1945, p. 6.

17. One of the few noteworthy cooperative acts was the joint signing by prominent Roman Catholics, Jews, and Protestants of a public statement, "Pattern for Peace," issued on 7 October 1943. See Macfarland, *Pioneers,* 221-3; Samuel McCrea Cavert, *The American Churches in the Ecumenical Movement, 1900-1968* (New York: Association Press, 1968), pp. 176, 180; and Cavert, *Church Cooperation and Unity in America* (New York: Association Press, 1970), pp. 179, 283. In 1941 a Jesuit publication carried an article indicating why some Catholics abhorred cooperation: "If it be urged that this is not a time for controversy, and that we should forget our differences in order to unite as far as possible in a common fight against paganism, the disturbing thought comes that Protestantism has really proved to be the ally of paganism. . . . The Protestant churches are dying, and we cannot save them, even if we would." C. Leslie Rumble, "Are American Catholics Growing Soft and Satisfied?" *America* 64 (1941): 343-4. See also Francis M. Connell, "Catholics and 'Interfaith' Groups," *American Ecclesiastical Review* 105 (1941): 336-53. *Theological Studies* articles developing the principles of cooperation (in addition to those already cited in notes 2 and 14) were John LaFarge, "Some Questions as to Interdenominational Cooperation," 3 (1942): 315-32; T. Lincoln Bouscaren, "Co-operation with non-Catholics: Canonical Legislation," 3 (1942): 475-512; Murray, "Co-operation: Some Further Views," 4 (1943): 100-11; and Murray, "Intercredal Co-operation: Its Theory and Its Organization," 4 (1943): 257-86.

18. For example, early in 1945, shortly before the end of the war, the new Catholic bishop of Nottingham announced that Catholics who had been in the Leicester Christian Council since 1942 could no longer participate in the Council's silent opening prayer. When Anglicans and Free Churchmen insisted that such prayer was a necessary part of the Council's existence, Catholics withdrew their membership. *ICNIS*, No. 17, 1945.

19. Mersch, *The Theology of the Mystical Body*, trans. Cyril Vollert (St. Louis: B. Herder Book Co., 1958), p. 504. See also Tomkins, "Catholic Church," p. 699; Henri Bruston, "Rapports actuels entre catholiques romains et protestants en France," *Foi et vie* 57 (1958): 345; Michael van der Plas and Henk Suer, eds., *Those Dutch Catholics* (New York: The Macmillan Co., 1967), p. 42.

20. From a letter by an anonymous author, printed in *The World Council Courier*, March 1942. Cf. Guitton, *Journal de captivité*, pp. 174, 180. The hope of a postwar federated Europe had emerged in various resistance groups, and a key role in coordinating their thought about the future was played by ecumenical leader W. A. Visser 't Hooft. See his *Memoirs*, pp. 177-81.

21. *World Council Courier*, March 1942.

22. Important analyses of the Catholic biblical renewal include Jean Levie, *The Word of God and Words of Men* (New York: P. J. Kenedy & Sons, 1961), pp. 1-199; Roger Aubert, "La théologie catholique au milieu du XXe siècle: I. Le renouveau biblique," *La revue nouvelle* 17 (1953): 561-76; Roland E. Murphy, "Old Testament Studies," and John J. Collins, "New Testament Studies," in Elmer O'Brien, ed., *Theology in Transition* (New York: Herder and Herder, 1965), pp. 41-77, 78-119. All of the Catholic intellectual developments discussed in this chapter are provocatively analyzed in VanderGucht and Vorgrimler, eds. *Bilan*, by Roger Aubert, "La théologie catholique," 1: 448-74, and Joseph Comblin, "Depuis la fin du pontificat de Pie XII," I: 479-86.

23. Gustave Thils, *Orientations de la théologie* (Louvain: Editions Ceuterick, 1958), pp. 21-3; Gustave Weigel, *Catholic Theology in Dialogue* (New York: Harper & Row, 1961), pp. 14-5.

24. M. Villain, "Les renouveaux de l'église et l'oecuménisme," in Roger Aubert et al., *Le Christ et les églises* (Paris: Editions universitaires, 1961), p. 12. The importance of the Bible for Catholics was forcefully expressed by a distinguished German Jesuit in 1962: "All true Catholicism is and should be based on the Word of God in Scripture. Scripture should be the source of spiritual life for every Catholic and especially for every priest." Eugene Bianchi, "A Talk with Cardinal Bea," *America* 107 (1962): 589-90.

25. Among the most helpful studies of the liturgical renewal are Roger Aubert, "La théologie catholique au milieu du XXe siècle: II. Les renouveaux liturgique et patristique," pp. 38-46; John H. Miller, "Liturgical Studies," in O'Brien, ed., *Theology in Transition*, pp. 174-211; and Ernest Koenker, *The Liturgical Renaissance in the Roman Catholic Church*, 2nd ed. (St. Louis: Concordia Publishing House, 1966).

26. Aubert, "La théologie catholique," pp. 38-46; Walter J. Burghardt, "Patristic Studies," in O'Brien, *Theology in Transition*, pp. 120-73; Thils, *Orientations*, pp. 43-9; Jean Daniélou, "Patristic Literature," in Daniélou, A. H. Couratin, John Kent, *Historical Theology*, The Pelican Guide to Modern Theology (Baltimore: Penguin Books, 1969), pp. 25-32.

A major demonstration of patristic authors' relevance to modern issues was the influential work of Henri DeLubac, *Catholicism: A Study of Dogma in Relation to the Corporate Destiny of Mankind*, trans. by L. C. Sheppard (New York: Sheed and Ward, 1958).

27. Aelfred H. Tegels, "St. Sergius Conferences," *Worship* 33 (1958-59): 550-1; I. H. Dalmais, "Le renouveau liturgique dans le protestantisme d'expression française," *La Maison-Dieu* (1950), 48-53; J. M. Droin and A. Senaud, "Renouveau liturgique catholique et renouveau liturgique réformé," *Paroisse et liturgie* (1956), 11-17; C. J. Dumont, "Worship in the Roman Church Today," *Ecumenical Review* 7 (1954-55): 367-73; Michael J. Taylor, "Preface," Taylor, ed., *Liturgical Renewal in the Christian Churches* (Baltimore: Helicon, 1967), pp. 5-13.

28. Considerable data supports the conclusion of two Catholic biblical specialists (voiced well before such statements became commonplace): "All modern Catholic exegetes are indebted to the tremendous stream of non-Catholic works on biblical subjects, which flow universally over the Western world, for their suggestive ideas, scholarly exegesis and broad and bold hypotheses. These, when tested and examined by the touchstone of the Rule of Faith, have yielded, and continue to yield, valuable lights and fresh illustration of the truth of God's Word." Bernard Orchard et al., "The Place of the Bible in the Church," *Catholic Commentary on Sacred Scripture* (New York: Nelson, 1953), p. 8.

29. S. de Dietrich, "The Bible as a Force for Unity," *Ecumenical Review* 1 (1948-49): 410-16; Jean Daniélou, "Holy Scripture: Meeting Place of Christians," *Crosscurrents* 3 (1953): 251-61; Raymond E. Brown, *New Testament Essays* (Milwaukee: Bruce Publishing Co., 1965), pp. 17-35.

30. Reginald Fuller, "The Revised Standard Version Catholic Edition and Its Ecumenical Significance," *One in Christ* 1 (1965): 360-66. The RSV Catholic edition of the New Testament had been published the preceding year.

31. *Ecumenical Press Service*, No. 47, 1956. (EPS, sponsored by the World Council of Churches, is the successor of *ICNIS*.)

32. Abbott, "The Bible is a Bond," *America* 102 (1959): 100-2. Cf. Bernard Orchard and Edmund Flood, "Sharing the Same Book," *Worship* 33 (1958-59): 530-36; and Abbott, *The Bible . . . Road to Unity* (New York: The America Press, 1961).

33. *EPS*, No. 40, 1960. The first volume published was *Genesis*, Introduction, Translation and Notes by E.A. Speiser (Garden City, New York: Doubleday, 1964).

34. "Towards a Common Bible," *One in Christ* 1 (1965): 401-404; *EPS*, No. 13, 1961; *EPS*, No. 15, 1962; *EPS*, No. 21, 1962; Ward, *Documents*, pp. 231-6; David Noel Freedman, "Toward a Common Bible?" in Leonard Swidler, ed., *Scripture and Ecumenism* (Pittsburgh:Duquesne University Press, 1965), pp. 133-50.

35. Bruston, "Rapports actuels"; George A. Lindbeck, "The Evan-

gelical Possibilities of Roman Catholic Theology," *Lutheran World* 7 (1960-61): 141-52. The extent of Catholic interest in Protestant thought is suggested by the 1960 report of Ernst Kinder that over half of the doctoral dissertations being written by Catholic priests in West Germany dealt with some aspect of Protestant theology. *EPS*, No. 8, 1960.

36. Küng, *The Council, Reform and Reunion*, trans. Cecily Hastings (Garden City, New York: Doubleday Image Book, 1965), pp. 112-13. René Girault, *Pour un catholicisme évangélique* (Paris: Les Editions Ouvrières, 1959) expressed many of the elements of the new spirituality.

37. Robert McAfee Brown, *The Ecumenical Revolution: An Interpretation of the Catholic-Protestant Dialogue* (Garden City, New York: Doubleday Anchor-Image Book, 1969), pp. 104-21. Catholic discussion of the "development of dogma" necessary for such reform is summarized in Schoof, *Survey*, 194-224.

38. Walter Ong, "The Religious-Secular Dialogue," in John Cogley, ed., *Religion in America* (New York: Meridian Books, 1958), pp. 180, 207.

39. The term was employed by Pope John XXIII to describe this sociological phenomenon in *Mater et Magistra* (New York: America Press, 1961), p. 18.

40. The cultural currents and mood of the postwar decades are provocatively analyzed by Jean-Marie Domenach, "Le visage du monde contemporain," in VanderGucht and Vorgrimler, eds., *Bilan*, 1: 13-62.

41. Caroline Ware, K. M. Panikkar, and J. M. Romein, eds., *The Twentieth Century*, vol. 6 of History of Mankind: Cultural and Scientific Development (New York: Harper and Row, 1966), p. 1317.

42. Cited from Joseph W. Evans and Leo R. Ward, *The Social and Political Philosophy of Jacques Maritain* (New York: Charles Scribner's Sons, 1955), p. 8.

43. Léonard, *Dialogue des chrétiens et des non-chrétiens* (Brussels: La Pensée Catholique, 1959), pp. 21-2, 58-61.

44. "Réflexions philosophiques sur la vérité," in Dondeyne and Jean Giblet, *Christianisme et vérité* (Brussels: La Pensée Catholique, 1959), pp. 63-4. The same note had been sounded in Dondeyne's earlier work, *Foi chrétienne et pensée contemporaine*, 2nd ed. (Louvain: Publications Universitaires de Louvain, 1952).

45. Congar, "Le Concile, l'église, et 'les autres,' " *Lumière et vie* 8 (1959): 75. Cf. *Dialogue between Christians*, pp. 65-8. The point was put simply by a declaration printed in bold letters on an undated leaflet circulated by the "Movement Without Name" of Brussels: "Sans les autres, je me détruis" ("Without others, I destroy myself").

46. *The Future of Man*, trans. Norman Denny (New York: Harper and Row, 1964), p. 72.

47. Schillebeeckx, *Christ the Sacrament of the Encounter with God* (New York: Sheed and Ward, 1963), p. 8.

48. A. F. Carrilo de Albornoz, *Roman Catholicism and Religious*

Liberty (Geneva: World Council of Churches, 1959); Patricia Barrett, *Religious Liberty and the American Presidency* (New York: Herder and Herder, 1963); Eugene Bianchi, *John XXIII and American Protestants* (Washington: Corpus Books, 1968), pp. 95-132. The contributions to this new stance of Catholics noted for their ecumenical work include Congar, "A Letter on Religious Liberty with Reference to the Position of Protestants in Spain," (1948) *Dialogue Between Christians*, pp. 312-32; J. C. Murray, "Freedom of Religion," *Theological Studies* 6 (1945): 229-86; Pribilla, "Dogmatische Intoleranz und bürgerliche Toleranz," *Stimmen der Zeit* 144 (1949): 27; Couturier, ed., *Unité Chrétienne et tolérance religieuse* (Paris: Editions du Temps Present, 1950); R. Aubert et al., *Tolérance et communauté humaine* (Tournai-Paris: Casterman, 1952); Gustave Weigel, "The Church and the Democratic State," *Thought* 27 (1952): 165-84; H. van der Linde and F. Thijssen, *De Situatie van de Protestanten in Spanje* (Utrecht: Het Spectrum, 1950).

49. The Council's development of this theme is discussed in George A. Lindbeck, *The Future of Roman Catholic Theology* (Philadelphia: Fortress Press, 1970). Its presence in preconciliar Catholic thought can be detected in, e.g., Baum, *Progress and Perspectives*, p. 19.

50. Suhard, *Growth or Decline? The Church Today*, trans. James A. Corbett (South Bend, Indiana: Fides Publishers, 1948), p. 56.

51. Among the most useful analyses of this missionary ferment are Adrien Dansette, *Destin du catholicisme français, 1926-1956* (Paris: Flammarion, 1957); Jean-Marie Domenach and Robert de Montvalon, *The Catholic Avant-Garde: French Catholicism Since World War II* (New York: Holt, Rinehart and Winston, 1967); R. Aubert, "La théologie catholique . . . III. Ouverture au monde moderne," *La revue nouvelle* 18: 161-81, and "La théologie catholique . . . IV. Face à l'existentialisme et à l'oecuménisme," pp. 272-88; Kenneth S. Latourette, *Christianity in a Revolution-Age*, 5 vols. (New York: Harper and Row, 1961) 4: 71-88.

52. *Growth or Decline*, p. 31. See also Jean Bruls, "Ouverture au monde et esprit catholique," *Eglise vivante* 11 (1959): 317; and Ronan Hoffman, "Some Missiological Reflections on Current Theology," in William J. Richardson, ed., *Revolution in Missionary Thinking* (Maryknoll, New York: Maryknoll Publications, 1966), pp. 97-113.

53. A linkage of missionary and ecumenical interests characterized the literature prepared by Courturier for the Week of Prayer for Christian Unity; Curtis, *Couturier*, pp. 102, 105. During the pontificate of John XXIII that tie became prominent in the thought of several Catholic ecumenical leaders; see Jean Daniélou, ed., *Union des chrétiens et conversion du monde* (Paris: Editions du Centurion, 1962), and M. J. LeGuillou, *Mission et unité: les exigences de la communion*, Unam Sanctam, vols. 33 and 34 (Paris: Editions du Cerf, 1960). Several European journals which circulated in Catholic missionary circles gave periodic attention to ecumenical matters {e.g. *Eglise vivante, Rhythmes du Monde*, and *Parole et Mission*). One may surmise that among the reasons for the slowness with

which Catholic ecumenical interest developed in the traditional mission fields were less contact there with the currents of renewal; greater attention to the evangelistic task and to its potentially divisive implications ("which church shall I enter?"); and the relative abundance of Protestants reared in an anti-Catholic atmosphere and the relative scarcity of persons influenced by the movements for renewal within Protestantism.

54. E.g. A. Nijman, "L'activité missionaire protestante en 1952," *Eglise vivante* 5 (1953): 230-51; S. Delacroix, ed., *Histoire universelle des missions catholiques* 3: 237-69; Küng, *The Council in Action* (New York: Sheed and Ward, 1963), pp. 244-60. During the 1960-61 academic year at the Catholic University of Louvain the author observed (and participated in) several instances of a mounting reciprocal interest: a French Protestant from the Taizé Community visited Louvain and Brussels to receive sociological information about Latin America from Catholic specialists; Catholic students invited a Baptist executive of the International Missionary Council to discuss developments in Protestant missionary and ecumenical circles; representatives of the World's Student Christian Federation (Protestant and Orthodox) and of Pax Romana (Roman Catholic) met together for the first time to discuss the Christian witness in a technological society.

55. John B. Sheerin, "The Laity, Our Ecumenical Hope," *Catholic World* 192 (1961): 324-8; John B. Mannion, "The Layman and the Dialogue," *Catholic World* 193 (1961): 280-87. It must be remembered, however, that the critical formative figures in Catholic ecumenical development were priests. Protestant lay ecumenical pioneers John R. Mott, Robert Gardner, and J. H. Oldham did not have Catholic counterparts.

56. Le Guillou, "Le Conseil oecuménique des Eglises," *Lumière et vie* 4 (1955): 95-6: "We forget too often that the ecumenical problem and the missionary problem are only the two faces of a fundamental requirement which is 'to bring the dispersed children of God to unity.' " In the 1950s a close relationship between these two interests was evident in the writings of such influential scholars as Jean Daniélou, Charles Moeller, Jean Guitton, Hans Urs van Balthasar, and Karl Rahner.

57. Elmer O'Brien, "Theology in Transition," in O'Brien, ed., *Theology in Transition*, pp. 247-9.

58. François Biot, *Communautés Protestantes* (Paris: Editions Fleurus, 1961). The theological writings of Max Thurian, subprior of Taizé, were a major expression of the brothers' bridge-building efforts: e.g. *Confession*, trans. Edwin Hudson (London: SCM Press, 1958), *Marriage and Celibacy*, trans. Norma Emerton (London: SCM Press, 1959).

59. Adolph Schalk, "Reformation in Germany, 1958" *Commonweal* 69 (1958): 229-31; Eva-Marie Jung, "Pastor Lackmann's Way to Unity," *Catholic World* 193 (1961): 381; Swidler, *Ecumenical Vanguard*, pp. 246-52; Lackmann, "Toward Corporate Reunion," *Perspectives* 7 (1962): 3; G. A. Pottebaum, "Interview with Pastor Max Lackmann," *Catholic World* 195 (1962): 210-18.

60. "Report of the General Secretary," *Ecumenical Review* 2 (1949-50): 64.

61. Weigel, "Faith and Order at Oberlin," *America* 98 (1957): 71.

62. Important volumes published by Catholics prior to Vatican II that treat the ecumenical movement include Gustave Thils, *Histoire doctrinale du mouvement oecuménique* (Louvain: Warny, 1955); Thomas Sartory, *The Oecumenical Movement and the Unity of the Church*, trans. from the 1955 German ed. (Westminster, Maryland: Newman Press, 1963); Edward Duff, *The Social Thought of the World Council of Churches* (New York: Association Press, 1956); W. H. Van der Pol, *The Christian Dilemma: Catholic Church—Reformation*, trans. from the 1948 Dutch ed. by G. Van Hall (London: G. M. Dent, 1952); Gustave Weigel, *A Catholic Primer on the Ecumenical Movement*, Woodstock Papers, No. 1 (Westminster: Newman Press, 1957); J. P. Michael, *Christen Suchen Eine Kirche* (Freiburg: Verlag Herder, 1958); Le Guillou, *Mission et unité*; George Tavard, *Two Centuries of Ecumenism*; Maurice Villain, *Unity: A History and Some Reflections*, trans. by J. R. Foster from the 1961 3rd French ed. (Baltimore: Helicon Press, 1963); Bernard Lambert, *Le problème oecuménique*, 2 vols. (Paris: Editions du centurion, 1962). Catholic responses to World Council conferences are summarized in "The Roman Catholic Church and the First Assembly of the World Council of Churches," *Ecumenical Review* 1 (1948-49): 202-12; W. G. Menn, "Roman Catholic Voices on the Lund Conference," *Ecumenical Review* 4 (1952-53): 294-8; Eva-Maria Jung, "Roman Catholic Impressions of the Evanston Assembly," *Ecumenical Review* 7 (1954-55): 169-71; "Survey of Press Comments on the Third Assembly," *Ecumenical Review* 7 (1961-62): 480-7.

63. Lukas Vischer, "The Ecumenical Movement and the Roman Catholic Church," in Harold E. Fey, ed., *The Ecumenical Advance: A History of the Ecumenical Movement, Vol. 2, 1948-1968* (Philadelphia: Westminster Press, 1970), p. 320. See also Stephen Neill, *Brothers of the Faith* (New York: Abingdon Press, 1960), p. 173, and Visser 't Hooft, *Memoirs*, p. 320.

64. Congar, *Dialogue Between Christians*, pp. 36-8, 71; *Ecumenical Review* 1 (1948-49): 197-201; "Dr. Visser 't Hooft's Reply to Cardinal Stritch," *Ecumenical Review* 7 (1954-55): 169-71; Tavard, *Catholic Approach*, p. 115; John Sheerin, *Christian Reunion: The Ecumenical Movement and American Catholics* (New York: Hawthorn Books, 1966), pp. 65-6; Vischer, "Ecumenical Movement," pp. 316-28; Visser 't Hooft, *Memoirs*, pp. 206-8, 323-9.

65. "L'église catholique et l'oecuménisme," in *Le Christ et les Eglises*, pp. 233-6. Cf. *EPS*, No. 6, 1961.

66. From a tract published by the French "Union of Protestant Defense." Cited by John Wilkinson, "An Answer of Peace," *Faith and Unity* 6 (1960): 22. See also Bianchi, *John XXIII*, p. 54; Brown, *Ecumenical Revolution*, pp. 5-7; and Curry, *Protestant-Catholic Relations*, pp. 36-60.

67. "The Roman Catholic Church and the Ecumenical Movement," in *Man's Disorder and God's Design: The Amsterdam Assembly Series* (New York: Harper, 1948), p. 168.

68. *One in Christ*, trans. Axel C. Kildegaard (Philadelphia: Muhlenberg Press, 1957), p. 49.

69. Kinder, "Protestant-Roman Catholic Encounter an Ecumenical Obligation," *Ecumenical Review* 7 (1954-55): 339, 346. In 1955 the World Council-sponsored Graduate School of Ecumenical Studies included "Roman Catholicism" as one of the subjects treated by its students. *Ecumenical Review* 7 (1954-55): 180.

70. Skydsgaard, ed., *The Papal Council and the Gospel* (Minneapolis: Augsburg Publishing House, 1961). Later the commission was succeeded by the Lutheran Foundation for Ecumenical Research, and a research institute was established in Strasbourg.

71. Especially prominent among the Protestant writings serving this purpose were Walther von Loewenich, *Modern Catholicism*, trans. from the 1955 German ed. by Reginald H. Fuller (New York: St. Martin's Press, 1959); Roger Mehl, *Du Catholicism romain* (Neuchâtel: Delachaux et Niestlé, 1957); G. C. Berkouwer, *Recent Developments in Roman Catholic Thought*, trans. J. J. Lamberts (Grand Rapids, Michigan: Eerdman's, 1958); Jaroslav Pelikan, *The Riddle of Roman Catholicism* (New York: Abingdon Press, 1959); Robert McAfee Brown (and Gustave Weigel), *An American Dialogue* (Garden City, New York: Doubleday, 1960). The articles and reviews of George A. Lindbeck belong in such a listing (e.g., see note 35). Von Loewenich, Pelikan, and Lindbeck are in the Lutheran tradition; Brown, Mehl, and Berkouwer in the Reformed.

72. One finds that theme recurring in articles published in *Dialog* 1 (1962): Skydsgaard, "Why Lutherans Must Talk With Rome," pp. 12-20; Paul Tillich, "The Permanent Significance of the Catholic Church for Protestants," pp. 22-25; E. Kinder, "The New Encounter in Germany," pp. 34-39. Cf. Vittoria Subilia, *The Problem of Catholicism*, trans. Reginald Kissack (Philadelphia: Westminster Press, 1964), p. 182. A somewhat similar position was reflected in works by two Catholic scholars: Ludwig Lambinet, *Das Wesen des Katholisch-Protestantischen Gegensatzes* (Einsiedeln/Cologne: Verlagsanstalt Benziger, 1946); Jose Luis L. Aranguren, *Catolicismo y Protestantismo Como Formas De Existencia*, 2nd ed. (Madrid: Revista de Occidente, 1957).

73. F. Leenhardt, *Two Biblical Faiths: Protestant and Catholic*, trans. Harold Knight (Philadelphia: Westminster Press, 1964), p. 117.

VII
Toward a Promised Land

For four hundred years Catholics and Protestants had wandered in a wilderness of personal estrangement and ecclesiastical division. Prophetic spirits occasionally had awakened hopes of reaching a "promised land" where the gift of reconciliation was lived among all Christians, but for most it had seemed an impossibly distant, even illusory goal. By the early years of this century, however, the flow of history had begun to favor those willing to journey toward that land. After 1945, in the wake of mankind's most destructive war, a growing and determined band of Catholic pilgrims embarked toward its ever more alluring frontiers.

We now must look more directly at the voyagers' progress between the end of World War II and the beginning of Vatican II. The four-century separation had placed formidable obstacles in their path. Most Catholics remained unaware that some had set out on so daring a journey; until Pope John's pontificate, those who were aware frequently evidenced suspicion of the ecumenical vanguard. Their pilgrimage could not fail to attract papal attention, for it raised issues of great magnitude for the entire Roman Church. Pope Pius XII found it necessary to restrain the most innovative features of Catholic ecumenical effort, but, fatefully, his successor supported ecumenism and created an official home for it within the Roman Church.

Peacetime Acceleration

In the first five years following World War II a flood of ecumenical activity burst among Catholics in several European lands. In Germany its scope and impact were prodigious. Again the passions of men unwittingly served the ecumenical cause. Some 6400 German churches had been destroyed or damaged during the war,

and many that still stood became tangible signs of freshly discovered bonds between Catholics and Protestants. Joint usage of
those facilities was occasioned by the sudden arrival of 11 million
German refugees, most of whom had been expelled from their
homes in eastern Germany or the Czechoslovakian Sudetenland
and had fled into West Germany. The massive displacement of
population upset religious boundaries that for centuries had determined that Protestants preponderated in some areas of Germany
and Catholics in others. "By a strange kind of providence," reported Ernst Kinder, "it happened that almost always Catholic refugees fled into Protestant territories and vice versa."[1] With worship
facilities scarce, members of the host group frequently offered refugees use of their churches. Protestant and Catholic worship in the
same sanctuaries continued in many communities well into the
1950s.

German Catholics and Protestants who used the same buildings for worship often found other bonds. Some cooperated in
relief programs for suffering victims of the war and its aftermath.
In West Germany many joined the new Christian Democratic
Union which, though not free of wrangling between Protestants
and Catholics, provided an effective framework for their first political coalition.[2]

The realm of most intensive Catholic-Protestant rapprochement in divided postwar Germany was the Una Sancta Brotherhood. Interconfessional circles, many of them formed earlier
under Metzger's guidance, were active in some forty cities and
towns. Coordination was provided by Dr. Matthias Laros, a priest
from the Rhineland. Normally clergy and laity participated in the
same circle and met at least monthly. Occasionally large audiences
were attracted to public events planned by Una Sancta members.
Some circles sponsored more intensive conferences and retreats
lasting several days.[3]

Una Sancta activity quickly attracted the German hierarchy's
attention. In 1946 Archbishop Lorenz Jaeger of Paderborn was appointed to give episcopal oversight to the Una Sancta program in
behalf of all German bishops. That year Jaeger sponsored a discussion among twenty-four prominent Catholic and Protestant theologians at Paderborn. So fruitful was their session that every year

subsequently the Evangelical-Catholic Ecumenical Work Circle gathered at Paderborn for five days of amicable and vigorous theological discussion. Until 1957 they also met a second time annually in a session hosted by Protestant theologians. Archbishop Jaeger and Lutheran Bishop Wilhelm Stählin regularly attended and kept their episcopal colleagues informed of the theologians' progress.[4]

Initiation of another academic project was symptomatic of those hopeful years. In 1946 the Institute for Reformation Research was established by Protestants and Catholics to foster a cooperative study of disputed historical issues. One of its leaders, Lutheran historian Karl August Meissinger, explained that the Institute was dedicated to "a clear delineation of the doctrinal differences on both sides, not however for the selfish purpose of controversy, but rather in a believing common seeking for the one truth."[5]

An expanding body of articles and books on ecumenical themes appeared. A contribution of wide impact was made by the veteran Tübingen theologian Karl Adam. Lectures delivered in 1947 at large Una Sancta gatherings in Stuttgart and Karlsruhe were published later that year and translated subsequently into several languages. Adam eloquently summarized christological and ecumenical perspectives shaped in Catholic circles during the past two decades: "We must give ourselves unconditionally to Christ and His holy will; and, inspired by this love of Christ, we must root out of ourselves all loveless prejudice." Adam urged that Protestants consider the papacy in this spirit, for then they would discover it to be the indispensable servant of unity rather than a barrier; they would see that "the way to unity is. . . . from Christ to Peter." The reunion that ensued would mean mutual enrichment, "giving and receiving on both sides."[6] He renewed the claim made periodically in the past that Catholic disciplinary regulations might be altered in such matters as clerical celibacy in order to facilitate a corporate reunion of Protestant groups with the Roman Church.

A fresh burst of ecumenical activity also occurred in France following the war. The pattern there contrasted with the German one because of differing historical, sociological, and ecclesiastical factors. In West Germany (the area of greatest ecumenical ferment among German Catholics), the number of Protestants and Catholics was nearly equal, while in France Protestants constituted only two per cent of an overwhelmingly Catholic population. The opportunities for direct French Catholic encounter with Protestants were thus more limited. Also, in Germany the Protestant population was predominantly Lutheran, whereas in France it was predominantly Reformed. The distinct histories and theological accents of the two Protestant traditions meant that their modern-day representatives would differ somewhat in their estimation of the issues most urgently in need of discussion with Catholics. The presence of articulate Orthodox theologians in Paris also tended to turn French Catholic ecumenists to certain theological (especially ecclesiological) issues less critical for their German counterparts not as normally engaged in Catholic-Protestant-Orthodox dialogue.[7]

The creative hand of Paul Couturier touched most phases of postwar French Catholic ecumenical activity. The Lyons priest gave himself unstintingly to year-round promotion of the Week of Prayer for Christian Unity. By 1945 Cardinals Gerlier of Lyons, Saliège of Toulouse, and Liénart of Lille had endorsed the Week, and it soon flourished in those cities and their environs. Abbé Couturier's failing health prohibited extensive travel, but other Catholic ecumenical leaders (chiefly Fathers Maurice Villain and Congar) spoke widely during the Week. At times Protestant leaders also spoke and Protestant parishes were invited to attend. Couturier personally arranged such Protestant participation in Lyons and encouraged it elsewhere, but it was not a necessary ingredient, and the Week often proceeded without direct Protestant involvement, especially in areas where relations were strained or Protestants scarce.[8]

The annual tracts and frequent letters written by Couturier conveyed essentially the same positions he had enunciated before the war, but with some now given added or clearer emphasis. Fundamental to the pursuit of unity, he insisted, is a proper "orientation of the inner life." Christians must genuinely open themselves to God, for only as his life enters theirs will they be capable of the love essential for unity. The supreme way of opening the self to God is prayer. So important is prayer for unity, Couturier believed, that it must be more than an annual act; for persons truly committed to Christian unity there must be "habitual prayer and penitence." Such persons constituted what Couturier called the "Invisible Monastery."[9]

His conviction grew that the renewal underway among the churches was contributing powerfully to their eventual reunion. As each reorients its corporate life in the light of fresh perceptions of the divine will, and as divided Christians engage in what Couturier called "spiritual emulation," the churches will move nearer one another, for among them now are convergent understandings of Christ's intention for his people. Unity will result from the churches' mutual transformation according to the will of Christ. That "sanctification" of the entire Christian family should be uppermost in the hopes and prayers of Christians eager for unity. In 1946 Couturier altered the daily prayer intentions of the Week of Prayer for Christian Unity to express this conviction. Persons participating in the Week prayed first for the unity of all Christians as willed by Christ, then on successive days for the sanctification of Catholics, Orthodox, Anglicans, Lutherans, Calvinists, and "all other Protestants." Couturier's commitment to the larger unity of mankind was expressed in the last day's intention: the "unity of all men in the charity and truth of Christ."[10]

Couturier also played a critical role shaping the interconfessional "Group of the Dombes" that he had helped organize earlier. Beginning in 1946, it met annually, alternating its meeting place between the Trappist monastery of Les Dombes (near Lyons) and several Protestant centers. At each session a dozen theologians and pastors from Swiss and French Protestant (mostly Reformed) churches met for several days with a like contingent of Catholics. Every year a person from each side presented a paper on the topic chosen for discussion. The ambience of early gatherings (and Couturier's influence) is suggested by a 1947 report: "The meeting took place in a spirit of fervent prayer. Every member thinks essential to remain true to his own tradition and to deepen it in a spirit which grows more and more obedient to Scripture and to the demand for unity with which God confronts His Church today."[11]

As Catholics' interest in unity mounted, Couturier realized that most priests were ill-equipped for the ecumenical leadership that growing numbers of them wished to provide in their parishes.

He welcomed the proposal made by his associate Maurice Villain that an annual week-long session be held for priests who desired a rudimentary education in ecumenism. In 1945 a beginning was made near Grenoble; thereafter such opportunities were offered annually during the summer in a Lyons suburb.[12]

Belgian Catholics were exposed to ecumenical perspectives by a handful of laymen and priests. In 1942 the Benedictine Monks of Union began hosting an annual theological discussion, which by 1947 included Catholic, Orthodox, Reformed, and Anglican theologians from several countries. The spark for this venture came from several of Beauduin's Benedictine associates and from two young Belgian scholars, Charles Moeller and Roger Aubert. Reports of their discussions appeared periodically in *Irénikon*.[13] This group, like comparable ones in Germany and France, continued to meet into the 1960s, and its participants, too, played critical roles in illumining the common theological ground shared by Catholics and Protestants, as well as in identifying and assessing differences. In 1945 the Belgian Committee for Religious Documentation for the East was established in Brussels. Chiefly through the labors of its lay leaders, Lucien and Hélène Morren, the Committee encouraged Catholic generosity toward East European refugees and introduced Couturier's Week of Prayer into Belgian seminaries and parishes.[14]

In the Netherlands memories of wartime bonds were nourished by annual commemorations of liberation from Nazi rule. Those occasions, observed widely throughout the country and directed jointly by priests and pastors, included Scripture-reading, preaching, and prayer. Some Protestants and Catholics who had begun meeting during the war continued to gather for regular discussion of common pastoral and theological concerns. Heightened Catholic interest in Protestantism was expressed and promoted by the 1948 establishment of a chair in the Phenomenology of World Protestantism at the Catholic University of Nijmegen. Its first occupant, W. H. Van der Pol, a former Protestant, soon was recognized as a leading interpreter of Protestantism. The following year a major shift occurred in the Apologetic Association of Peter Canisius, an organization of Catholic clergy and laity formed in the early 1900s. Its purpose was redefined as the reunion of the churches and the rechristianization of Holland, and its name was changed to the Association of St. Willibrord (Willibrord was an eighth-century pioneer of Dutch Christianity, admired by Catholics and Protestants alike). Leaders of the Association, especially Frs. Frans Thijssen and Jan G. M. Willebrands, channeled into Dutch Catholic circles the ecumenical and missionary currents that had arisen in neighboring lands.[15]

Elsewhere in the world scattered efforts were made to continue fraternal relationships begun during the war or to take the first cautious steps toward them. In the United States, for example, a Catholic agency co-sponsored an interchurch relief program that sent heifers to despoiled agricultural areas of Europe. A small group of Catholic, Orthodox, and Protestant intellectuals in the New York City area began meeting for discussion of religious issues in 1945; their circle took as its name "The Third Hour." Christian leaders in Cairo continued the gatherings begun during the war; in 1946 Jewish and Muslim participants joined them in a discussion of "Religion and World Order." Protestant and Catholic relief agencies in Budapest cooperated in the distribution of scarce food supplies to needy persons. Catholics and Protestants in London met to discuss unity during the Week of Prayer. Some Anglo-Catholics sponsored annual observances of the Octave. A group of Catholic, Anglican, Orthodox, and Free Church theologians that had been first convened in 1944 met annually at Oxford under the leadership of Dom Bede Winslow. In 1945 the Unitas Association was inaugurated in Rome to facilitate rapprochement among Christians. Its founders hoped that national committees would be formed in other lands, and that their membership would include both Catholics and other Christians. Czech Roman Catholic leaders joined counterparts from Orthodox, Protestant, and Old Catholic churches in a 1948 plea for world peace. Twenty Catholic, Lutheran, and Orthodox clergymen shared a two-day conference in Sweden during the 1948 Week of Prayer for Christian Unity.[16]

Affirmation of Christian solidarity was not the sole stance taken by Catholics toward Protestants in the first years of peacetime. Bitterness erupted in several Catholic-dominated lands, especially Spain.[17] In 1947 Protestantism was denounced as the "new enemy" of Spanish Catholic unity, and Protestants there remained a persecuted minority for over a decade.[18] This denial of religious liberty aroused Protestant resentment elsewhere, intensified fear that world Catholicism was irreversibly committed to the positions taken by Spanish Catholics, and heightened the difficulties facing Protestants committed to fostering rapprochement with the Roman Church.[19] Moreover, in some Catholic circles where ecumenical ventures had developed rapidly after the war, second thoughts about such innovation became persuasive. The announcement early in 1946 that only Roman Catholics could become members of the Unitas Association presaged a more far-reaching reaction soon to issue from the Vatican.[20]

Pius XII and Catholic Ecumenism

Pope Pius XII shared his predecessor's interest in the achievement of reunion, and periodically he issued appeals for a return of non-Catholics to Roman unity. Although the approach to unity taken by the Vatican under Pius XII incorporated several of the breakthroughs made by Catholics north of the Alps, more characteristically the pronouncements of Pius and the Holy Office revealed anxiety over avant-garde Catholic ecumenists' too radical distancing of themselves from traditional hallmarks of Catholic unionist activity. Guardians of tradition in the Eternal City feared that should the transformationist course of the Congars and Couturiers go unchecked, they would jeopardize perilously the treasure entrusted to the Roman Church.

Four pronouncements directly or indirectly affecting ecumenism were made between 1948 and 1950. The first, a brief *Monitum* ("warning"—also known as *Cum compertum*) was issued by the Holy Office on 5 June 1948. It reminded Catholics of canonical prohibitions against unauthorized participation in "so-called 'ecumenical' meetings" with non-Catholic Christians and in shared worship (*communicatio in sacris*). Most viewed the *Monitum* as a proscription of Catholic attendance at the forthcoming Amsterdam Assembly of the World Council of Churches. Some considered it also aimed at Una Sancta meetings in Germany, and a marked decline of that activity ensued in the months following the *Monitum*'s appearance. The gloom brought to Una Sancta circles by the June statement, however, soon was dispelled by more elastic interpretations. One commentator noted that the *Monitum* was not directed against private meetings where Catholics and Protestants engaged in rigorous discussion of theological issues. A Holy Office official explained that even for certain public interconfessional meetings, Catholic participation was possible, provided prior papal or episcopal approval had been secured. Less than two months after the *Monitum*'s appearance, Archbishop Jaeger wrote Matthias Laros that the German bishops were seeking ways to continue Una Sancta activity within the framework of canon law. Some French interpreters regarded the *Monitum* as forbidding active participation in other Christians' worship services but not in less formal acts such as praying the Lord's Prayer together.[21]

On 1 March 1950 a more comprehensive *Instructio* (also referred to as *Ecclesia Catholica* and *De Motione Oecumenica*) was published by the Holy Office. In some quarters the brief *Monitum* had created uncertainty and consternation regarding Rome's position toward Catholic encounter with other Christians, and requests had been made for a more complete explanation of the possibilities and limitations of Catholic ecumenical endeavor.[22]

The *Instructio* opened with a statement that was the most positive official Roman response to the ecumenical movement yet made:

> The present time has witnessed in different parts of the world a growing desire amongst many persons outside the Church for the reunion of all who believe in Christ. This may be attributed, under the inspiration of the Holy Ghost, to external factors and the changing attitude of men's minds but above all to the united prayers of the faithful. To all children of the true Church this is a cause for holy joy in the Lord; it urges them to extend a helping hand to all those sincerely seeking after the truth by praying fervently that God will enlighten them and give them strength.[23]

The *Instructio* directed Catholic bishops to make efforts for reunion "a special object of their care and attention." Each bishop should inform himself about ecumenical activities underway in his diocese; provide facilities for non-Catholics wishing to learn about

Catholicism; authorize attendance by qualified priests and laymen at those ecumenical meetings in his diocese which give promise of good results; allow them to "meet as equals" with non-Catholics to discuss matters of faith and morals; report all such activity annually to the Holy Office; instruct the faithful in ecumenical matters; and encourage the clergy to pray and work for this cause. Permission from the Holy Office would be required for Catholic attendance at interdiocesan, national, or international ecumenical conferences dealing with doctrinal matters, but no prior hierarchical approval would be necessary for Catholic participation in "mixed gatherings" treating problems of the social order. The document reiterated the *Monitum*'s prohibition against *communicatio in sacris*, but with the significant exception granted that the Lord's Prayer or another approved prayer could be jointly recited at meetings with other Christians.

The *Instructio* also directed bishops to guard against certain dangers the Holy Office believed to attend ecumenical ventures. They must beware the "indifferentism" fostered when similarities among Christians are exaggerated and differences minimized. Persons of an irenic spirit must not be allowed so to blend Catholic and dissident doctrines that they jeopardize the purity of Catholic teaching and obscure its true meaning. The full seriousness of the reformers' defection from Catholic teaching must not be blinked or the faults of sixteenth-century Catholicism exaggerated. Catholic teaching regarding the church, the papacy, and the necessity for non-Catholic Christians' return to the Roman Church must be stated uncompromisingly and unambiguously. And non-Catholics must not be misled in their expectation of what that return will entail: "Non-Catholics may certainly be told that, should they return to the Church, such good as the grace of God has already wrought in their souls will not be lost, but will be completed and brought to perfection. But they must not be given the impression that by their return they are contributing to the Church something essential which formerly she lacked."[24]

Among Catholics and Protestants alike the *Instructio* provoked a mixed reaction. Most Protestant comment reflected fear that Catholic ecumenical initiative might now be stifled by episcopal control; but some also welcomed the guarded approval given Catholics to engage in discussion and prayer with other Christians.[25] Several German Catholics publicly lamented the possible dampening effect of the Holy Office's statement.[26] Some British Catholics were stunned at its approval of common prayer.[27] Charles Boyer, a leader among Catholics whose approach to other Christians followed traditionalist lines, hailed the *Instructio* as "the great charter" of Catholic unionist activity.[28] Paul Couturier, though less elated than Boyer, also considered it an important advance. In comparison with the *Monitum* it "encourages what the first one scarcely tolerated. . . . This document inaugurates a new era. It half-opens the ecumenical gates and that is immense."[29]

Couturier's optimism is intriguing. In certain crucial respects the *Instructio* merely echoed *Mortalium animos*. Especially was it clear that return to the Roman Church was still the normative Catholic definition of the way to Christian unity, and that the Holy Office would tolerate no re-interpretation of Catholic teaching for the sake of unity. But the *Instructio* revealed that the transformationist motif had gained a beachhead in Rome. For the first time Roman officials cautiously encouraged Catholic dialogue with other Christians. The latter's pursuit of unity was attributed to the Holy Spirit. Their reunion with Rome was conceived as a fulfillment. The cause of unity was judged important enough to be made a responsibility of bishops. This decentralizing thrust of the *Instructio* would allow Spanish bishops to pursue ecumenism in their way and German bishops in theirs. Couturier doubtless hoped that now that bishops were encouraged to play an active role promoting unitive efforts with other Christians, they actually would do so. However, there is no evidence that the *Instructio* stimulated appreciable episcopal effort on behalf of the Catholic ecumenical cause. The time was not yet ripe for that. Nevertheless, the document did provide a measure of official approval to Catholics already engaged in the often suspect pursuit of unity, and it encouraged them, within tolerable limitations, to continue their labors.[30]

Later that year the course of Catholic-Protestant rapprochement was gravely threatened by two other statements issued in Rome.

On 12 August 1950 the encyclical *Humani generis* warned

against dangers Pius believed to have been created by attempts to adapt Catholic truth to the modern mind. Although Catholic ecumenism was not the pope's major target, it did fall among the subjects he treated. Pius cautioned Catholics whose "imprudent irenicism" leads them to attempt to reconcile opposing dogmatic positions. Some, he claimed, now seek to free Catholic dogma from its expression in a traditional philosophical idiom and to return to biblical and patristic modes of thought so that they may reach "a mutual assimilation of Catholic dogma with the tenets of the dissidents."[31] Against this practice Pius insisted that Catholics respect scholastic presentations of Catholic dogma, and he reiterated the continuing relevance of Thomistic philosophy.

During the early 1950s the restraining hand of Rome was to be extended to other innovating groups within the Roman Church (most of them, like the worker-priests, French).[32] A number of high-placed officials believed that Catholic radicals, like the Modernists earlier, had gone too far in their flirtation with the seductive liberal forces of the time. The faith itself could be compromised and ordinary Catholics confused by the innovators. Hence, they must be called back to the tested and stable ways of the past. This conservative stance spread widely throughout the Catholic Church during the later years of Pius' pontificate. Called "integralism" (like the reaction to modernism earlier), it was characterized by a French Catholic publication as a "horror of all novelty, of all innovation, of all modernity. . . . This scorn of the new is general, reaching to theology, to politics, to social life, to literature and to the arts."[33] Wherever that mood prevailed, no Catholic ecumenical endeavor that appeared novel could prosper.

Pope Pius XII and his advisers judged that it was not enough to warn against deviations; positive statements of Catholic teaching must also be provided. The major dogmatic pronouncement of Pius' pontificate was issued less than three months after *Humani generis*. On 1 November 1950 the apostolic constitution *Munificentissimus Deus* was promulgated, in which Pius infallibly declared that at her death, the Virgin Mary "was assumed body and soul into heavenly glory." The definition both climaxed a mounting wave of Marian devotion among the Catholic faithful and contributed to a further exaltation of Mary during the 1950s.

Roman officials had been warned of the negative response that the definition would likely provoke in Protestant circles, but that possibility had had no dissuasive effect upon Pius.[34]

The Marian declaration aroused vigorous objections from Protestants. No scriptural warrant, they claimed, could be found for the new dogma; and by elevating Mary (in the pope's first use of his alleged infallible teaching authority since its definition by the First Vatican Council) the Roman Church had gravely obscured the salvific significance of Jesus Christ. Nor could Protestants accept Pius' claim that should anyone deny or doubt the dogma, "let him know that he has fallen away completely from the divine and Catholic faith." The theological distance between Protestantism and Catholicism now seemed hopelessly vast.[35]

The publication of *Munificentissimus Deus* (together with other objectionable Roman pronouncements and acts in this period) brought a noticeable cooling among Protestants who earlier had evidenced interest in rapprochement with Catholics. In some communities Una Sancta circles and the Week of Prayer either collapsed or declined markedly in popularity.[36] Remonstrances by some Protestant bodies sharply asserted traditional Protestant objections to Catholic teaching and practice. In these years of ecumenical crisis, however, several prominent voices also were raised on both sides to encourage continuation of the quest for unity. Karl Rahner, a leading member of the Paderborn theological group, wrote that Catholics and Protestants must always openly declare their beliefs to one another, and that they must not shrink from dialogue when disagreement becomes pronounced. Catholics especially hope, he added, that the Marian definition will not deter Protestants from a continued pursuit of Catholic-Protestant unity.[37] Augustine Bea, the German Jesuit head of Rome's Pontifical Biblical Institute, argued that Protestants' reactions had the salutary effect of revealing the depth of their interest in Roman Catholic doctrinal commitments.[38] Pastor Marc Boegner maintained that the Marian definition and the Protestant response to it had enhanced the quality of the dialogue:

At least we know the truth about each other; Protestants no longer can have the illusion that the Roman Church will at-

tenuate her doctrinal intransigence to facilitate their return;
Catholics no longer can nourish the dream that the churches
of the Reformation will accept papal infallibility and the
Marian dogma. Our reciprocal loyalty is the only solid foundation of the common labor to which we know we are called
by a compelling demand of God.[39]

Because men such as Boegner, Bea, and Rahner had already
recognized the presence both of common theological ground and
major differences, they were not crushed by pointed reminders of
the differentia. And because these men pursued unity in response
to what they believed was "a compelling demand of God," they
were prepared to persist in their quest regardless of the difficulties.
Thus, while popular interest in Protestant-Catholic rapprochement
waned in the early 1950s, the persons whose interest had been
more profoundly rooted were not swayed from their course.[40]
    The papal and curial statements were welcomed by some
Catholics as bearing decisive direction for their ecumenical pursuits. Believing that Couturier, Congar, and their kind had strayed
into an "imprudent irenicism," the more conservative ecumenists
were encouraged to develop an alternative posture more in keeping
with the outlook of Pius XII and his predecessors. The preservationist motif dominated their position, which usually was developed without benefit of the progressive perspectives that had
emerged in recent Catholic scholarship. A major rallying point for
their work was the annual Octave of Prayer for Church Unity
founded earlier by Wattson (and re-named the Chair of Unity Octave in 1949). The Atonement Friars, who continued to direct the
Octave, found support in France from some Augustinians of the
Assumption and in Rome from the Unitas Association. The latter
group's president was Charles Boyer, a French Jesuit and dean of
the faculty of the prestigious Gregorian Pontifical University in
Rome. In 1946 Fr. Boyer founded and became editor of a quarterly journal, *Unitas*; within a few years it appeared regularly in Italian, English, and French editions. Through *Unitas* and his other
writings, Boyer became a principal spokesman of the more conservative Catholic ecumenists.
    In the 1940s and 1950s disagreement rarely surfaced publicly
between those who stressed the preservationist motif and those

who stressed the transformationist motif. Occasionally, however, the illusion of Catholic unanimity on ecumenism was broken. In 1954 Fr. George H. Tavard, a French Assumptionist scholar living in the United States, charged that "unionist integralism . . . is a very strange phenomenon since it is generous in its intentions and right in its ultimate goals, but incapable of serving the idea to which it is devoted." Tavard sharply criticized a book by Fr. Edward Francis Hanahoe, a leader of the Society of the Atonement, in which he had attempted to establish the principles of Catholic ecumenism upon documents issued by the Holy See. To employ that procedure, charged Tavard, is to misunderstand the roles both of the theologian and of the pope. The former's inquiries and reflections, though obviously respecting papal directives, range over the entire Christian tradition in search of light. His questions and constructive formulations necessarily will relate to issues not yet treated by the popes. Tavard also contended that Hanahoe showed too little respect for non-Catholic Christians and an inaccurate understanding of them.[41]

The Couturier-inspired Week of Prayer was the chief target for critics of the progressive Catholic ecumenists. Occasionally during Pius XII's pontificate it was publicly criticized.[42] In 1960 (when its popularity was unprecedented) the most severe attack yet made was launched by Fr. Boyer. He charged that although Couturier had believed that the locus of eventual unity would be the Roman Church, too often that fact was obscured by stress upon the gradual sanctification and convergence of all Christians, including Catholics, as the way to full unity. Moreover, the Week created the illusion that dogmas and other essentials of the Roman Church could be changed in order to facilitate union. That misconception, Boyer insisted, will be avoided only by firm, unambiguous statements of unchanging Catholic faith, whose acceptance must be proclaimed as the only way to Christian unity. He also disagreed with Couturier's claim that divided Christians properly can use the same prayer for unity. As long as Christians are divided, they will differ in their understandings and articulations of the unity for which they pray. The alternative proposed by Boyer was that Protestants and Catholics offer their different prayers for unity simultaneously.

The sympathy of most non-Catholic Christians aware of the

distinctions existing within the Catholic ecumenical spectrum was with the Couturier approach rather than the Wattson one. The prospect of growth by mutual sanctification toward a unity not yet fully perceived was congenial to the Protestant ecumenical outlook, as was the recognition that eventual unity will be built upon what the divided churches now preserve of their authentic inheritance from Christ. Protestants did, perhaps, tend to "deRomanize" Couturier, but in him and in those grouped with him they met spokesmen of the Roman Church with whom they could engage expectantly in dialogue and prayer. Such was not their response toward those who clustered around the other pole of the Catholic ecumenical problematic. Typically, Visser 't Hooft said of Hanahoe's volume that it "really . . . puts an end to any conversation between Roman Catholics and non-Roman Catholics."[44]

Boyer and his colleagues did little either to excite Protestant interest in Protestant-Catholic unity or to shape a fresh Catholic ecumenical perspective. Their commitment to the preservationist task could not be faulted by Christians eager to maintain the church's apostolic foundation, but their execution of that task through the instrumentality of an outdated conceptual framework tended to obscure the proper role of theological preservation and to make unduly competitive a relationship between positions and persons that could have been richly complementary. The conservative ecumenists did, however, enable large numbers of Catholics to discover that they must work and pray for Christian unity. As exemplars of Pius XII's approach to unity, they were especially adept at arousing interest in ecumenical issues among conservative Catholics in Rome and elsewhere who were suspicious, even scornful, of the more venturesome Catholic ecumenists.[45]

The Pace Quickens

The postwar rise of Catholic-Protestant rapprochement, though decelerated in 1950, was resumed by the mid-1950s. Later in the decade, after Angelo Roncalli became Pope John XXIII, the quest for Christian unity became a major, official priority for the Roman Church, and the promised land of reconciliation beckoned more appealingly than ever before.

German Catholics remained among those in the vanguard of

the Roman Church's ecumenical progress. The virility of the Una Sancta movement was especially evident in Berlin, where circles met regularly and sponsored occasional public gatherings throughout the divided city. In 1957, Julius Döpfner, one of the German bishops most sympathetic toward Una Sancta activity, became Archbishop of Berlin. The following year Lutheran and Catholic officials in Berlin created a joint committee to direct the Una Sancta program there, a step hailed by Una Sancta leaders as a model for other cities.

In 1953 the *Una Sancta Rundbriefe*, which helped link scattered Una Sancta circles throughout Germany, became the responsibility of Thomas Sartory, a member of the Benedictine community at Niederaltaich. Under Sartory's editorial direction the newsletter was transformed into a quarterly ecumenical journal and renamed *Una Sancta*. Sartory's work reflected the long-standing ecumenical interest of the Niederaltaich Benedictines (which had been stimulated by Pius XI's *Equidem verba* in 1925) and especially of their abbot, Emmanuel Heufelder. That interest also was demonstrated by establishment at the abbey in 1956 of a hostel which provided library, discussion, and living facilities for Catholics and Protestants who came in pursuit of increased mutual understanding. The Benedictine monks also continued manufacture of "unity candles," intended for use on Thursdays in conjunction with prayers for unity.[46]

In January 1957 the Johann-Adam Möhler Institute was inaugurated at Paderborn under the sponsorship of Archbishop Jaeger and the direction of Professor Eduard Stakemeier. The Institute fostered study of Protestant theology, assumed the editing of *Catholica* (established earlier by Robert Grosche), issued a small periodical bulletin, and published major scholarly monographs on ecumenical themes. As befitted an institute bearing Möhler's name, its program increasingly provided a substantial theological base for Catholic ecumenical initiatives.[47]

Cooperation between Protestants and Catholics in nontheological realms also characterized German Christianity in these years. Church buildings continued to be shared. In 1954 religious journalists began periodic discussions of their common vocational and ecumenical responsibilities. When need arose, each side supplied supplementary housing for the large crowds that gathered for the other's massive rallies, the Catholic Katholikentag and the Protestant Kirchentag.[48]

In France the Week of Prayer for Christian Unity remained the focal point of Catholic ecumenical enterprise. Following the death of Paul Couturier on 24 March 1953, Cardinal Gerlier of Lyons assigned direction of the Week first to Jean-Paul Vincent, then to Pierre Michalon, a priest of the Society of Saint-Sulpice. Under Michalon's direction (and with the support of the Christian Unity Association in Lyons) the Week was continued along lines charted by Couturier, emphasizing what Michalon called "spiritual ecumenism." Pamphlets were published regularly for use in conjunction with the Week. During January the religious and secular press featured articles on Christian unity, and Catholic ecumenical specialists traveled widely to address interested groups.[49] Numerous parishes throughout France observed the week. Never before had large numbers of Catholics encountered the transformationist motif in such an appealing form. Couturier's vision of unity through mutual renewal fit the emerging evangelical-ecumenical mood of Catholics as aptly as Wattson's had the mood that prevailed four decades earlier.[50]

From Michalon's office tracts and posters increasingly were sent throughout the world. In 1953 some 63,000 documents were requested and distributed. In 1956 the number had reached 220,000 and in 1957 430,000. In 1959 it jumped to more than 700,000; by 1961 it was 920,000.[51] The impact of the Week outside France grew markedly. The attention Michalon, Villain, and their associates gave to French and Belgian seminaries and missionary journals substantially furthered the global spread of Couturier's vision, for the worldwide deployment of Catholic missionaries from the two lands far exceeded that of other nations. By 1955 translations of the prayer pamphlets for the Week were made into English, Arabic, Malagasy, and Portuguese, and by 1960 into a dozen languages. Observance of the 1958 Week was reported to have occurred in more than forty lands and of the 1962 Week in more than fifty.[52] The Week of Prayer was quietly preparing Catholics around the world for the ecumenical vision eventually affirmed by Vatican II.

Couturier and later Michalon were in close touch with pro-
moters of the week of ecumenical prayer sponsored by the World
Council of Churches Faith and Order Commission, and the two
periods of prayer more and more reflected the convergent convictions of their sponsors. In 1960 Michalon and other Catholics participated in a World Council consultation that stimulated even
closer coordination among persons responsible for the two periods
of ecumenical prayer.[53]

The Catholic and Protestant teachers active in the Christian
Association of Professors (usually called "Amitié"—Friendship—
after the name of the Association's bulletin) helped spread mutual
understanding among French Christians. Begun in the late 1920s,
the organization by 1959 counted nearly 800 members and associates scattered in 230 French communities (with another two
dozen in the French-speaking regions of Belgium and Switzerland).
The group's purpose was to develop a common Christian understanding of vocational and philosophical issues arising within their
profession. Amitié's ecumenical stance had been decisively shaped
by Couturier, and often members initiated or helped arrange observances of the Week of Prayer.[54] Their influence upon successive
generations of students, though not subject to precise measurement, was considerable.

Significant ecumenical ferment also was stimulated by the
Dominican priests who operated the Istina Study Center in Paris.
During the early 1950s, the focus of their work shifted from the
Russian Orthodox Church to a wider range of churches and ecumenical issues. The name of their journal accordingly was changed
in 1954 from *Russie et chrétienté* to *Istina*. It and the Center's
smaller publication, *Vers l'unité chrétienne* (begun in 1948), regularly contained analyses of current ecumenical events and questions by the Center's leader, Christophe J. Dumont, a younger associate, M.J. LeGuillou, and other Catholic ecumenists. A second
Dominican institution for ecumenical study, the Saint Irenaeus
Center, was established in Lyons in 1953 and more directly addressed itself to Catholic rapprochement with Protestants than did
its sister organization in Paris. Its director was René Beaupère, a
former student of Paul Couturier and editor of a new Catholic
theological journal, *Lumière et vie*.

In 1959 fourteen Benedictine monasteries around the world were asked by their order to give close attention to ecumenism. In France the ancient monastery of Saint-Martin de Ligugé (near Poitiers) was chosen for this assignment, and a team of monks began attempting to awaken Catholic interest in rapprochement with Protestants in French communities where little ecumenical interest had yet been manifested.[55]

A new pattern of Protestant-Catholic encounter was begun by a group from Lyons in 1961. Seventy-four laymen from Protestant and Catholic parishes in France and Switzerland made a two-week Easter "pilgrimage" to the Holy Land. Guided by two Catholic priests (including Fr. Beaupère) and two Protestant pastors from the Lyons area, they visited biblical sites such as Jerusalem, Nazareth, and Bethlehem. The success of the first ecumenical pilgrimage encouraged its leaders to offer similar opportunities regularly.[56]

In France as elsewhere, the quest for Christian solidarity during the 1950s was furthered especially by theological dialogue and prayer. Patterns of joint secular action that had arisen during the war were rarely revived. Toward the end of the period, however, greater interest was shown in common action: Catholics and Protestants who had arrived at new theological agreement and personal trust believed that they should give expression to their common faith through shared ameliorative action for disadvantaged people. In France that turn was encouraged by a 1959 joint appeal made by Pastor Marc Boegner and Cardinal Feltin of Paris on behalf of the one million Algerians placed in refugee camps by the French government.[57] Protestants and Catholics in some communities were spurred to common action also by a proposal made by Professor Oscar Cullmann. The Protestant biblical scholar wrote that St. Paul's collection among Gentile churches for the Jerusalem church suggested a comparable affirmation of Christian solidarity by Protestants and Catholics: could they not manifest their solidarity by exchanging offerings for each other's poor? Occasionally Cullmann's proposal was accepted in amended form; rather than Protestants and Catholics giving to each other, a single Protestant-Catholic offering was given to needy persons without regard for their religious affiliation.[58]

Catholics in other lands followed their pace-setting brothers in Germany and France at varying distances. In Belgium the Monks of Union's ecumenical competence was acknowledged in 1959 by the request that they guide the efforts of the fourteen Benedictine monasteries chosen for ecumenical specialization.[59] Professor and Madame Lucien Morren became the first directors of the St. John House, an international student hostel established in Héverlée in 1956 to foster ecumenical awareness among lay and clerical students who attended the Catholic University of Louvain. During the 1959-60 academic year, the University established the Pope Adrian VI Chair for the study of non-Catholic churches and of Christian unity.[60]

Discussion increased sharply among Catholics and Protestants in the Netherlands during the late 1950s. Monsignor Jan G. M. Willebrands, president of the St. Willibrord Association, was asked by the Dutch hierarchy in 1958 to assume full-time supervision of expanding Catholic ecumenical activity. On the first Sunday of May 1959 Catholics and Protestants across the country shared intercessory prayers for peace. Prayers used the following January during the Chair of Unity Octave were amended to conform more closely to the language and spirit of the Week of Prayer for Christian Unity. In 1960 teams of Protestants and Catholics went from door-to-door in several cities selling Bibles. By 1962 twenty-five Protestant-Catholic Bible study groups were known to be meeting throughout the country.[61]

In England the degree of cooperation reached early in the war was not recaptured, but Catholics, Anglicans, and Free Churchmen in London continued to observe the Week of Prayer for Christian Unity. In 1961 the British Catholic hierarchy established an episcopal Commission for Fostering Unity among Christians and named Archbishop John Heenan of Liverpool its chairman.[62]

In January 1953 persons attending a public meeting in Vienna heard a Lutheran bishop and a Catholic bishop call for "religious peace." A step toward that peace was taken the following year by construction of a "double church" in Hochleiten, Austria; Protestants used one side of the building and Catholics the other.[63] Swiss Catholics were periodically reminded of their ecumenical responsibilities by François Charrière, bishop of the Geneva-Lausanne-

Fribourg diocese (in which the World Council of Churches head-quarters was located). In December 1956 Catholics joined other Swiss Christians in a cooperative approach to religious programming for television. In 1962 a new hymnal was published for Catholics in German-speaking Switzerland which included an appendix containing sixteen hymns used by the Evangelical Reformed Church of the area.[64]

Catholics outside Europe moved more slowly toward new relations with Protestants, but occasional acts of solidarity did occur in such diverse lands as India, Lebanon, Pakistan, New Zealand, Australia, and Malaya.[65] Heightened religious cooperation among Americans was portended in September 1957 when forty Protestant, Catholic, and Jewish clergymen in Little Rock, Arkansas jointly sought to promote the peaceful racial integration of that embittered city's public schools.[66] In May 1958 leading Protestant, Catholic, Jewish, and secular scholars participated in a five-day seminar on "Religion in a Free Society"; their papers were subsequently published and read widely. One contributor, the Jesuit theologian Gustave Weigel (1906-1964), became increasingly influential among American Catholics as an interpreter of ecumenism and among Protestants as a spokesman for Catholicism.[67] In the autumn of 1958 a small group of Protestant and Catholic graduate students and younger theological professors (most of them associated with Yale and Fordham Universities) began meeting periodically for private discussion of theological questions.[68] In December 1960, following several years of intensifying activity among Protestants and Catholics in the area, St. John's Benedictine Abbey in Collegeville, Minnesota hosted a three-day conversation among eight prominent Protestant and Catholic theologians.[69] The following September, forty-five Protestant ministers participated in a three-day retreat with Catholic priests in Kentucky. The first diocesan ecumenical commission in American Catholicism was established by Archbishop Lawrence Shehan of Baltimore in January 1962.[70] In the United States, as in most other lands, Catholics had come belatedly to the ecumenical journey, but by the eve of Vatican II a growing minority of them were eager voyagers.

The most dramatic changes in Catholic patterns occurred in

Latin lands where conflict between Protestants and Catholics often had been bitterest. In June 1959 a three-day study conference for Protestants and Catholics was planned at the Benedictine monastery of Montserrat in Spain. Even though the conference (to which Karl Barth had been invited) was cancelled by the Holy Office, a Baptist official testified to the presence in Spain of "an intangible, yet noticeable change of attitude on the part of many Catholics toward Evangelicals."[71] The following year a Spanish Catholic ecumenical bulletin, *Orientation y Informacion Ecumenica*, was inaugurated, but it was forced to cease publication after only two issues; its squashing too originated in Rome.[72] A Waldensian leader in Italy reported in 1961 that a "wind of change from Rome" had produced closer ties between Protestants and Catholics; later that year common Bible study developed in some Italian communities.[73] In 1960, 9,000 Colombian Protestants and Catholics attended a meeting in Cali at which Catholic and Protestant clergymen spoke. Similar instances of more cordial relations between Latin American Christians were reported in Chile, Brazil, Peru, and Argentina.[74]

The foregoing pages have provided only a sampling of the diverse Catholic ecumenical activities underway by the eve of Vatican II. The total number of Catholics involved in them cannot be known. The number was growing rapidly by 1962, but it constituted only a small minority of the Roman Church's membership. Significantly, this minority included persons in positions from which they could influence large numbers of other Catholics. Their assessments of their encounters with Protestants doubtless varied. The character of the breakthrough that many agreed had occurred was suggested by the 1958 report of an American Catholic lay journalist: "Somehow or other, what had been an acrimonious debate had been transformed into a Protestant-Catholic conversation. The differences between us were still real enough, and they would not be easily resolved, but on each side we were recognizing those who spoke with truly Christian accents. The miracle was that across centuries of misunderstanding and suspicion Christian spirit spoke to Christian spirit."[75]

As changed sociological patterns brought a greater intermingling of Protestants and Catholics, and as reports spread of new theological and spiritual accord, the number of marriages between young Catholics and Protestants rose sharply.[76] Such "mixed marriages" normally were discouraged by ecclesiastical leaders on both sides. Catholic canon law allowed Catholics to marry non-Catholics, but only under conditions often painful to Protestants (e.g., written agreement to rear the couple's children in the Catholic Church). Some officials conceded that Catholic-Protestant marriages bore salutary possibilities and local policies occasionally were altered within the limits allowed by canon law.

The shift that began to occur was typified by developments in Poitiers, France. In 1951 the diocesan synod ruled that in regions where Protestants predominated, mixed marriages could be performed in a Catholic church with use of the same rites normally reserved for the wedding of two Catholics (save for a nuptial mass). In 1957 the same practice was extended throughout the diocese. In 1960 priests were urged to give the marriage ceremony of such couples a spiritual dignity in which the non-Catholic was not humiliated, to provide continuing pastoral support as husband and wife faced the inevitable tensions rising in their marriage, and to try "to make them know in their married life both the tragedy and the blessed experience of the diverse Christian communities engaged in the ecumenical movement."[77] In some communities, moreover, Protestant pastor and Catholic priest began to consult each other about their counseling of the partners of a mixed marriage. And the conviction grew among some Catholic leaders sensitive to the anguish frequently created in mixed marriages that Catholic canonical regulations governing those marriages were "the salt in the wound of Christian disunity" and that they must be changed.[78]

Emerging Catholic ecumenical interest remained within a fundamentally coherent framework partly because of an organization created in 1952. Fr. Congar earlier had tried unsuccessfully to form an association of Catholic ecumenical specialists.[79] In September 1950 Fr. Boyer had assembled twenty-five Catholic ecumenists at Grottoferrata, Italy, but no permanent structure had emerged.[80] In 1951 Mgr. Willebrands and Fr. Thijssen traveled through Europe to canvass opinion on the desirability of a continuing organization for such persons. The interest they met prompted another meeting of Catholic ecumenical specialists in August 1952 at Fribourg, Switzerland. Here, with the strong support of Bishop Charrière, the "Catholic Conference for Ecumenical Questions" was born. Under the leadership of Willebrands and a small executive committee, the Conference met periodically at European sites to which it was invited by the local bishop.

Subjects considered at those sessions closely paralleled questions under discussion in the World Council of Churches, and in 1954 the Conference made its reflections on Christian hope, the theme of the Council's second Assembly, available to that body; thereafter its leaders were regularly in touch with the Council's Geneva staff.[81] Close communication also was maintained with the Holy Office. Appointment by Pope John of key Conference members to the Secretariat for Promoting Christian Unity gave the conciliar agency a nucleus of ecumenical specialists who over the previous decade had moved toward significant agreement regarding an ecumenical stance for Catholics. Through them the harvest of the quiet labors of past years would be brought directly to the Second Vatican Council.

Pope John XXIII (1881-1963)

When Angelo Roncalli was elected to succeed Pius XII on 28 October 1958, most Roman insiders expected a short and undistinguished pontificate from the relatively unknown seventy-seven-year-old Italian prelate. Most of his adult life had been spent in ecclesiastical service in Bulgaria, Turkey, and France. There a spontaneous affection for people had brought him into sympathetic contact with a wider spectrum of non-Catholic life than was normally known by high-ranking Roman officials.

The world quickly became aware of Pope John's winsome humanity. Numerous pastoral visits outside the Vatican—to churches, schools, prisons, and hospitals—revealed a man strikingly different from his predecessors. Leaders from other churches were among the prominent non-Catholic visitors warmly received in the Vatican by the pope. His December 1960 reception of the Archbishop of Canterbury was hailed as a major thawing of ecclesiastical relations. His ministry of love won him a degree of respect and admiration from non-Catholics never before accorded a pope.

For many Protestants John gave the papacy an evangelical character they had not believed possible. "In him," said American Presbyterian Robert McAfee Brown at John's death in 1963, "we have heard the voice of the Good Shepherd, solicitous for those outside as well as inside the sheepfold. Catholics have lost a pope; we have lost a friend and brother."[82]

Pope John's most momentous act was the convoking of the Second Vatican Council. Like Pope Leo XIII earlier, John believed that the Roman Church must break from inherited ways that hampered her ministry in the modern world. Such change, he knew, would not be generated or encouraged by the tradition-bound officials of the Roman Curia. Intelligent, loyal voices were being raised throughout the church on behalf of Catholic renewal. He concluded that bishops from around the world must be brought together to take stock of the church's plight, to listen to the spokesmen of "aggiornamento," and to plot a fresh course for the Church of Rome. On 25 January 1959 John set in motion the process that resulted in the opening of the Second Vatican Council nearly four years later.

From the outset Pope John associated the Council with the cause of Christian unity. His decision to convoke the Council was announced to surprised curial cardinals on the last day of the 1959 Chair of Unity Octave. After an initial period of uncertainty regarding the Council's ecumenical objective and methods, successive statements explained John's hope that the Council would bring such revivification to the Roman Church that other Christians would find their traditional objections removed and thus could claim her once again as their own. Their return, he said, would be a kind of "homecoming" prepared by brothers for brothers: "Please note that when we call you tenderly to the unity of the true Church, we are not inviting you to a strange home, but to your very own, the common home of our Father."[83]

Two major steps, both unprecedented, were taken to help the Council move Christians toward greater unity. On 5 June 1960 announcement was made of the creation of the Secretariat for Promoting Christian Unity. Its immediate purpose was to help prepare the Council's deliberations upon ecumenical matters; its broader purpose and eventual wide-ranging labors were hinted at in John's charge that it "manifest in a special way our love and good will towards those who bear the name of Christ, yet who are separated from this Apostolic See."[84] The person John named president of the Secretariat was Cardinal Augustine Bea (1881-1968), former confessor to Pius XII, head of the Pontifical Institute for Biblical Study, and key liaison person between ecumenical leaders and Vatican officials.[85] Chosen to head the Secretariat's executive staff was the Dutch ecumenist, Jan Willebrands. Members and consultants of the Secretariat included Catholics experienced in ecumenical relations such as Bishops Jaeger and Charrière, and Fathers Dumont, Baum, Hamer, Thils, Weigel, Tavard, and Boyer. With unusually able leadership and the pope's firm backing, the Secretariat was destined for an unexpectedly active role.

The second critical step taken by Pope John to ensure the Council's ecumenical orientation occurred in the summer of 1962. After discreet private inquiries had assessed the likely responses, twelve non-Catholic churches and ecclesiastical associations were invited to appoint "delegated observers" to the Council. The "Rules and Regulations regarding Delegated Observers" stated blandly that they had been invited in order that they "may be better informed on the work of the Second Vatican Council." They could have neither voice nor vote in official sessions, but they could attend plenary assemblies in St. Peter's Basilica, receive all schemata, and discuss conciliar proceedings regularly with the Secretariat for Promoting Christian Unity.[86] Soon after the first session began, however, the delegated observers were encouraged to assume a more creative role than that originally envisaged for them.

In the years between the Council's announcement and commencement, its impact upon the imagination of hopeful Catholics mounted. The accelerated pace of Catholic ecumenical initiative after 1958 was directly stimulated by Pope John's ecumenical intentions for the Council. Ecumenism began to be fashionable, and some became euphoric in their expectation of imminent union. Most Catholic ecumenical leaders recognized, however, that the demands placed upon Catholics by the quest for unity were severe, for the pope (like Mersch, Congar, Couturier, and other pioneers) had tied it directly to the quest for renewal. It would be no easy matter for Catholics to make the Roman Church sufficiently habitable for other Christians to embrace it as "the common home of our Father." Change of accustomed ways was required, and that process, rarely comfortable for human beings inside or outside the churches, had been shown to have powerful opponents in the Roman Church.

Numerous voices began to elaborate what they regarded as implications of the new direction in which Pope John had turned his church. None expounded the theme of unity through mutual renewal with greater impact than Hans Küng, dean of the Tübingen Catholic theological faculty. In a widely read book, *Konzil und Widervereinigung* (first published in 1960 and translated the following year as *The Council, Reform and Reunion*), Küng gave incisive expression to the ecumenical bearings of conclusions reached in recent scholarship. The Catholic Church, he claimed, is too encrusted with the vestigial forms of earlier ages to allow her to be fully effective today. Her thought, organizational structure, discipline, liturgy, and piety must be reformed and renewed according to the gospel. What Christ has given her is irreformable but not its historical expressions. Until such changes are made, the Roman Church will not have adequately fulfilled her ecumenical responsibility. Especially must Catholics take to heart the impediments to reunion caused by the papacy. The young theologian acknowledged that regrettably some popes have seemed to bear little resemblance to the good shepherd portrayed in the Gospels, and he urged that as Catholics seek to make the papacy's pastoral, servant character more manifest, Protestants must give closer attention to the New Testament account of the Petrine office and to that office's indispensability for the total community of Christians.

Küng's picture of eventual union was sketchy. His accent (as had been the case among most Catholic ecumenists since the late 1920s) fell upon the next steps necessary on both sides for the sake of unity. Courageous voices from the past echoed in his charge to divided Christians:

If Catholics carry out Catholic reform and Protestants carry out Protestant reform, both according to . . . [the] Gospel image, then, because the Gospel of Christ is but one, reunion need not remain a utopian dream. Reunion will then be neither a Protestant "return" nor a Catholic "capitulation," but a brotherly approach from both sides, with neither consciously calculating, on the other's behalf, which of them has more steps to take; an approach penetrated through and through with love, and wholly determined by truth.[87]

Prophetic words that ring clearly and forcefully on mountaintops often fade into apparent irrelevance by the time they reach busy arenas of decision-making in valleys below. But by 1962 Küng did not stand alone, nor could he and other advocates of unity through mutual renewal be kept on academic niches or in monastic retreats safely distant from centers of power and decision. In Pope John they had a friend, in growing numbers of Catholics an eager audience. And in the Second Vatican Council they would have a unique opportunity for their positions to be heard, evaluated, and—to the degree that they were persuasive— assimilated into the life of the Roman Catholic Church.

* * *

Catholics and non-Catholics alike have credited Pope John with a major role in thrusting his church into the ecumenical era. Persons aware of the courageous, unheralded labors of such precursors as Couturier and Congar may be tempted to regard as excessive the acclaim given John for his ecumenical feat. John, they well may argue, only gave the pioneers a platform; a man of limited theological interest and acumen, he merely endorsed ideas they had struggled successfully to mould. Up to a point that contention is true. Nevertheless, it must be acknowledged that Pope John belongs among the prominent figures of ecumenical history. For it was John who decisively brought the issue of the Roman Church's unitive responsibility from the periphery of her concern to its center. By placing that issue inescapably before the Council, and by publicly affirming much of the outlook of the progressive ecumenists, John overrode the nearly unanimous tradition of post-Tridentine Catholicism, the policy of his revered predecessor, and the judgment of most of his curial associates. Enormous authority rested in his hands, and his innovative action was fully consonant with the privilege the Roman Church accorded him. But rarely have even popes so completely asserted their independence of the people and traditions that have surrounded them. Pope John refused to be a prisoner of his church's sectarian history. Instead he associated himself and sought to associate the entire Roman Catholic Church with the vision and hopes of her ecumenical pioneers. And once John had taken that course, he would allow neither alarmed conservatives nor failing health to deter him from it.

John doubtless knew that risks were involved in whatever he might do as pope, and he concluded that it was a less acceptable risk to maintain his church's accustomed fortress mentality than it was to build bridges toward the non-Catholic world. In taking the latter course John exemplified a rare style of papal leadership. Like other popes, he knew that treasures from the past must be guarded. But, unlike most others, he also knew that a vicar of Christ must be committed to helping his flock find pathways among outsiders, for there God beckons them and prepares new treasures for them. "The whole world is my family," John wrote in his diary in 1959, and with the "strength of daring simplicity" he believed God had given him, he acted to implement that conviction.[88]

NOTES

1. Kinder, "The New Encounter in Germany," p. 36; *ICNIS*, No. 6, 1945; *EPS*, No. 1, 1951; Swidler, *Ecumenical Vanguard*, 167-9; Geoffrey Murray, "Joint Service as an Instrument of Cooperation," in Fey, ed., *Ecumenical Advance*, p. 206.

2. *ICNIS*, No. 12, 1947; *EPS*, No. 48, 1948; Swidler, *Ecumenical Vanguard*, pp. 172-3.

3. Ibid., pp. 173-90.

4. Among the Protestant members (mostly Lutheran) were Edmund Schlink, Hans von Campenhausen, and Ernst Kinder; Catholic members included Josef Lortz, Hermann Volk, Karl Rahner, and Michael Schmaus. Ibid., pp. 190-92, 199-200; Grosche, "La Situation oecuménique en Allemagne," pp. 14-5; Schlink, "A Report of an Ecumenical Group of Protestant and Catholic Theologians," *Dialog* 2 (1963): 320-28. The original German version of Professor Schlink's report included a bibliogra-

phy of papers presented to the group: *Kerygma und Dogma* 4 (1962): 221-35 Some of the papers have been published in Schlink and Volk, eds., *Pro Veritate, en theologischer Dialog* (Münster-Kassel, 1963).

5. Swidler, *Ecumenical Vanguard*, p. 187. At Meissinger's death in 1950 the Institute collapsed.

6. *One and Holy*, trans. Cecily Hastings (New York: Sheed and Ward, 1951), pp. 105, 111, 127.

7. Thomas Sartory, "L'esprit de l'oecuménisme en Allemagne," *Istina* 7 (1960): 17-8; Swidler, *Ecumenical Vanguard*, pp. 269-70; René Beaupère, "Notes sur le protestantisme français," *Lumière et vie* 7 (1958): 44-54; François Biot, "Le protestantisme allemand," Ibid., 55-72.

8. Villain, *Couturier*, pp. 86-93; Curtis, *Couturier*, pp. 123-30.

9. Curtis, *Couturier*, pp. 100-101, 351, 353-4.

10. Villain, *Couturier*, pp. 73-6. An alternative set of prayer intentions included prayers for the sanctification of Jews and all non-Christians, making the universality of Couturier's ecumenical vision even more explicit. The convergence of his thought with that of non-Roman ecumenical leaders is suggested by two statements issuing from the 1948 World Council of Churches Assembly: "Our first and deepest need is not new organization, but the renewal, or rather the rebirth, of the actual churches." "We pray for the churches' renewal as we pray for their unity. As Christ purifies us by His Spirit we shall find that we are drawn together and that there is no gain in unity unless it is unity in truth and holiness."

11. *ICNIS*, No. 41, 1947. Among the Catholic participants were Frs. Martelet, de Baciocchi, and Villain; among the Protestants were Pastors Thurian, Roux, and Bosc (and occasionally executives from the nearby Geneva office of the World Council of Churches). A full report of the Dombes group's progress is published in Patrick C. Rodger, ed., *Ecumenical Dialogue in Europe*, Ecumenical Studies in History (Richmond: John Knox Press, 1966). Like comparable theological discussion circles at Paderborn and Chevetogne, the Dombes group continues to meet.

12. Curtis, *Couturier*, p. 236; Villain, *Unity*, pp. 278-85.

13. E.g., Charles Moeller, "Bible et l'oecuménisme," 23 (1950): 164-88, and "Tradition et l'oecuménisme," 25 (1952): 337-70; see also C. Moeller and G. Philips, *The Theology of Grace and the Oecumenical Movement* (London: A. R. Mowbray and Co., 1961). Other prominent Catholic scholars who participated in this group were Congar, Jérôme Hamer, Gustave Thils, and Jan Willebrands. See O. Rousseau, "Les journées d'études oecuméniques de Chevetogne (1942-1967)," in L. Cerfaux et al., *Au Service de la Parole de Dieu* (Gembloux: Editions J. Duculot, 1968), pp. 451-86.

14. Interview with Canon Roger Aubert, December 1960, and Professor and Madame Morren, April 1969.

15. Leo G. M. Alting von Geusau, "Pays-Bas," in *Situation oecuménique dans le monde*, pp. 55-84; Jan Grootaers, "Jan Cardinal Willebrands," *One in Christ* 6 (1970): 24.

16. *ICNIS*, Nos. 13-14, 1947; "From the Editors," *The Third Hour* IX (1970): 5; *ICNIS*, No. 23, 1947; *ICNIS*, No. 2, 1947; *ICNIS*, No. 4, 1947; *EPS*, No. 6, 1948; Winslow, "An Oecumenical Study: Catholic, Dissident, Oriental, Anglican," *Unitas* 3 (1951): 3-8; *ICNIS*, No. 40, 1945; *EPS*, No. 5, 1948; *EPS*, No. 6, 1948.

17. Old antagonisms also were revived in Poland (*ICNIS*, No. 7, 1946), Mexico (*ICNIS*, No. 32, 1946), and Brazil (*ICNIS*, No. 8, 1947). In the 1950s Colombia became the scene of a major persecution of Protestants, which was intimately entangled with that nation's economic and civil strife. See *EPS* No. 24, 1956; A. F. Carillo de Albornoz, *Religious Liberty* (Geneva: World Council of Churches, 1964); E. K. Culhane, "Colombia and U.S. 'Missionaries,' " *America* 98 (1957): 656-9.

18. *ICNIS*, No. 42, 1947. A 1950 catechism on Protestantism for Spanish children asked, "How can foreign propagators of Protestantism be recognized?" The answer: "As for the English, who are like birds of prey who swoop down everywhere to seize their victims, they appear at first sight to be devout and religious . . . and always carry their Bibles or prayer-books under their arms." Members of the Reformed tradition were described in less complimentary fashion: "They are generally ignorant fanatics, given over to hating Catholics. They do not know what they believe and what they do not believe. They only know how to hate Catholicism." Jacques Delpech, *The Oppression of Protestants in Spain* (Boston: The Beacon Press, 1955), p. 41.

19. American Protestant anxiety was evidenced by the 1947 creation of Protestants and Other Americans United for the Separation of Church and State, and by Paul Blanshard's volumes: *American Freedom and Catholic Power* (Boston: Beacon Press, 1949) and *Communism, Democracy and Catholic Power* (Boston: Beacon Press, 1951).

20. *ICNIS*, No. 13, 1946.

21. The Latin text of the *Monitum* is in *AAS* 40 (1948): 257; the English text is in G. K. A. Bell, ed., *Documents on Christian Unity*, Fourth Series, 1948-57 (London: Oxford University Press, 1958), pp. 16-17. Reactions are indicated in "The Roman Catholic Church," *Ecumenical Review* (1948): 197-201; *EPS*, Nos. 24/25, 1948; Swidler, *Ecumenical Vanguard*, pp. 206-12; Max Thurian, "L'église romaine et l'oecuménisme," in J. Cadier et al, *Unité chrétienne*, pp. 183-210; Villain, *Couturier*, pp. 242-3.

22. Villain, *Couturier*, pp. 243-4.

23. *AAS* 42: 142; the English text is cited from Bell, ed., *Documents*, p. 22. The *Instructio* was first published in the March 1 issue of *Osservatore Romano*; it was dated 20 December 1949, and presumably had been sent at that time to Catholic bishops.

24. Bell, ed., *Documents*, p. 24. This statement recalls positions taken by Mersch, Adam, and Congar before World War II. Even though their thought is here appropriated as part of a restrictive disciplinary

ruling, progress in developing an official Roman Catholic ecumenical position is marked by the fact that it *is* appropriated.

25. Swidler, *Ecumenical Vanguard*, pp. 219-21; Tomkins, "Catholic Church," p. 692; "De Motione Ecumenica," *Ecumenical Review* 2 (1949-50): 296-8.

26. Swidler, *Ecumenical Vanguard*, pp. 221-2.

27. Maurice Bevenot, "Communicatio in sacris," in John C. Heenan, ed., *Christian Unity: A Catholic View* (London: Sheed and Ward, 1962), pp. 114-25.

28. Boyer, *One Shepherd*, trans. Angeline Bouchard (New York: P. J. Kenedy and Sons, 1952), p. 63; Boyer's judgment was seconded by English Jesuit Bernard Leeming, *The Churches and the Church* (London: Darton, Longman and Todd, 1960), p. 264. Cf. Francis J. Connell, "An Important Roman Instruction," *American Ecclesiastical Review* 112 (1950): 321-30.

29. Cadier et al., *Unité chrétienne*, p. 300. These words appear in an introduction to the *Instructio* and, though unsigned, were likely penned by Couturier, the editor of the volume; see Curtis, *Couturier*, pp. 274-5.

30. Thomas Sartory, a German Benedictine ecumenist, wrote of the *Instructio* in 1955: "It has relieved Catholic oecumenical theologians from the pressure of uncertainty from which their work had frequently suffered. They now know that their labours are safe and they are encouraged to seek for a mutual understanding on an unequivocal basis." *The Oecumenical Movement*, p. 96. Cf. Villain, *Couturier*, pp. 245-6, and Tavard, *Two Centuries of Ecumenism*, pp. 230-1.

31. *Humani Generis: Encyclical Letter of Pope Pius XII* (New York: Paulist Press, 1955), p. 6; *AAS* 42: 561-78.

32. James M. Connolly, *The Voices of France* (New York: Macmillan, 1961), pp. 173-202; Dansette, *Destin*, pp. 261-305.

33. This statement was made by the Centre d'information Catholique, and cited by G. Mury, *Essor ou declin du catholicisme français* (Paris, 1960), p. 317. See also Congar, *Vraie et fausse réforme dans l'église*, pp. 605-22; and W. A. Purdy, *The Church on the Move* (New York: John Day & Co., 1965), pp. 276-7, 283-4.

34. *The Dogma of the Assumption* (New York: Paulist Press, 1951), p. 22; *AAS* 43: 753-771. Prior discussion for and against the definition is summarized in Swidler, *Ecumenical Vanguard*, pp. 224-5; Villain, *Couturier*, 248-9; "The New Dogma from a Protestant Standpoint," *Ecumenical Review* 3 (1950-51): 159-63; "The Assumption and Unity," *America* 83 (1950): 664; Leon Gauthier, "The Dogma of the Assumption and Mariology," *Ecumenical Review* 4 (1951-2): 91-5.

35. "Répercussions du dogme de l'Assomption hors de l'Eglise catholique," *La documentation catholique* 48 (1951): cols. 235-50; Giovanni Miegge, "La définition du dogme de l'assomption et ses répercussions oecuméniques," *La revue réformée* 12 (1961): 1-18; Miegge, *The Virgin*

Mary: The Roman Catholic Marian Doctrine, trans. Waldo Smith (Philadelphia: Westminster, 1955); Von Loewenich, *Modern Catholicism*, pp. 188-239.

36. Swidler, *Ecumenical Vanguard*, pp. 231-2; M. J. Congar, *Le Christ, Marie et l'église* (Paris: Desclée de Brouwer, 1955), pp. 9-10; A. J. Maydieu, "Chrétiens en quête de l'unité: la route barrée," *La vie intellectuelle* (1953), pp. 8-9.

37. Rahner, "Das 'neue' Dogma," *Wort und Wahrheit* 5 (1950): 819-20.

38. Augustine Bea, "La definizione dell'Assunta e i Protestanti," *Echi e Commenti della Proclamazione del Domma della Assunzione*, Studia Mariana 8 (1954): 75-92; cited in George H. Williams, "Introduction," in Samuel H. Miller and G. Ernest Wright, eds., *Ecumenical Dialogue at Harvard: The Roman Catholic-Protestant Colloquium* (Cambridge: Belknap Press of Harvard University Press, 1964), p. 20.

39. *La documentation catholique* 48 (1951): col. 238. Comparable responses were made by some German Protestant leaders; see Swidler, *Ecumenical Vanguard*, pp. 227-9.

40. Significantly, the Chevetogne, Dombes, and Paderborn theological groups met regularly during the "crisis" period. Also, a smaller group of European Catholic and Anglican theologians actually began a series of private meetings in 1950; six sessions were held between then and 1962. Chadwick, "The Church of England," pp. 94-100.

41. *A la rencontre du Protestantisme*, "Le poids du jour" (Paris: Le Centurion, 1954), p. 80. Cf. the somewhat milder language of Fr. Tavard's English translation of his book: *The Catholic Approach to Protestantism*, p. 94. He also wrote that "to underestimate non-Catholic Christians in an attempt to make our task easier is a kind of apologetical duplicity that runs afoul of the truth. It is not compatible with a Catholic ecumenism or, simply, with mere honesty." Ibid., p. 99. The book criticized was Hanahoe, *Catholic Ecumenism: The Reunion of Christendom in Contemporary Papal Pronouncements*, Studies in Sacred Theology, No. 76 (Washington: Catholic University of America Press, 1953). Hanahoe was a student of Joseph C. Fenton, an influential conservative theologian and editor of the *American Ecclesiastical Review*.

42. E.g., Boyer, "Fr. Paul Wattson's Concept of the Unity Octave," *Unitas* 8 (1956): 199-202; Gustave Weigel, "American Catholicism and Ecumenism," *Lutheran World* 5 (1958): 36, 331-2.

43. Boyer's case was originally argued at a 1960 conference of Catholic ecumenists sponsored by the Atonement friars; it then was published as "Current Trends in Catholic Ecumenism," *Unitas* 13 (1961): 81-91; see also Boyer, "The Intentions for the Unity Octave of Prayer," *Unitas* 12 (1960): 81-92.

44. "Notes on Roman Catholic Writings Concerning Ecumenism," *Ecumenical Review* 8 (1955-56): 193.

45. Fr. Boyer's prestige and influence were vividly demonstrated in

Rome in 1955. Six cardinals were among a distinguished international group participating in a program which marked the tenth anniversary of the founding of the Unitas Association. Their program included an address by Fr. Ciappi, the "Master of the Sacred Palace," and, on the final day, a personal papal blessing for members of the Association. Leeming, *Churches*, pp. 263-4.

46. Swidler, *Ecumenical Vanguard*, pp. 233-64; Sartory, "L'esprit," pp. 27-9; Avery Dulles, "Protestants and Catholics in Germany," *America* 100 (1959): 493-5; Emmanuel Maria Heufelder, "The Council and Reunion," in Heufelder, ed., *In the Hope of His Coming*, trans. Otto M. Knab (Notre Dame: Fides Publishers, 1964), pp. 241-61.

47. Swidler, *Ecumenical Vanguard*, p. 240; *EPS*, No. 7, 1957; Albert Brandenburg, "Roman Catholic Institute for Confessional and Diaspora Research," *Lutheran World* 5 (1957-8): 73-4.

48. *EPS*, No. 41, 1954; Swidler, *Ecumenical Vanguard*, pp. 266-7; Antoine Wenger, "Catholic-Protestant Tensions in Germany," *Catholic World* 195 (1962): 281-8; *EPS*, No. 31, 1953; *EPS*, No. 42, 1957; Wolfgang Haendly, "Catholiques et protestants dans l'Allemagne centrale," *Istina* 7 (1960): 37-42.

49. *Un dans le Christ* (Paris: Centre de Pastorale Liturgique and Istina, 1954); Aubert, *Unité: la semaine de prière pour l'unité chrétienne*, rev. ed. (Brussels: Editions Pro Apostolis, 1959); Michalon, *Oecuménisme spirituel*, Pages Documentaires, No. 5 (Lyons, 1960); Minus, "Catholic Reconsideration," pp. 242-3.

50. In February and March 1962 the author conducted a survey among Catholics in French-speaking Europe in an attempt to determine local ecumenical practices and attitudes. With the able and indispensable assistance of Fr. François Houtart, Director of the Centre de Recherches Socio-Religieuses, a questionnaire was sent to a random selection of 1000 priests and lay people in Belgium, France, and Switzerland; of these, 356 were returned. One of the twelve questions inquired about observance of the Week of Prayer. The answers to that question reported the practice of 210 parishes; 90% of that number indicated that they did observe the Week (presumably in January 1962). Another question asked respondents to indicate which of two statements appearing on the questionnaire better described their understanding of the "way toward the full unity of Protestants and Catholics." One alternative plainly reflected the spirit of Fr. Wattson's earlier Octave, the other that of Couturier (a third alternative allowed the respondent to indicate that he thought that another statement would have better described that "way"). Approximately 23% chose the first alternative; 70% the second; and 7% the third. See Minus, "Catholic Reconsideration," pp. 405-10. As in my dissertation, so now I gratefully acknowledge Canon Houtart's assistance.

51. These figures are based upon reports shown the author by Fr. Michalon, February 1961.

52. *EPS*, No. 6, 1955; *EPS*, No. 46, 1960; *EPS*, No. 45, 1958;

194   THE CATHOLIC REDISCOVERY OF PROTESTANTISM

"Unité Chrétienne," *Ecumenical Notes* 2 (1963): 11.
53. Curtis, *Couturier*, pp. 278-80; *EPS*, No. 10, 1960; Vischer, "The Ecumenical Movement," in Fey, *Ecumenical Advance*, p. 322.
54. Curtis, *Couturier*, pp. 126-7; *Irénikon* 30 (1957): 239-41; *L'amitié* (April 1959), 39-43; Etienne Fouilloux, "Genèse et premières années d'un groupement oecuménique français 'l'amitié,' " *Revue d'histoire de l'Eglise de France* (1967), pp. 269-88.
55. Minus, "Catholic Reconsideration," pp. 273-5, 391-3.
56. René Beaupère, "Ecumenical Pilgrimages to the Lands of the Bible," *Eastern Churches Quarterly* 14 (1961-62): 425; Beaupère, ed., *Protestants et catholiques en marche: Les pèlerinages oecuméniques au Pays de la Bible* (Paris: Cerf, 1967).
57. *EPS*, No. 22, 1959; Minus, "Catholic Reconsideration," pp. 283-4.
58. *EPS*, No. 4, 1957; *EPS*, No. 45, 1958; Swidler, *Ecumenical Vanguard*, p. 265. The Cullmann proposal (originally made in 1957) was translated into English as *Message to Catholics and Protestants*, trans. Joseph A. Burgess (Grand Rapids: Eerdmans, 1959).
59. "L'ordre bénédictin et l'unité chrétienne," *Irénikon* 32 (1959): 488. Two smaller Benedictine institutions in Belgium, the monastery of Christ-Roi de Gelrode (near Louvain) and the Vita et Pax center at Schotenhof (near Antwerp), also concerned themselves actively with ecumenism.
60. J. Coppens et al., *Union et désunion des chrétiens*, p. 9; *EPS*, No. 31, 1959; Minus, "Catholic Reconsideration," p. 394. The St. Chrysostem Center was established in Brussels in 1958 to develop ecumenical interest in the Belgian capital.
61. *EPS*, No. 33, 1958; *EPS*, No. 17, 1959; *EPS*, No. 43, 1959; *EPS*, No. 3, 1960; Walter Abbott, "Bible, Laity, Unity," *America* 106 (1962): 560; *EPS*, No. 6, 1962; *EPS*, No. 4, 1961; *EPS*, No. 4, 1962.
62. Michael de la Bedoyere, "From My Window in Fleet Street," *Catholic World* 170 (1950): 303-6; *EPS*, No. 5, 1953; *EPS*, No. 4, 1954; *EPS*, No. 4, 1958; *EPS*, No. 36, 1957; *EPS*, No. 18, 1958; *EPS*, No. 42, 1960; Heenan, "Catholics and the Dialogue," *Clergy Review* 47 (1962): 1-5.
63. *EPS*, No. 5, 1953; *EPS*, No. 44, 1954; *EPS*, No. 26, 1956.
64. *Unitas* 11 (1959): 49; *EPS*, No. 26, 1960; Ward, *Documents*, pp. 90-91; *EPS*, No. 49, 1956; *EPS*, No. 15, 1962.
65. *EPS*, No. 14, 1952; *EPS*, No. 33, 1953; *EPS*, No. 10, 1952; *EPS*, No. 44, 1953; *EPS*, No. 2, 1960; *EPS*, No. 46, 1953; *EPS*, No. 44, 1960.
66. *EPS*, No. 37, 1957. Instances of earlier cooperative action in the United States are reported in *EPS*, No. 43, 1952; *EPS*, No. 42, 1953; *EPS*, No. 17, 1955; *EPS*, No. 4, 1956; and Kane, *Catholic-Protestant Conflict*, pp. 207-13.
67. John Cogley, ed., *Religion in America*. See James O'Gara, "Catholics and the Dialogue," *Commonweal* 68 (1958): 228. Several

works by Fr. Weigel are mentioned elsewhere in this book; another sign of his impact in the United States was a collection of essays, *Faith and Understanding in America* (New York: Macmillan Paperbacks Edition, 1962).

68. The author was the Protestant coordinator of the group, which met five times over a two-year period.

69. Abbott, "Bible, Laity, Unity," p. 560; E. E. Malone, "An American Ecumenical Colloquy," *American Benedictine Review* 12 (1960): 1-12. Papers presented at that meeting subsequently were published as *Christians in Conversation* (Westminster, Maryland: Newman Press, 1962). A similar discussion was held at Notre Dame University in 1961, and plans were made for its annual renewal; some of the papers read at the Notre Dame Colloquia were published in K. E. Skydsgaard, Barnabas Ahern et al., *The Church as the Body of Christ*, The Cardinal O'Hara Series, vol. 1 (Notre Dame: University of Notre Dame Press, 1963).

70. *EPS*, No. 35, 1961; *America* 107 (1962): 432; Ward, *Documents*, pp. 120-21; *America* 106 (1962): 493-4.

71. *EPS*, No. 25, 1959; *EPS*, No. 22, 1959.

72. *EPS*, No. 25, 1960; *Irénikon* 35 (1962): 246.

73. *EPS*, No. 14, 1961; *EPS*, No. 33, 1961; *EPS*, No. 50, 1961.

74. *EPS*, No. 48, 1960; *EPS*, No. 33, 1961; *EPS*, No. 1, 1962; *EPS*, No. 29, 1962.

75. O'Gara, "Catholics and the Dialogue," p. 288.

76. For example, in Germany in 1910, 14% of the marriages performed were between Catholics and Protestants; by 1957 25% of them were. Paul Zieger, "What the Statistics Say About Mixed Marriages," *Lutheran World* 5 (1958-59): 393-4. See also *EPS*, No. 3, 1958; and Beaupère, "La 'politique extérieure' de l'Eglise Réformée de France vis-à-vis du Catholicisme," *Istina* 2 (1955): 463.

77. "Notre attitude devant le renouveau oecuménique," Supplement to *La semaine religieuse* (27 November 1960), p. 9.

78. Minus, "Catholic Reconsideration," pp. 290-91; *EPS*, No. 36, 1962; Küng, *Council*, p. 175.

79. Congar, *Dialogue Between Christians*, pp. 27-8.

80. *Unitas* 2 (1950): 303.

81. C. J. Dumont, "La Conférence Catholique Internationale pour les questions oecuméniques," *Vers l'unité chrétienne* 14 (1961): 18-20; Congar, *Dialogue Between Christians*, p. 41; Minus, "Catholic Reconsiderations," pp. 395-6; Grootaers, "Willebrands," pp. 24-5.

82. Ward, *Documents*, p. 20. The literature on Pope John continues to grow. The two volumes perhaps providing the best overall view are Meriol Trevor, *Pope John* (Garden City: Doubleday, 1967) and E. E. Y. Hales, *Pope John and His Revolution* (Garden City: Doubleday Image Books, 1966). The exact course of the development of Roncalli's ecumenical perspective has not, to my knowledge, been closely studied. Among the key influences upon him were his years in Eastern Europe which brought

close ties with Orthodox Christians; a long-standing friendship with Lambert Beauduin; and close contact with French Catholic ferment when he served as Apostolic Nuncio in Paris following World War II.

83. *Ad Petri cathedram* (29 June 1959), *AAS* 51 (1959): 515. Cited in Skydsgaard, "The Coming Council," in Skydsgaard, ed., *Council*, p. 115 (where one finds many pertinent texts collected and analyzed).

84. *AAS* 52 (1960): 436. Cited in Bea, *Ecumenism in Focus* (London: Geoffrey Chapman, 1969), p. 29.

85. George H. Williams, "Introduction," in Miller and Wright, eds. *Ecumenical Dialogue*, pp. 3-24. After the Council, Bea wrote that in 1960 he had received a request "from Germany" that Pope John create a "Commission for the Union of Christians." The proposal was transmitted by Bea to the pope on 11 March 1960, and the two men discussed it on 13 March. See Bea, *Ecumenism in Focus*, p. 29.

86. Documents indicating the original conception of the role of delegated observers are reproduced in *Lutheran World* 9 (1962): 330-34. The non-Catholic bodies represented at the beginning of the Council were the Anglican Communion, World Presbyterian Alliance, Evangelical Church in Germany, World Convention of the Churches of Christ (Disciples), Friends' World Committee for Consultation (Quaker), International Congregational Council, World Methodist Council, World Council of Churches, Old Catholic Church (Utrecht), Coptic Church of Egypt, Syrian Orthodox Church, and Lutheran World Federation.

87. Küng, *The Council, Reform and Reunion*, p. 100.

88. Pope John XXIII, *Journal of a Soul*, trans. Dorothy White (New York: McGraw-Hill Book Co., 1965), p. 299.

VIII
Conceptual Reformulation

Catholic ecumenical activities in the postwar years were supported by a prodigious intellectual effort. Feeding the scholars' conceptual labor was a growing conviction that the fresh foundations and new directions established in the late 1930s, however advanced for Catholics then, must be rethought and reformulated in light of what was being learned from the surging movements for Catholic renewal and the accelerating pace of ecumenical experience. The concepts of an earlier day did not adequately express present perceptions or serve present opportunities.

Persons aware of the necessity of updating theological perspectives undertook four major tasks: determining the status of the individual Protestant and his church; reassessing the Reformation; clarifying the Catholic vision of unity; and restating traditionally controverted doctrines. By the time of the Second Vatican Council they had produced conceptual tools with which the fathers of the Council could, if they wished, effect a major renovation of the official Catholic stance toward Protestantism.

The Protestant and His Church

Congar had proposed in *Chrétiens désunis* that the present-day Protestant be considered a "dissident" rather than a "heretic," and that by virtue of his baptism and good faith he be regarded as an incomplete member of the true church. Although, predictably, few Protestants showed interest in the postwar Catholic debate about their religious status, that discussion (especially of the second issue) represented an important stage in Catholics' attempt to give precise definition to the Christian reality they acknowledged to be present among Protestants.

Like many shifts marking the rise of Catholic ecumenism, acceptance of a new nomenclature for Protestants resulted from adaptation of an ancient one. The usage rejected by Congar had risen following the Reformation when Catholics began to distinguish between two types of heretics: *formal* heretics who maliciously and knowingly reject articles of the true faith; and *material* heretics who inherit the fruit of their forebears' heretical rejections. Theologians had explained that because formal heretics commit grave sin, their prospects for eternal salvation are dim. Material heretics retain a mixture of truth and error in good faith, are reached by grace, and thus can be saved. An important distinction had been intended between the two, but use of the word "heretic" for both groups had tended to obscure the distinction. Congar's proposal was to eliminate the formal-material terminology and (following Augustine) simply call the one person "heretic" and the other "dissident." In 1951 Congar's alternative won the significant support of Charles Journet. With the word "heretic" suggesting a judgmental posture that ill accorded with the mood of mid-twentieth-century Catholics, it increasingly fell into disuse. According to Congar's definition the word still applied to Luther and other converts from Catholicism, but it tended to be used sparingly even for them. The word "dissident" normally was employed only in technical theological discussions. Among growing numbers of Catholics, "separated brothers" and "Christian brothers" became commonly accepted designations of Protestants.[1]

Of keener interest to Catholic theologians was the relationship of the dissident Christian to the Roman Catholic Church. Discussion of that subject was precipitated by Pope Pius XII's 1943 encyclical *Mystici Corporis Christi*. Here a brief reference was made to persons (presumably non-Catholic Christians) who are "unsuspectingly . . . related to the Mystical Body of the Redeemer [identified by the encyclical as the Roman Catholic Church] in desire and resolution." So tenuous is that link that presently they cannot "be sure of their salvation;" hence they should become members of the Roman Church. Some interpreted the encyclical's equivocal language as requiring that non-Catholic Christians be considered as belonging among the multitudes whose only effectual link with Christ's church is a fragile "desire and resolution." Although some Catholic scholars argued that the text supported a more positive appreciation of other Christians, they could not deny that nothing had been said to acknowledge explicitly that dissidents' baptism and other distinctly Christian characteristics avail to join them to Christ's mystical body. Protestant interpreters inferred that Rome regarded as equally precarious the spiritual state of Protestants, Orthodox, Muslims, Jews, and all other non-Catholics possessing the proper subjective attitude.[2]

A similar response was provoked by the 1949 Holy Office statement, *Suprema haec sacra*. The document's purpose was to deny the claim of Fr. Leonard Feeney of Boston that the traditional Catholic teaching of *extra ecclesiam nulla salus* means that all non-Catholics are deprived of salvation. The Holy Office insisted that persons "invincibly ignorant" of the true church can nevertheless be linked to her by an "implicit intention which is so called because it is included in that good disposition of the soul whereby a person wishes his will to be conformed to the will of God."[3] The *votum ecclesiae* concept seemed generously to open wide the gates of the Roman Church and thus of salvation; but in doing so, it ignored—and some thought it implicitly denied—the Christian realities existing among Protestant and Orthodox believers and their ecclesial communities.

The two Roman statements prompted numerous articles by Catholic theologians on the question of the multiple links by which persons are joined to the Catholic Church. The intricacy of their arguments created what German Lutheran theologian Peter Brunner termed "a jungle of distinctions and conditions."[4] Nevertheless, the issues at stake in that discussion were important for the development of Catholic ecumenical thought. Most theologians broaching the subject proposed formulae that acknowledged the closer proximity of Orthodox and Protestant Christians to the Catholic Church than of non-Christians. Many continued to use the word "members" to describe dissidents' relation, though qualified to show the incompleteness of membership. Others preferred to speak of them as "belonging" to the Roman Church, but not to the extent of being members. Most maintained the closer proximity of Orthodox Christians to the Roman Church than of Protestants; others made little of the distinction. Some stressed that dissidents' precarious link with the Roman Church (and hence with the saving grace of Christ) was established principally by an implicit "desire"; most followed Congar's lead in stressing the durable role of baptism in incorporating the dissident into the Catholic Church. Significantly the latter position won the public endorsement of Cardinal Bea in 1961: "Non-Catholic Christians must not, therefore, be put on the same plane as the non-baptized; for they always bear, not only the name of Christ on their foreheads, but his actual image in their souls, deeply and indelibly imprinted there by baptism. From a more positive point of view, in virtue of baptism, they are subjects and members of the Church. And this effect of baptism is not removed by heresy or schism. . . . Because fundamentally, even if not fully, they belong to the Church, they also have the benefit of the influence of God's grace."[5] But the presence among them of baptism and grace, Bea added, does not entitle dissidents to remain separated from the Roman Church. Because grace is incompletely present among non-Catholic Christians, Catholics must attempt to lead them back to the Roman Church, "so that they may have life in its fullness and enjoy in full all the rights and privileges of sons."[6]

Acknowledgment of the effective presence of baptism among non-Roman communities raised the critical question of their churchly status, and Catholic theologians turned increasingly in the 1950s to a determination of the exact ecclesial standing of the corporate bodies in which dissident Christians encounter God's grace. Congar had already posed the question and proposed an answer in *Chrétiens désunis*. In articles written in 1950 and 1952 he developed further his explanation of why Roman documents apply the term "church" to some communities of non-Catholic Christians but not to others. Christ's church, he contended, is realized among local communities of Christians in more and less perfect ways. It is perfectly realized where all the elements that give it structure are present. Such elements—the teaching, sacraments, and ministry received from Christ and the apostles—are found in their plenitude only in the Roman Church; hence she alone is the true church. When elements are separated from that plenitude, they may continue to be used by God as instruments of grace; when they are sufficiently present in a community of Christians, one may properly speak of the presence of Christ's church there.

Orthodox communities, hence, are local, albeit imperfect, realizations of the true church. Because the elements are so minimally present in Protestant bodies, especially because they lack a ministry in apostolic succession, Congar again denied the word's applicability to them; it is not proper theologically to speak of a Protestant *church*. One would better refer to each Protestant body as a "communion," a term Congar thought rich in religious meaning.[7]

Some Catholic theologians granted even less positive significance to non-Catholic Christian communities than had Congar. Their positions reflected sympathy with sentiments expressed in a letter to an English bishop: If Catholics and Protestants share as much as some now claim, "then why have I, my husband, and many converts who have sacrificed so much in order to become Catholics ever bothered to do so? . . . Surely what we need now is more encouragement to hold the true Faith and more clear exposition of the reasons for the truth of the Catholic Church and the untruth of the Protestant churches."[8] The Calvinist concept of "vestigia ecclesia," which had been revived in 1950 by the World Council of Churches Central Committee to explain the character of mutual ecclesial recognition implied in Council membership, was employed by conservative Catholic theologians to propose a minimal valuation of the mere "vestiges" of the true church preserved by non-Catholic bodies. Fr. Edward Hanahoe stressed that the very poverty of the vestigia plays a role in turning non-Catholics toward the Roman Church: The vestigia "do not satisfy the soul searching for truth; they only elicit a hunger and thirst for the reality itself. . . . It does not please us, their brethren, that . . . [non-Catholic Christians] continue to try to sustain themselves on crumbs while the full festive board awaits them."[9]

Other theologians sought to move Catholic thought toward maximal acknowledgment of the richness of dissidents' corporate life; if they possess vestigia, full account must be taken of the fact that these genuinely are vestigia *ecclesia*. The progressive theologians were discovering among Protestant churches the "separated particles of gold-bearing rock" that Pius XI earlier had acknowledged among Eastern Orthodox churches. They found a helpful resource in recent exegetical and systematic discussions interpreting the church as the People of God. Especially significant for the ecclesiological foundations of ecumenism was the stress placed by the People of God motif upon the church's unfinished pilgrimage toward her eschatological destiny (hence her present incompleteness) and upon the value of charisms dispersed throughout the entire church (including those outside the hierarchy and priesthood).[10] Progressive theologians also tended to be sensitive to developments among other churches. They did not ignore convictions mounting within the ecumenical movement, such as that reflected in the forceful words of Lesslie Newbigin, a bishop of the Church of South India:

> No one who is not spiritually blind or worse can fail to acknowledge that God has signally and abundantly blessed the preaching, sacraments, and ministry of great bodies which can claim no uninterrupted ministerial succession from the apostles, but who have contributed at least as much as those who have remained within it to the preaching of the Gospel, the conversion of sinners, and the building up of the saints in holiness. Any theology which tries in any way to evade the most complete acknowledgment of that fact is self-condemned. Like the Church in Jerusalem listening to Paul and Barnabas, we must at this point simply be silent and hearken to what God has done.[11]

Progressive Catholic theologians who wished to acknowledge "what God has done" among non-Roman bodies were unwilling to allow that acknowledgment to compromise Catholic teaching about Christ's true church. That church, they believed, is found in its plenitude uniquely within the Roman Catholic Church. But because they could perceive something of the same reality existing outside the Roman Church, they made no absolute, unqualified identification of the true church with the Roman Church. They believed, nevertheless, that the identification exists to such a degree that Catholics may properly evaluate other churches according to their approximation to the Roman Church. By that standard of measurement Orthodox churches were rated "higher" than Protestant ones. Implicit or explicit distinctions also were made among Protestant bodies; the Church of England normally was considered more nearly a church than other ecclesiastical descendants of the Reformation. Lowest on the scale presumably were the sectarian Protestant bodies among whom a catholic tradition could not be discerned. Very little attention was paid them by Catholics engaged in the rediscovery of Protestantism.

Some progressive theologians proposed concepts that allowed a more positive judgment of Protestant bodies than had been made by Congar (though none went so far as to argue that they may properly be called churches). Istina director Christophe Dumont wrote in 1950 that "elements" of Christ's powers of governing, teaching, and sanctifying his church are found in diverse degrees in each of the separated Christian confessions. Their presence means that those bodies "*possess* something of what, existing in its essential perfection in the Roman Church, makes her the church of Christ." The Catholic may go further to say that those "confessions *are* in a certain sense (and, once again, in diverse titles and degrees) *something* of this church inasmuch as she is the church of Christ."[12]

Five years later Louvain theologian Gustave Thils maintained that if an element of the church be regarded as containing something "essential to the true church of Christ," there is no *a priori* reason for insisting (as Congar had done) that elements belong only to the realm of the church's visible structure. For when the total reality of the church is considered, one must acknowledge that the presence of the Holy Spirit, though invisible, clearly is essential for the church. Thils observed that to regard elements of the church as belonging to the realm of its visible structure alone would limit the number found in non-Roman bodies, whereas to include the invisible realm would increase it.[13]

Thils did not argue for the latter option, but in 1960 French Dominican René Beaupère contended that should Catholics limit their evaluation of Protestant churches to doctrinal and disciplinary elements, they would overlook that which constitutes the essence of a Christian church, "its being in Christ." Especially through its "life of prayer," Beaupère wrote, a Christian community places itself most profoundly into relationship with Christ.[14]

Catholic theologians had found that they could admit a positive value in Protestants' baptism more readily than in their celebrations of the eucharist. But in 1960 Edward Schillebeeckx, adapting positions of St. Thomas, maintained that although baptized Protestants' eucharist is not valid and does not bestow the fullness of eucharistic grace, it does retain some of the "fundamental aspects of the Catholic Eucharist," and is "a quasi-sacramental manifestation of an explicit eucharistic desire which . . . implicitly looks forward to the true fruits of the Catholic Eucharist." Through it Protestants "really grow in unity with Christ and with men."[15]

In 1960 American Jesuit theologian Avery Dulles contended that through their baptisms Protestants receive a share in Christ's threefold office of prophet, priest, and king. Dulles's consideration of Protestant ministers' preaching authority led him to acknowledge that the Holy Spirit bestows prophetic charisms upon them. Moreover, claimed Dulles, although their ordination is not a true sacrament, the Catholic must recognize the critical importance of the ministerial office within Protestant communities. Here an "ordination in desire" may exist, and through that *votum* for the sacrament some of its fruits may be received. "The minister would in consequence be able to proclaim the word of God with something of the power corresponding to the priestly office"[16]

Two years later, on the eve of the Council, Gustave Thils expressed the consensus arising among theologians who had carried Catholic ecumenical thought to the farthest frontier yet reached: non-Catholic communions, he wrote, are "means of salvation" by virtue of the Word of God proclaimed there, the sacraments administered, and the ministry exercised.[17]

A wide gap separated Catholics who stood with Thils from those who supported Hanahoe's contention that Protestants feed upon "crumbs." Both groups would be present at the Second Vatican Council, and both would be eager to have their views expressed by its pronouncements.

Reassessing Luther

In the years between World War II and Vatican II, traditional polemical evaluations of Luther's teaching continued to be repeated in Catholic theological manuals, and some authors publishing new historical studies of Luther contented themselves with merely rehearsing well-worn positions.[18] However, most Catholic scholars who freshly studied Protestant origins showed their independence of the older traditions and explored the new realms pioneered by Lortz. Several gave their attention to figures who had rarely received serious scrutiny from Catholics (e.g., Zwingli, Calvin, Wesley), but most followed Lortz's lead and concentrated upon Luther. Nearly all of that scholarship proceeded in Germany.

The ground had been helpfully prepared for fresh interpretations by Paderborn professor Adolf Herte's analysis of the traditional Catholic rejection of Luther. In 1943 he published a three-volume study tracing the pernicious influence upon Catholic Luther study of the 1549 work by John Cochlaeus, *Commentarii de actis et scriptis Martini Lutheri*. Until the twentieth century, claimed Herte, Catholics had repeatedly drawn their pictures of Luther on the basis of such slander as Cochlaeus's contention that "Luther is a child of the devil, possessed of the devil, full of falsehood and pride. . . . Luther lusted after wine and women; he had no conscience and every means was good in his eyes."[19] Herte urged Catholics aware of their forebears' shameful distortion of history to make fairer evaluations of Luther. Hopefully, he added, a Protestant scholar will undertake a comparable study of traditional anti-Roman polemic in order to promote a fairer Protestant assessment of the Roman Catholic Church. But, as French Protestant scholar Richard Stauffer has recently noted, there is "no Protestant self-criticism corresponding to Romanist self-criticism."[20]

Josef Lortz continued to explore themes enunciated in *Die Reformation in Deutschland*. The major conclusions of that work were more sharply delineated and their ecumenical implications more provocatively developed in numerous articles and in several small books. The young Luther, wrote Lortz in 1948, "was a great and fervent believer, filled with the faith that moves mountains. He burned with love for the Lord Jesus and his zeal for preaching the Gospel was unquenchable." Deplorable conditions existing in the Catholicism of his day made reformation a "historical necessity." But if reformation was necessary, Luther's schism was not; the church was split because, after his authentic evangelical discovery, Luther tragically misunderstood Catholic doctrine and bequeathed that misunderstanding to his followers. Catholics and Protestants today share responsibility for the resulting split. Reconciliation will be furthered as they recognize that each side stands with Luther in such evangelical affirmations as these: "Without faith there is no Christian life and all justification comes from faith. . . . God's grace is absolutely indispensable not only for the beginning of Christian existence but also for its continuance and development. . . . God's grace is always a free gift. . . . In preaching and in theology, the Lord Jesus, the Person of the Lord, is to have absolute primacy."[21]

From that common ground Catholics and Protestants must view the barriers created in the sixteenth century. They will see that Luther not only failed to recognize that "his" evangelical affirmations belonged to the Catholic tradition, but he also concluded that to defend them he must deny the sacramental priesthood, the binding power of tradition, man's role in the achievement of salvation, and papal infallibility. Luther's fourfold denial has continued in Protestantism and poses a grave obstacle to reunion. But it should be possible, Lortz claimed hopefully, for Protestants to be shown that the sacramental priesthood is not in fundamental opposition to what Protestants affirm about the universal priesthood, nor tradition to what they affirm about Scripture; properly understood, each of those realities exists conjunctively with its complement. Luther's rejection of man's cooperative role in the process of salvation, Lortz argued, is contrary both to Scripture and to the experience of devout Christians—a fact, he added, that some Protestant theologians fortunately are beginning to admit. It is especially difficult to convince Protestants that they err in rejecting the pope's infallible teaching authority. But hopefully they will discover that Protestantism's tragic abandonment of Reformation principles has been "a logical consequence of the rejection of an infallible teaching authority in the Church."[22] Strange though it may seem to Protestants, only an infallible pope can preserve the Reformation's authentic gospel message. The way to Protestant fulfillment and Christian reunion is the way of Protestant return to Rome.

Lortz's theme was elaborated in a slightly different key by French scholar Louis Bouyer. In 1939 Bouyer had left Protestantism to embrace the Roman Church; fifteen years later in *Du Protestantisme à l'Eglise* he prescribed the same course for what he diagnosed as a badly ailing Protestantism. Bouyer's inventory of the positive principles discovered by Luther and Calvin echoed Lortz: "Salvation as the pure gift of God in Christ, communicated by faith alone, in the sense that no other way can be thought of apart from faith or even along with faith; justification by faith in its subjective aspect, which means that there is no real religion where it is not living and personal; the absolute sovereignty of God, more particularly of His Word as contained in the inspired writings—all these principles are the heart of Protestantism as a reforming movement."[23] What the reformers "discovered" is the authoritative teaching of Catholic tradition and of the Roman Church today. Regrettably, in the heat of controversy and through the pernicious influence of nominalism, the reformers' teachings became gravely distorted: the principle of *sola gratia* was erroneously interpreted to mean that man's justification is extrinsic only, producing no real change in him; the principle of God's sovereignty to imply a debasement of man; and the principle of submission to Scripture to entail rejection of the teaching authority of tradition and the hierarchy. Those "negative elements" were rejected by the Roman Church but retained by Protestants, among whom they subsequently undermined the original evangelical treasures of the Reformation. Protestants will regain those treasures only by returning to the Roman Church. Catholics, Bouyer concluded, must prepare the way for their Protestant brothers by freshly understanding and affirming the profound truths of the Reformation, truths that though preserved by the church too frequently have been overlooked by her members.

Three additional studies attracted wide attention and foreshadowed increasing diversity among Catholic interpreters of Luther. In 1947 Johannes Hessen, a professor of religious philosophy at Cologne, maintained that the Catholic Church of Luther's day was threatened by intellectualism, moralism, sacramentalism, and institutionalism. Hessen likened Luther to an Old Testament prophet recalling men to the essentials of religion. "His struggle to put the Gospel back on the lampstand, to make it again the throbbing heart of the Christian religion, was, in view of the contemporary state of Catholicism, only too justified."[24] But in the heat of battle Luther went to extremes; hence Protestants today must examine their rich inheritance from Luther with a critical eye. Catholics too must play a part in this "reforming of the Reformation," for they also can learn much from the German reformer.

In 1960 German scholar Albert Brandenburg published a probing, appreciative study of Luther's 1513-1515 lectures on the Psalms. Whereas Lortz and his disciples were committed to a biographical analysis of Luther, seeking to explain his total theological and reformative perspectives in relation to his developing career and historical milieu, Brandenburg's volume moved in a fresh direction by focusing on only one segment of Luther's thought, exploring it in depth, and admitting the permanent value both of the questions it raised and the direction it offered. Moreover, Brandenburg's interpretation of Luther in existentialist categories linked him with a different school of Protestant Luther scholarship than that with which Catholic scholars usually had sympathized.[25]

The following year Thomas Sartory gave four radio lectures (later published in *Una Sancta*) that provocatively affirmed the continuing relevance of Luther for Catholics: "Down the centuries we Catholics have been indoctrinated against Luther, to our loss. . . . In spite of our reservations, in spite of the 'No' spoken against him by the Church, we Catholics wish to hear his word insofar as it is a witness to the Gospel, so that we too may be inflamed with the love of God which burns in him."[26] Subsequently Karl Rahner commended Sartory's evaluation of Luther and warned Protestants against discounting it as contrary to an assumed official Roman position, for Trent had not condemned Luther by name; "there is no official judgment on Luther to which the Catholic is bound by his Church." Rahner's statement suggested that the Catholic reassessment of Luther had not yet reached its full potential.[27]

The positions sketched in these pages increasingly provoked Protestant responses. Appreciation was expressed for Catholics' attempt to assess the richness of the Reformation heritage, but the theme of Reformation-fulfillment-by-return grated upon Protestant sensitivities. The seeming fairness of Lortz's work, wrote German Lutheran Walther von Loewenich, made it "more dangerous" than the obviously flawed account of a Denifle; the Protestant eager for unity might be led by Lortz to see only the positive features of the Roman Church and to overlook essential distinctions between Catholicism and Protestantism. Some charged that Catholics' attempts to explain and even to excuse Luther's pilgrimage prevented them from taking seriously the criticisms he still addresses to the Roman Church. Bouyer was answered by the rejoinder from some Protestants that the Reformation gospel he had applauded was more visible in Protestantism than in Catholicism, that he had caricatured the reformer's alleged negative elements, and that agreements he had affirmed between Reformation and Roman teachings were verbal only. The attempt to interpret Luther without a thinly veiled conversionist intent was more appreciatively received by Protestant scholars. Lutheran Peter Meinhold wrote that in Sartory's lectures "the continual misinterpretations of Luther have been decisively cleared away and . . . a new road has been driven through in the attempt to understand Luther." Richard Stauffer concluded a comprehensive analysis of the Catholic rediscovery of Luther with the acknowledgment that recent Catholic study of Luther contains criticism that is fair and honest. It must be answered, he urged, by Protestant recognition of Luther's limitations, but chiefly by a more rigorous testing of Protestant positions by the touchstone of Scripture.[28]

Catholic study of the Reformation also contributed an important strand to the vision of renewal and reunion that emerged prior to the Council. Historians had argued that the lamentable condition of sixteenth-century Catholicism made the Roman Church partially responsible for the outbreak of the Reformation and the division of Christians. That responsibility had been confessed in 1522 by Pope Adrian VI but rarely by members of the hierarchy since. On 29 January 1959 Pope John XXIII, speaking with reference to the Eastern churches, declared that "we do not wish to put anyone in history on trial; we shall not seek to establish who was right and who was wrong. Responsibility is divided. We only want to say: Let us come together, let us make an end to our divisions." Stirred by John's example, other Catholic leaders began to sound the same note and to extend it more broadly. In January 1962 Cardinal Paul-Emile Léger, Archbishop of Montreal, urged that "all Christians must become aware of their common infidelity to the will of Christ, not to accuse one another, but to implore with one heart God's collective pardon for their common guilt."[29] Here was frank, authoritative acknowledgment that Catholics are united with other Christians in sin against unity and in the need for pardon. Wherever that conviction arose, it bespoke a mood of humility and contrition which, Couturier had claimed, was the beginning of ecumenical wisdom.

The Emerging Catholic Vision of Unity

By 1962 Catholics' understanding of Christian unity was in flux, and varied currents competed to shape the mind of their church. Some persons continued to view the Catholic ecumenical task essentially as the Holy Office's 1950 *Instructio* had described it, but others had moved differing distances beyond it. Consequently, a position such as Cardinal Bea's regarding dissident baptism would be viewed by some Catholics as a dangerous hypothesis, by others as a daring insight, and by yet others as a self-evident truth. At the Second Vatican Council all the variants met, and the Council's *Decree on Ecumenism* was an attempt to bring them into as harmonious and constructive a relationship as was then possible.

On a fundamental point the Catholics most responsible for shaping a fresh understanding of Christian unity remained in agreement with their conservative opponents: the church's unity has been divinely established, is divinely upheld, and thus cannot be lost. But they were unwilling to accept all traditional assumptions about how that unity is to be understood or what demands its full realization places upon Catholics. Theologians who approached these issues in fresh ways were no less committed than traditionalists to the preservation of what Christ has given his church. But they conceived that endowment and its preservation in terms more consonant with perspectives emerging from the ferment in Catholic scholarship. Because those perspectives closely paralleled ones concurrently evolving in some Protestant circles and affecting Protestant ecumenism, certain features of the emergent Catholic vision of unity significantly resembled positions developing among Protestants most involved in articulating the ecumenical movement's theological foundations.

Catholics responsible for shaping that vision approached their task from varying experiences and outlooks, and their accents consequently were placed at different points. In the ecumenical perspective that had emerged among them by 1962 six complementary notes were stressed: mystery, mission, plenitude, renewal, dialogue, and pluralism.

The fundamental unity that God has given, Catholic ecumenists affirmed, is the unity of his own triune life. Men are granted the awesome privilege of participating in the profound unity existing among Father, Son, and Spirit. Its theocentric source accounts for the essential *mystery* of the unity given Christ's church. Christians' growth in unity therefore is growth into the fullness of God's infinitely rich truth and love. That fullness has not yet been attained. It is, wrote Fr. Michalon, an "eschatological reality . . . which the Church prays for unceasingly because it will not reach its consummation until Christ gives back the kingdom into His Father's hands." Even as men grow ever more completely into this unity, its further dimensions elude human understanding, and its future visible expressions defy the imagination. The Catholic Church, wrote Fr. Michalon, "has not yet sounded all the depths of the mystery of the unity by which she exists."[30]

The unity that God gives is not for Catholics alone, nor is it only for Christians. To the church he has entrusted Christ's *mission* of healing the wounds of mankind and restoring the unity of the entire human family. The church's unity therefore exists for the world; it is "outgoing, dynamic, and missionary," reaching (as the word "ecumenical" implies) toward the whole inhabited earth.[31]

The fullness of the divine life to which all men are called is given through the Roman Church alone. Only she is endowed with the *plenitude* of means by which the *plenitude* of God's life is communicated to men; hence, full growth into the mystery of God's life is possible only through full participation in the life of his church. All Christian values and churchly elements dispersed outside her visible boundaries belong rightfully to the Catholic plenitude. Only when reincorporated into the whole will the parts find their proper harmony and fulfillment. In dispersion they retain within themselves a movement toward the true church, causing dissident Christians to turn knowingly or unknowingly toward her.[32]

During her earthly pilgrimage the Roman Church imperfectly expresses her endowment from Christ. Modern theology and piety have been colored too determinatively by polemical reactions against dissident Christians, and many forms of the church's faith and action fashioned in other ages do not adequately serve her mission today. The task of Catholic *renewal* is to re-center the Roman Church's thought and life upon the gospel of Christ, thereby more perfectly expressing the truth and grace entrusted to her. Such renewal is a fundamental Catholic contribution to the quest for Christian unity, for by it the Roman Church's true nature becomes more evident and other churches are prompted to a like deepening and purification of their own life.[33]

An indispensable instrument of renewal is *dialogue* with other Christians. As Catholics and Protestants seek to be conformed more perfectly to the gospel, each side must be attentive to what it can learn from the other about the gospel's demands. Catholics must be sensitive to evangelical insight and practice that have been obscured in their church and that now can be assimilated into restatements of Catholic doctrine and repatternings of Catholic life. They also must endeavor to help Protestants discover that their serious questions and concerns are addressed by the Catholic tradition. In dialogue, too, both sides must seek to determine which differences are only apparent and which are real; and among those that do exist they must discover which destroy unity and which enrich it.[34]

The unity to which the Roman Church invites men is distinct from uniformity. As the divinely-intended spiritual home of the entire human family, she must demonstrate that she is able to embrace and fructify the profound diversities existing among men. The church's unity of worship, faith, and order are to be expressed through a *pluralism* of liturgies, theological systems, dogmatic formulations, and canonical forms. Too long dominated by Latin ways, the Roman Church has only recently begun to take the steps necessary to make her catholic, pluralistic ideal operative. The future unity of the universal church may be conceived as a communion of diverse local churches presided over by bishops, with each of the churches embracing authentic expressions of the manifoldness of the gospel, and all sharing the same faith and accepting

the pope's teaching and governing authority. Although this conception of future unity encompassed chiefly Orthodox and Roman
churches, some Catholic ecumenists publicly extended it to include
the Anglican church, and some doubtless privately projected it to
include Protestant communions that eventually might evolve sufficiently to be considered churches.[35]

Doctrinal Restatement

The attraction of Catholic theologians to the task of doctrinal
renewal produced a flood of scholarly articles and books. A wide
range of issues was treated, including those traditionally debated
most heatedly with Protestants. At several junctures a considerable
distance was traveled toward theological rapprochement. At
others, even though a wide gap still existed, significant steps were
taken to begin to narrow it. It must be remembered that the rapid
evolution of Catholic theological thought was accompanied by a
similar ferment in many Protestant circles. Scholars on both sides
followed paths newly opened within their respective traditions and
found themselves upon a convergent course.

The effort of progressive Catholic theologians to establish a
fresh approach to the church's knowledge of revelation was a key
shift helping to stimulate others. It was precipitated chiefly by the
contention of several scholars that the Council of Trent, contrary
to a long-standing interpretation, had not taught that God's truth
is communicated partly in Scripture and partly in tradition. They
argued that the *partim-partim* position should be rejected in favor
of one that acknowledges the normative role of Scripture for the
church's understanding of revelation. Although theologians who
moved in this direction did not agree upon a single alternative to
the dominant Counter-Reformation position, there was growing
consensus among them that Scripture contains all revealed truth
and that tradition is the authentic interpreter of Scripture. Some
even affirmed the traditional Protestant watch-word, *sola scriptura*
(though not all its Protestant content).[36]

Catholic sacramental theology also moved perceptibly toward
themes stressed among Protestants. An important step was the
reappropriation of an earlier understanding of the sacraments as
signs that both announce and present Christ's saving acts to be-

lievers. In this view the sacraments' impact depends not solely upon their valid performance, but as well upon their declaring Christ's acts in such fashion that they can be understood and actively responded to by the worshipping community. In sacramental worship the people enter upon a "personal encounter with the risen Lord by which he sovereignly acts in us through the sacred rite instituted by him."[37]

The most dramatic doctrinal rapprochement occurred in the two traditions' understanding of the process by which man is saved. For four hundred years Protestants and Catholics had seemed irreversibly committed to opposing positions. Protestants had stressed the decisive role of God in man's justification, and Catholics the essential role of man. In 1955 the possibility of reconciliation was signaled by Belgian scholar Charles Moeller. Reflecting interconfessional discussion that had occurred at Chevetogne the preceding year, Moeller admitted that some medieval formulations of the doctrine of "created grace" had made subsequent Catholic teaching often minimize dangerously the primacy of God's action in effecting man's salvation. A proper theology of grace will insist "both on the primacy of God, who justifies and sanctifies man, and at the same time on the reality of regeneration." Moeller maintained that though Protestants and Catholics now agree on the first point as well as on the fact that God effects some change in man, they do not yet agree regarding the regeneration accomplished through justification. Protestant teaching, he contended, stops short of affirming the justified man's "real sharing in the divine life." That failure is the consequence of a too pessimistic view of sin and, more fundamentally, of a Christology that inadequately acknowledges the continuing significance for man's regeneration of the glorified humanity of Jesus Christ.[38]

In 1957 a provocative study of justification by Hans Küng elicited wide scholarly interest in the prospects for theological accord. The young theologian first analyzed Karl Barth's position on justification and then evaluated it in the light of Catholic teaching. Küng concluded that when one looks carefully at the supposedly irreconcilable differences between Barth and the Catholic tradition, one surprisingly finds *fundamental* (though not *total*) agreement between them. Roman Catholic theology agrees with Barth in taking "justification seriously as the gracious act of God's sovereignty in Jesus Christ," and Barth agrees with Catholics in taking "justification seriously as the justification of man." Although some trends in Barth's thought separate him from certain theological schools within Catholicism, the same trends align him with other Catholic schools (notably the Thomistic). At least on this one doctrine the agreement of Barth and the Roman Church gives the Protestant theologian "no genuine argument for separation from the ancient church."[39]

Küng's approach recalls earlier generations of hopeful Catholics who had affirmed a fundamental unity of faith beneath conflicting formulations. Never before, however, had the climate for such an endeavor been so favorable nor the intellectual tools so plentiful. Küng's argument reflected shifts that had occurred within some European theological circles regarding both the method of theology and the doctrine of justification. He contended that Trent's pronouncements and role have been misunderstood by those Catholic theologians who have found in the Tridentine dogmatic decrees an extreme stress upon the human role in man's salvation and have considered that position to be normative Catholic teaching. Not even Trent, Küng argued, should be given a decisive role in determining the content of Catholic truth. The Tridentine decrees, though irreformable, are marked by the inevitable limitations of all historical statements. They are polemical pronouncements against what the Tridentine fathers believed to be the reformers' heretical disregard for the human role in salvation, and they properly accent that role. But they are not intended to provide a full and balanced presentation of Catholic teaching on justification. Dogmatic statements point beyond themselves to the fundamental source of Catholic teaching: they are "living signposts for continued research into the inexhaustible riches of the revelation of Jesus Christ." The locus of those riches is Sacred Scripture. Only here do "we possess the outright and unmediated testimony of God Himself, and in its original idiom and its primal source. . . . It is the theologian's primary norm, even when it irks him."[40] Read in the light of the church's living tradition, Scripture teaches the entirety of Catholic truth—including a view of justification in fundamental agreement with Barth's.

Küng's volume stimulated wide discussion. Barth had already publicly acknowledged that Küng's interpretation of his teaching was accurate, and virtually all Catholic reviewers agreed that the position Küng had espoused was, as J. L. Witte of the Pontifical Gregorian University wrote, "a theological interpretation which is, at least, a possible one in the Catholic Church . . . understood by all as truly Catholic."[41] Some Catholic theologians, though not attacking Küng's position as unCatholic, worked from theological perspectives which allowed limited appreciation of it. Most Protestant commentators echoed Barth's pleasure at Küng's restatement of Catholic teaching regarding justification. American Lutheran theologian George Lindbeck saw an acute challenge posed to Protestantism by Küng: "In effect . . . this most irenic of books contains a devastating attack on the Reformation, for it does not attempt the impossible task of convincing the Reformers and their heirs that they are in error, but rather seeks to prove that their central protest against the Roman Church is a mistake because based on a tragic misunderstanding of what it really teaches."[42] Some Protestants insisted that Trent had correctly judged the Reformation's view of justification to conflict fundamentally with Rome's; the gap between Roman and Protestant teaching on this issue, they contended, is still vast.[43]

Catholic theologians also gave fresh consideration to traditional doctrines of Mary and the papacy, but by 1962 considerably less ecumenical convergence was visible in these realms than in the three already discussed. In 1952, in one of the first ecumenically sensitive studies of Mariology, Congar maintained that Catholic spiritual theology had too uncritically supported the acceleration of honors and attributes accorded Mary by pious Catholics. Theology and piety alike must constantly be tested by the "sovereign rule of the objective data of Revelation." Measured by that rule, he contended, the Catholic must admit that some Marian developments cloud dangerously the Scriptural affirmation of Jesus Christ as the sole mediator between God and man.[44] The need for Christological correction also was voiced by Cardinal Montini of Milan (later to become Pope Paul VI): devotion to Mary, he urged, must be made to recover "its real function of bringing souls to Jesus."[45]

Febronius's eighteenth-century attempt to promote union by re-interpreting the papacy had taken him far afield of acceptable

Catholic teaching. We have noted the efforts of Beauduin, Adam, and Lortz to bring that issue to the arenas of twentieth-century ecumenical encounter. By the time of the Council most Catholic ecumenists agreed that among the difficult issues standing in the way of Protestant-Catholic rapprochement that of the papacy was the thorniest. The "key question for reunion," wrote Hans Küng in 1960, is "Do we need a Pope?"[46] Catholics who addressed that question took into account a probing 1952 study by Protestant scholar Oscar Cullmann entitled *Peter*.[47] Here Cullmann had gone further than most Protestants by admitting that Jesus gave a certain primacy to the apostle Peter, but he denied that there were exegetical or historical grounds for concluding that Peter's unique apostolic office in the primitive church had been transmitted to successors.

Küng agreed with German theologian Otto Karrer that arguments about the Petrine office will be less persuasive to non-Catholic Christians than the actual manner in which it is exercised. In the pope other Christians unfortunately do not yet hear the voice of the "good shepherd," nor do they perceive him as the "servant of the servants of God." Fixed in their minds instead is an image of Peter's successor as one who restricts Christian freedom and makes pretentious spiritual claims. Küng contended that a fundamental step can be taken both to answer Protestants' protest and to promote the health of the Roman Church by restoring the full value of the episcopal office. As the proper role of Catholic bishops is recovered, the structure of Roman hierarchical authority will be decentralized and the diversification of Catholic life enhanced. Others shared that hope, and the approach of the Second Vatican Council found prominent Catholic scholars seeking to lay exegetical, historical, and theological foundations for conciliar recognition of the divine institution and collegiality of the episcopate.[48] They were preparing the way for what proved to be one of the major struggles and achievements of Vatican II.

* * *

Although most Protestants found newer presentations of Catholic teaching on controverted issues less objectionable than older ones, they nevertheless believed that they must continue to voice serious objections. Evangelical renewal of Roman doctrine had not yet produced what they could regard as a firm and comprehensive enough commitment to biblical truth. Nor had increased Protestant appreciation of the catholic dimensions of Christianity proceeded far enough to make attractive for most Protestants the prospect of their churches' integration into Roman Catholic wholeness. The theological division that remained was still acute, and at important junctures it was not yet possible to see how obstacles to unity would be overcome.

The more arresting fact by 1962 was that on both sides powerful movements of the intellect and the heart were leading Catholics and Protestants toward one another, and that the world which earlier had promoted their separation was now actively promoting their convergence. Some had begun to believe that the forces pushing toward unity were irreversible, and that no barriers could finally withstand the unitive pressures of the gospel and of the age.

We have seen that those pressures had issued from a variety of sources and had received multiform expression: both the gentle power of Paul Couturier and the violent power of Adolf Hitler had served the ecumenical cause. The present chapter has suggested the potency of the labors of Catholic scholars who refused to perpetuate concepts that had supported four centuries of division. They had glimpsed the possibility of a future different from the past, and their hours of quiet intellectual toil helped move their contemporaries toward that future. Their great accomplishment was to make it possible for the bishops of the Roman Church to discover that their church's acceptance of ecumenism was demanded by her service of Christian truth. One may regret that that acceptance was so long delayed, but it is to the Roman Church's credit that when its necessity was convincingly demonstrated at the Second Vatican Council, she moved deliberately and rapidly despite the difficulties that would inevitably result from so dramatic an about-face.

NOTES

1. Journet, *Eglise du Verbe Incarné*, 2 vols. (Paris: Desclée de Brouwer, 1951) 2: 708-17, 818-23. Several problems arising from the new

usage, including the questionable appropriateness of the word "heretic" for Luther (especially in view of the Catholic rediscovery of his true motives and teaching), are discussed in Minus, "Catholic Reconsideration," pp. 293-307. In the author's 1962 survey, respondents were asked to indicate which of six terms best applied to a Lutheran or Reformed Protestant. Only 1.2% chose the term "heretic"; 47.6% opted for "Christian brother," and 47.1% for "separated brother." See ibid., pp. 406, 408.

2. *The Mystical Body of Christ* (New York: Paulist Press, 1943), pp. 59, 14; *AAS* 35 (1943): 193-248. Instructive statements regarding the background and import of the encyclical appear in Jérôme Hamer, *The Church is a Communion*, trans. Ronald Matthews (New York: Sheed and Ward, 1964), pp. 13-25, and James O. McGovern, *The Church in the Churches* (Washington: Corpus Books, 1968), pp. 19-29. McGovern (p. 27) finds a recognition of dissidents' special status in the encyclical, but Lutheran scholar Peter Brunner, reading the same encyclical, states: "The conclusion we must draw from this doctrinal encyclical of the Roman Catholic Church is obviously this: Baptized Christians living outside of the boundaries of the Roman Catholic Church, as regards their possible association with the mystical body of Jesus Christ, are in principle, dogmatically speaking, no better situated than unbaptized Jews or heathens who consciously or unconsciously harbor the longing or desire that their wills may be in conformity with the will of God." Brunner, "The Mystery of the Division and the Unity of the Church," in Skydsgaard, ed., *Papal Council*, pp. 201-2; cf. Subilia, *The Problem of Catholicism*, p. 75. A like conclusion was reached by American Catholic theologian Joseph C. Fenton, *The Catholic Church and Salvation* (Westminster: Newman Press, 1958), pp. 94-9.

3. The Latin text and the official English translation of *Suprema haec sacra* appear in *American Ecclesiastical Review* 127 (1952): 307-15. An important antecedent of this statement was Pius IX's claim that "they who labor in ignorance of the true religion, if this ignorance is invincible, are not stained by any guilt in this matter in the eyes of God." Denziger, *Enchiridion*, 1947 (cf. 1677). See Boniface Willems, "Who Belongs to the Church?" in *The Church and Mankind*, Concilium, Dogma Vol. 1 (New York: Paulist Press, 1964), pp. 131-8.

4. Brunner, "Mystery of the Division," p. 201. That discussion and its antecedents have been closely analyzed by Ulrich Valeske, *Votum Ecclesiae* (Munich: Claudius Verlag, 1962). See also Minus, "Catholic Reconsideration," pp. 307-19; Berkouwer, *The Second Vatican Council and the New Catholicism*, trans. Lewis B. Smedes (Grand Rapids: Eerdmanns Publishing Co., 1965), pp. 186-201; and McGovern, *The Church*, pp. 29-38.

5. Bea, "The Catholic Attitude Toward the Problem," trans. and cited from *La Civiltà Cattolica* (14 January 1961) in Bea, *The Unity of Christians* (New York: Herder and Herder, 1963), pp. 32-3; cf. 82-3. It should be noted that Bea used another encyclical of Pius XII, *Mediator*

Dei (1947), as the point of departure for his argument about dissidents' baptism.

6. Ibid., p. 34.

7. Congar, "Notes sur les mots 'Confession,' 'Eglise,' et 'Communion,' " *Irénikon* 23 (1950): 3-36 (trans. in *Dialogue Between Christians*, pp. 184-213); "A propos des 'Vestigia ecclesiae,' " *Vers l'unité chrétienne* 39 (1952): 3-5. Much of the Catholic discussion of this issue is analyzed by Wolfgang Dietzfelbinger, *Die Grenzen der Kirche nach römisch-katholischer Lehre* (Göttingen: Vandenhoeck und Ruprecht, 1962); Emilien Lamirande, "La signification ecclésiologique des communautés dissidentes et la doctrine des 'vestigia ecclesiae,' " *Istina* 7 (1964): 25-58; Minus, "Catholic Reconsideration," pp. 319-52; and McGovern, *Church*, pp. 39-111.

8. John C. Heenan, "How the Heythrop Conference Came About," in Heenan, ed., *Christian Unity: A Catholic View* (London: Sheed and Ward, 1962), pp. 2-3.

9. Hanahoe, "Vestigia Ecclesiae," in Hanahoe and Cranny, eds., *One Fold*, p. 38.

10. The rise of the People of God motif is discussed in Congar, "The Church: The People of God," *Church and Mankind*, Concilium, Dogma Vol. 1, pp. 11-37.

11. Newbigin, *Household of God* (New York: Friendship Press, 1954), p. 344.

12. Fr. Dumont's 1950 article, originally published in *Vers l'unité chrétienne*, was reproduced in *Les voies de l'unité chrétienne*, Unam Sanctam No. 26 (Paris: Editions du Cerf, 1954), pp. 125-6. The statement quoted here from the French original was rather toned down in the Engl. trans. of Dumont's book: *Approaches to Christian Unity*, trans. H. St. John (Baltimore: Helicon Press, 1959), p. 133.

13. Thils, *Mouvement oecuménique*, 1955 ed., pp. 183-197.

14. Beaupère, "Requêtes de l'oecuménisme," *Lumière et vie*, 50: 99-100. In 1955 Thomas Sartory's *Oecumenical Movement* had moved in essentially this direction by including "the action of the Holy Spirit" within a ponderous consideration of vestigia ecclesiae (pp. 156-236).

15. Schillebeeckx, *Christ the Sacrament*, pp. 194, 195. Some aspects of Schillebeeckx's position had been anticipated by Otto Karrer, *Um die Einheit der Christen* (Frankfurt, 1953), p. 27; Sartory, *Oecumenical Movement*, pp. 179-80; and Lambert Beauduin, "Jubilé du Monastère de l'Union," *Irénikon* 23 (1950): 375-6.

16. Dulles, "The Protestant Preacher and the Prophetic Mission," *Theological Studies* 21 (1960): 578.

17. Thils, "Chrétiens séparés et 'éléments d'Eglise,' " *Collectanea Mechliniensia* 47 (1962): 475.

18. August Hasler, *Luther in der Katholischen Dogmatik,* (Munich: Max Hueber Verlag, 1968); Stauffer, *Luther*, pp. 71-2.

19. Herte, *Das Katholische Lutherbild im Bann der Lutherkommen-*

tare des Cochlaeus (Münster, 1943); cited in Stauffer, *Luther*, p. 43.
20. Stauffer, *Luther*, p. 44.
21. Lortz, *The Reformation: A Problem for Today*, trans. John C. Dwyer (Westminster: Newman Press, 1964), pp. 148, 213-4. The sixteen-year delay in translating this book into English is further indication of the slow pace of the pre-Vatican II development of Catholic ecumenism in Great Britain and North America.
22. Ibid., p. 242.
23. Bouyer, *The Spirit and Forms of Protestantism*, trans. A. V. Litterdale (Westminster: Newman Press, 1957), p. 137.
24. Hessen, *Luther in katholischer Sicht* (Bonn, 1947), p. 36; cited in Stauffer, *Luther*, p. 59. See also Congar, "Luther as Seen by Catholics," *Dialogue Between Christians*, pp. 367-8.
25. Brandenburg, *Gericht und Evangelium. Zur Worttheologie in Luthers erster Psalmenvorlesung* (Paderborn: 1960). See Walter Kasper, "The Dialogue with Protestant Theology," in Küng, ed., *The Church and Ecumenism*, Concilium, Ecumenical Theology Vol. 4, pp. 162-3; Otto H. Pesch, "Twenty Years of Catholic Luther Research," *Lutheran World* 13 (1966): 303-16.
26. Sartory, "Martin Luther in katholischer Sicht," *Una Sancta* 16 (1961): 54. Cited in Fred D. Meuser, "The Changing Catholic View of Luther," in Meuser and Stanley D. Schneider, eds., *Interpreting Luther's Legacy* (Minneapolis: Augsburg Publishing House, 1969), p. 52.
27. Rahner was quoted in "Evangelische und katholische Stellungnahmen zu 'Martin Luther in katholischer Sicht,' " *Una Sancta* 16 (1961): 195; cited in Stauffer, *Luther*, p. 54.
28. Von Loewenich, *Modern Catholicism*, p. 289. The two major Protestant critiques of Bouyer are Pierre Fath, *Du Catholicisme romain au Christianisme* (Paris: Editions Berger-Lebrault, 1957), and Rudolf J. Ehrlich, *Rome: Opponent or Partner?* (Philadelphia: Westminster Press, 1965), pp. 29-102. Meinhold's statement was included in "Evangelische und katholische," *Una Sancta*, p. 190. Stauffer's concluding point (in *Luther*, pp. 73-4) was seconded by Meuser, "Changing Catholic View," p. 54.
29. Gregory Baum, *Progress and Perspectives*, p. 90. Pope John's statement to the pastors of Rome was cited in *Herder Korrespondenz* 13 (1959-60): 274.
30. Michalon, "Spiritual Oecumenism," (Lyons, 1961), pp. 15, 27. Cf. Heufelder, "The Council and Reunion," in Heufelder, ed., *In the Hope of His Coming*, p. 251. A similar note was struck by the 1961 New Delhi Assembly of the World Council of Churches; see Vischer, *Documentary History*, p. 144.
31. Baum, *Progress and Perspectives*, p. 21. Cf. Willebrands, "Catholic Ecumenism," in Willebrands, S. G. Sheehan et al., *Problems Before Unity* (Baltimore: Helicon Press, 1962), pp. 3-8.
32. Hamer, "Mission de l'oecuménisme catholique," *Lumière et vie*

222   THE CATHOLIC REDISCOVERY OF PROTESTANTISM

19 (1955): 65-82; Le Guillou, "L'Eglise catholique et l'oecuménisme,"
pp. 230-53.
33. Villain, *Unity*, pp. 201-12; Küng, *Council*, pp. 23-67.
34. Gustave Thils, *La 'théologie oecuménique'* (Louvain: E.
Warny, 1960); Bea, *Unity of Christians*, pp. 94-110.
35. Küng, *Structures of the Church*, trans. Salvator Attanasio (New
York: Thomas Nelson and Sons, 1964), pp. 39-52, 385-9; Beaupère,
"Requêtes," pp. 105-20.
36. A helpful survey of the issue was provided by Josef R. Geisel-
mann, "Scripture, Tradition, and the Church: An Ecumenical Problem,"
in D. J. Callahan et al., eds., *Christianity Divided* (New York: Sheed and
Ward, 1961), pp. 35-72; see also Walter Kasper, "The Dialogue with Protestant Theology," *The Church and Ecumenism*, pp. 166-73. Cf. two Protestant analyses of the development of this issue in the Roman Church and
in the wider ecumenical discussion: Albert C. Outler, "Scripture, Tradition, and Ecumenism," in Swidler, ed., *Scripture and Ecumenism*, pp. 9-
22; and Berkouwer, *Second Vatican Council*, pp. 89-111.
37. Baum, *Progress and Perspectives*, p. 143. Schillebeeckx, *Christ
the Sacrament of the Encounter with God* was a major statement of this
view on the eve of Vatican II; but it had been emerging for several decades
among persons active in the liturgical renewal.
38. C. Moeller and G. Philips, *The Theology of Grace and the Ecumenical Movement*, pp. 4, 46; the substance of this book had been published by Moeller earlier in "Grâce et oecuménisme," *Irénikon* 28
(1955): 19-56. The same point regarding Protestant Christology was developed by Congar in another context: Congar, *Christ, Our Lady and the
Church: A Study in Eirenic Theology*, trans. H.P. St. John (London: Long-
mans, Green and Co., 1957), especially pp. 25-30. A helpful survey of recent
Catholic discussion of grace and justification is provided by Heribert
Mühlen, "Doctrine de la grâce," in VanderGucht and Vorgrimler, eds.,
Bilan 2: 371-411.
39. Küng, *Justification: The Doctrine of Karl Barth and a Catholic
Reflection*, trans. Thomas Collins, Edmund E. Tol, and David Granskou
(New York: Thomas Nelson and Sons, 1964), pp. 276, 277, 278. Two
other major Catholic studies of Barth's thought should be noted: Hans
Urs Von Balthasar, *The Theology of Karl Barth*, trans. John Drury (New
York: Holt, Rinehart and Winston, 1971), and Henri Bouillard, *Karl
Barth*, 2 vols. (Paris: Aubier, 1957). The Von Balthasar study was originally published in 1951.
40. Küng, *Justification*, pp. 101, 111, 112.
41. Ibid., p. xi. Cf. Callahan et al., eds., *Christianity Divided*,
pp. 307-8; and Karl Rahner, "Question of Controversial Theology on Justification," in Rahner, *Theological Investigations*, trans. Kevin Smyth
(Baltimore: Helicon Press, 1966), 4: 189-220.
42. George Lindbeck, "A New Phase in the Protestant-Roman Catholic Encounter?" *Ecumenical Review* 11 (1958-59): 339; Grover Foley,

"The Catholic Critics of Karl Barth," *The Scottish Journal of Theology* 14 (1961): 141-5.
43. Ehrlich, *Rome*, pp. 101-205. Cf. Mühlen, "Doctrine," pp. 403-4.
44. Congar, *Christ, Our Lady*, p. 82.
45. Cited in Küng, *Council*, p. 127. Mariological developments preceding and during the Council have been critiqued from a Protestant perspective by Berkouwer, *Second Vatican Council*, pp. 221-48.
46. Küng, *Council*, p. 132.
47. *Peter: Disciple, Apostle, Martyr*, trans. Floyd V. Filson (Philadelphia: Westminster Press, 1952; 2nd ed., 1962).
48. Among the chief works that appeared were Karl Rahner and Josef Ratzinger, *The Episcopate and the Primacy*, trans. Kenneth Barker (New York: Herder and Herder, 1962); G. Thils, *Primauté pontifical et prérogatives épiscopales* (Louvain, 1961); Y. Congar and B. D. Dupuy, eds., *L'Episcopat et l'Eglise universelle* (Paris: Editions du Cerf, 1962); Küng, *Structures of the Church*.

IX
The Council's
Ecumenical Achievement

When the Second Vatican Council began, few informed persons foresaw the magnitude of its eventual impact upon the Roman Church. Pope John had spoken boldly of "aggiornamento," but the way to it appeared blocked by determined partisans of an unchanging church. The continued influence of Curia conservatives had been demonstrated by a recent papal reaffirmation of Latin as the language of seminary instruction. More critically, their hands had decisively shaped conciliar preparatory documents. With little encouragement evident from Rome, it appeared doubtful that bishops trained in Counter-Reformation traditions would wish to venture far from them when they gathered in the Eternal City.[1]

The likelihood of far-reaching ecumenical advance also appeared slight. Preparatory drafts reflected only faint traces of the ecumenical currents flowing north of the Alps. An astute Lutheran observer wrote that the Council might produce an assessment of non-Catholic Christians more positive than the Holy Office's 1950 *Instructio*, but that with the creation of Cardinal Bea's Secretariat perhaps "most of what the Council will do towards better relations with other Christians has already been accomplished."[2] Some progressive Catholic theologians, fearing a conservative orientation in any conciliar pronouncements made upon ecumenical matters, preferred that only minimal attention be given to the quest for Christian unity.[3]

Rarely have ecclesiastical assemblies so confounded the expectations of close observers as did Vatican Council II. The Council's surprising ecumenical achievement was made possible by the interaction of currents that had begun to exert noticeable influence in the late nineteenth century. In recent decades the ecumenical experience and thought of a venturesome minority had matured sufficiently to become a valuable asset for the Roman Church. At the Council that asset was appropriated because the assembled bishops became convinced that the church must become a source of peace for the human family, and they knew that that mission cannot be effectively pursued until there is peace among Christians.

So recent is Vatican II and so massive is its continuing impact that one cannot yet adequately measure its total ecumenical achievement. We shall here undertake only a summary analysis of those features of the Council which made it the climactic event in the Roman Church's initiation to ecumenism. That task requires a focus of attention upon three realms: the processes within the Council that generated its ecumenical outlook; the constitutions, decrees, and declarations that deal secondarily but significantly with ecumenism; and the epochal *Decree on Ecumenism.*

A Schooling in Ecumenism

Most of the 2300 Council fathers brought to Rome only a slight acquaintance with the ecumenical perspectives that had emerged earlier among pioneering Catholics. At the Council they were exposed frequently to those perspectives and had repeated opportunity to test their authenticity. This schooling in ecumenism was a major ingredient in the remarkable process of episcopal re-education that occurred for four years in Rome.

Both Pope John and Pope Paul served as tutors in ecumenism. They kept the issue of Christian unity constantly before the Council and indicated by word and deed how unity should be pursued. In his opening address on 11 October 1962, John established theological guidelines that facilitated a fruitful consideration of ecumenism. His charge to the bishops recognized the indispensability of both a preservationist and a transformationist course for the Roman Church: "Our duty is not only to guard this precious treasure [of the patrimony of truth] as if we were concerned only with antiquity, but to dedicate ourselves with an earnest will and without fear to that work which our era demands of us." John urged that the church employ the modern intellectual tools that will allow her to understand and expound her treasure of faith afresh. The Council's early acceptance of the task of doctrinal renewal (and of its ecumenical consequences) was especially prompted by his acknowledgment of the critical distinction between "the substance of the ancient doctrine of the deposit of faith" and "the way in which it is presented."[4]

Pope John's goals for the Council were reaffirmed and developed by Pope Paul VI, who brought extensive Curia experience to the difficult task of implementing demanding ideals among a divided flock. Several features of the emergent Catholic vision of unity were strikingly expressed by Paul early in his pontificate. Only the Catholic Church, he declared at the beginning of the second session in September 1963, can offer divided Christians "the perfect unity of Christ." But possession of that gift is no warrant for self-righteous complacency. The Catholic Church looks ever to Christ to discern what she must be; should she discover that she does not conform to him, she must not hesitate to reform herself. Turning to the Protestant and Eastern Orthodox visitors in St. Peter's Basilica, Paul admitted the possibility of Catholic culpability for Christian divisions: "If we are in any way to blame for that separation, we humbly beg God's forgiveness. And we ask pardon too of our brethren who feel themselves to have been injured by us." Paul also acknowledged "with reverence . . . the true religious patrimony we share in common, which has been preserved and in part even well developed among our separated brethren."[5] Several weeks later, at a reception for the non-Catholic observers and guests (whom he addressed as "beloved brothers in Jesus Christ"), Paul urged all Christians "to listen to each other, to pray for each other, and, after such long years of separation and such painful polemics, to begin again to love each other." Their hopes and energies must be fixed "not on what has been, but on what ought to be. We must concentrate on bringing something new to birth, on realizing a dream."[6]

The pope himself now expressed convictions like those that earlier had placed such pioneers as Portal, Beauduin, and Congar under a Roman cloud. The powerful movement of history had made Pope Paul the sower of an ecumenical vision.

Popes John and Paul did not limit their ecumenical tutelage

to verbal pronouncements. Paul's January 1964 trip to the Holy Land and amicable meeting with the Ecumenical Patriarch Athenagoras symbolized his conviction that divided Christians must rediscover one another at the sources of their faith. At each of the four Council sessions the pope met with the whole corps of observers and guests from other churches. The mutual respect and affection developed during the Council were evident in their acts of shared worship. In October 1963, after greeting the Protestant and Orthodox leaders individually, Pope Paul asked them to pray the Lord's Prayer with him, each person in his own language. The following autumn Pope Paul received the group in the Sistine Chapel, where they recited together the *Gloria in excelsis Deo* and the Lord's Prayer. During the final week of the Council, on 4 December 1965, the observers and guests were invited to join Pope Paul and the Council fathers in a "sacred celebration for the promotion of unity among Christians." Several observers assisted in leading worship and Pope Paul delivered a homily; at the end the entire congregation sang "Now Thank We All our God." This event, called by Cardinal Bea "the finest ecumenical experience of the whole Council," was a fitting fruition for the labors of Paul Couturier who, thirty years earlier, had first urged divided Christians to pray together for unity.[7]

The two popes' emphasis of transformationist themes did not lead them to slight their preservationist task. As the outlook of most bishops grew steadily more progressive, Paul repeatedly asserted traditional positions that conservative bishops feared were being overlooked (especially the unique papal authority). Those positions were a part of traditional Catholic teaching and Paul judged that his preservationist responsibility required that he insist that they be maintained. Perhaps, too, he believed that their co-existence in conciliar documents with progressive positions increased the likelihood of the Council's psychological acceptability among his increasingly diverse flock. For ecumenically hopeful Catholics and Protestants the conservative texts were a reminder that however great the convergence of their churches, serious differences remained.[8]

Both popes publicly acknowledged the crucial importance of the Secretariat for Promoting Christian Unity. Soon after the

Council began, Pope John elevated the Secretariat to the rank of a conciliar commission.[9] This status allowed it to participate fully in the presentation and redrafting of schemas (functions it exercised with the *Decree on Ecumenism*, the *Declaration on the Relationship of the Church to Non-Christian Religions*, and the *Declaration on Religious Freedom*). In November 1962, when most Council fathers voted their disapproval of the conservatively-oriented schema on revelation, John remanded it to a mixed commission composed of members of the Theological Commission (which originally had drafted the document) and of the Secretariat. Increasingly, Cardinal Bea and his colleagues were viewed as major spokesmen for the progressive direction in which Pope John intended the Council to move. Throughout the four years of Vatican II, the theologians and bishops associated with the Secretariat worked effectively—in the aula of St. Peter's and in numerous informal settings—to stretch the ecumenical horizons of the Council fathers. Few persons were surprised that, as the Council neared its completion, Pope Paul made the Secretariat a permanent Vatican bureau.

During the four sessions of the Council, invited visitors from other churches also played key roles in introducing the bishops to ecumenism. Through encounter with these articulate Protestant and Orthodox leaders many bishops learned firsthand the rewards and agonies of the quest for Christian unity. The number and influence of the welcome "outsiders" grew as the Council progressed. Forty-nine observers (persons officially appointed by invited ecclesiastical bodies) and guests of the Secretariat (persons invited directly by the Secretariat) attended the first session, 103 observers and guests the final session. The number of ecclesiastical bodies that appointed observers rose from 17 at the first session to 29 at the fourth.[10] Among the group were men such as Oscar Cullmann, Edmund Schlink, and Kristen Skydsgaard whose theological skills had been employed for over a decade in Catholic-Protestant dialogue. From the beginning, the Secretariat had encouraged observers and guests to critique the schemas being considered by the bishops.[11] Weekly two-hour conferences gave them opportunity to discuss documents currently under consideration with members of the Secretariat and invited Council fathers. Their views were then transmitted to appropriate conciliar bodies. Occasionally their comments were echoed by bishops in subsequent sessions in St. Peter's. Doubtless some of the observers' and guests' suggestions affected both committee and plenary discussion of conciliar documents (especially the *Decree on Ecumenism*), but a complete assessment of their influence must await future research upon conciliar texts and processes.[12]

The visitors' impact upon the Council extended beyond the formal meetings arranged by the Secretariat. Their daily presence in the aula of St. Peter's kept the issue of Christian unity vividly before the bishops. Innumerable encounters occurred at informal moments in the basilica's two refreshment stands and throughout Rome. For most bishops this group of Protestant and Orthodox Christians provided their first sustained contact with responsible representatives of non-Roman churches. Friendships soon developed across the chasms of the centuries, and ecumenism was steered into the fertile realm of personal relationships. Congregationalist observer Douglas Horton spoke for many Catholics and non-Catholics alike who had discovered each other during the conciliar process: "Because you have made us your friends, nothing important to you can be unimportant to us: we shall never again be indifferent (however we may disagree) to anything in your theology, your polity, your liturgy. Let this relationship of simple human friendship be carried from the center you have created here to the boundaries of Christendom and we have at least the beginnings of ecumenism."[13]

Another group which played an important tutorial role was the articulate bishops whose public statements and private conversation helped move brother bishops toward a progressive ecumenical posture. Assisted by the large corps of theological specialists ("periti") brought to the Council, some bishops made statements in St. Peter's that reflected the convictions of ecumenical pioneers. Italian Archbishop Andrea Pangrazio, for instance, urged that conciliar documents acknowledge that there is a distinction between the primary and the subordinate truths of Christianity, and that Christians are united in the former realm and divided only in the latter. French Coadjutor Archbishop Leon Elchinger asked that the Council admit that some revealed truths have been upheld by other Christians better than by Catholics. And Venezuelan Cardinal Archbishop J. Humberto Quintero asked that the Council confess Catholic guilt for sixteenth-century division and ask pardon of other Christians.[14]

News of the ecumenical breakthroughs occurring in Rome between 1962 and 1965 was transmitted widely, and in numerous communities around the world Catholics and Protestants were initiated into the ways of dialogue, common worship, and common witness.[15] Catholic bishops, home between conciliar sessions, witnessed the enthusiasm with which most persons responded to the Council's bold ecumenical course. Some Catholic and non-Catholic leaders began to seek ways to continue high-level encounters after the Council's adjournment. A series of meetings initiated in April 1964 between representatives of the Secretariat and the World Council of Churches led the following winter to agreement to establish a Joint Working Group through which the Roman Church and the World Council would address issues of major ecumenical import.[16] In September 1964 the Executive Committee of the Lutheran World Federation proposed that an official Lutheran-Catholic bilateral conversation be inaugurated, and in August 1965 the first in a series of conversations occurred in Strasbourg between prominent Lutheran and Catholic theologians.[17] Before the Council's adjournment the following December, the possibility of similar dialogues with other Protestant bodies was actively under consideration. Also being considered was the establishment of a theological study center in Jerusalem directed jointly by Catholics, Protestants, and Orthodox.[18] Such developments helped ensure that once the exotic appeal of the new ecumenical situation faded, persons committed at deeper levels to the unity of all Christians would continue to labor for its realization.

A Pervasive Theme

The *Decree on Ecumenism* became the chief enduring expression of the bishops' collective mind regarding the pursuit of Christian unity, but so fundamental was the unity theme in their deliberations that varied facets of it were introduced into other conciliar documents. Because those documents embraced fresh theological perspectives that earlier had facilitated the rise of a Catholic ecumenical stance, ecumenism was given a firm rootage in official Catholic teaching and the likelihood of its postconciliar progress was markedly enhanced.

Numerous conciliar texts echo such pioneering theologians as Adam and Congar by affirming the God-given unity of mankind. The entire human family has been created by God, is moved and preserved by his grace, and will finally be perfectly united by him. Hence multiple bonds link Catholics and non-Catholics.[19] The pioneers' optimistic appraisal of outsiders was also incorporated into conciliar teaching: "The Catholic Church rejects nothing which is true and holy among other religions. . . . She looks with sincere respect upon those ways of conduct and life, those rules and teachings which, though differing in many particulars from what she holds and sets forth, nevertheless often reflect a ray of that Truth which enlightens all men."[20] The Council left no doubt that it believed that the fullness of enlightening truth is found uniquely in the gospel of Christ as it is known by the Roman Church. To Catholics falls the responsibility of entering into dialogue with outsiders, in order that their culture and wisdom may be utilized for the proclamation of Christ's message, that Catholics and non-Catholics may learn to labor together in tasks to which both are committed, and that what is good among non-Catholics may be healed and perfected.

Catholic appreciation of outsiders was extended eagerly to non-Roman Christians and their churches. Never had the Roman Church spoken so positively of them as she did in the Council's *Dogmatic Constitution on the Church:*

There are many who honor sacred Scripture, taking it as a norm of belief and of action, and who show a true religious zeal. They lovingly believe in God the Father Almighty and in Christ, Son of God and Savior. They are consecrated by baptism, through which they are united with Christ. They also recognize and receive other sacraments within their own churches or ecclesial communities. Many of them rejoice in the episcopate, celebrate the Holy Eucharist, and cultivate devotion toward the Virgin Mother of God. They also share with us in prayer and other spiritual benefits. Likewise, we can say that in some real way they are joined with us in the Holy Spirit, for to them also He gives His gifts and graces, and is thereby operative among them with His sanctifying power. Some indeed he has strengthened to the extent of the shedding of their blood (art. 15).

But preservationist themes also were sounded in the constitution, qualifying the affirmative stance that had been taken. The document noted, for example, that despite the presence of multiple gifts and graces among them, other Christian communities are flawed because they do not yet possess the entirety of faith nor do they participate in the Petrine unity intended by Christ for all his flock. The fullness of Christ's church is present only in the Roman Catholic Church. Because the treasures dispersed among non-Catholic Christians "possess an inner dynamism toward Catholic unity" (art. 8), and because the Holy Spirit now prompts them to pursue the unity willed by Christ, Catholics must endeavor to help their brothers reach that goal.

The urgency of the ecumenical task was underscored in conciliar texts far more emphatically than it had been in earlier Roman statements. Accounting largely for this fresh note was the bishops' mounting conviction that the centripetal flow of modern history was moving toward realization of God's intention that mankind be transformed into a single family yoked by bonds of love. Secular history had become markedly responsive to the hidden governance of the divine Spirit. But by itself mankind could neither accurately envision nor finally reach the unity for which it groped. The Council fathers concluded that at so critical a juncture of history, God summons his church to be a sign and instrument of the world's destined unity and peace. Mutual love among Christians must become a winsome foreshadowing of mankind's future and a creative leaven helping society to overcome its continued estrangements.[21]

The texts of Vatican Council II thus posed a challenge that had been recognized by pioneering Catholic ecumenists since the pontificate of Leo XIII: the unity of Christians must contribute to the wider unity of mankind. The Council fathers were not agreed about the exact character of that contribution, but the new direction of Catholic teaching gave an unmistakably high priority to the church's unitive task.[22] Faithfulness to her God-given mission to be a sign of unity among the nations requires that within her own ranks the Roman Church foster "mutual esteem, reverence, and harmony, through the full recognition of lawful diversity." And among divided Christians, it requires that she give herself with complete dedication to her ecumenical vocation, so that Christians' growing unity may become a ."harbinger of unity and peace for the world at large."[23]

The Council made a substantial contribution toward Christian unity by embracing doctrinal positions that had emerged under the influence of recent currents of renewal. Even though the progressive positions were modified in conciliar documents in an attempt to harmonize them with traditional theological patterns, their qualified acceptance led most knowledgeable commentators to judge that in the postconciliar period they would faciliate a continued convergence of Protestant and Catholic thought. Particularly responsible for Protestants' optimistic assessment of Vatican II's impact was the presence of biblical motifs in key conciliar pronouncements. Although he regretted that the Council had not been consistently governed by a biblical perspective, Oscar Cullmann judged that "on decisive points in the Council texts the Bible directly inspired the new reform thinking which is contained in the different constitutions and decress. . . . Return to the Bible is really the reforming principle of the Council."[24] The prospect of a continued reforming (and ecumenical) role for the Bible within the Roman Church was encouraged by the Council's *Dogmatic Constitution on Divine Revelation*. This document did not declare as normative a role for Scripture as many Protestants would have wished, but it did assert that Scripture is the Word of God, and it left the Scripture-Tradition question open for further theological reflection. Also auguring a future continued convergence with Protestant thought were the constitution's insistence upon the historical and personal character of God's revelation, its encouragement of scientific biblical scholarship, and its urging of attentive reading of Scripture among clergy and laity.[25]

The Council's desire to make Catholic life and teaching more reflective of Scripture was evident in large portions of the document most commentators have considered the Council's major theological achievement, the *Dogmatic Constitution on the Church*. Many of its emphases both embraced recent theological currents and moved Catholic thought nearer comparable Protestant positions. Such a summary judgment can be made, for example, regarding the constitution's view of the church's source in the life of the triune God; of the pilgrim people's movement through the trials of history toward their eschatological destiny; of the laity's participation in Christ's priestly, prophetic, and kingly functions; of the sacramentality and collegiality of the episcopacy; and of Mary as belonging within the church in the exercise of her salvific role.

Most Protestant commentators welcomed such positions as improvements upon previous official teaching, but they also contended that the new positions often fail to conform sufficiently to Scripture and even to reflect the best recent Catholic scholarship. For example, experienced Lutheran observers argued that the constitution stops short of acknowledging the church's full entanglement in the web of history and sin, that it makes excessive claims for the eminence of the episcopacy in the church, and that it fosters exaggerated views of Mary's role in Christ's redemptive work.[26]

Protestant scholars also welcomed the ecumenical advance brought by other conciliar documents, notably the *Constitution on the Sacred Liturgy*, the *Pastoral Constitution on the Church in the Modern World*, and the *Declaration on Religious Freedom*. But in those documents, too, they believed the Council had failed to follow all the implications of its evangelical insights.[27]

A further realm of the ecumenical impact of conciliar teaching was its accentuation of underlying concerns within the Roman Church similar to ones growing among Protestants. In the *Pastoral Constitution on the Church in the Modern World*, for example, the Council affirmed the Roman Church's desire to be involved in the struggles of contemporary man, and its stands on many particular issues were strikingly close to those taken by the World Council of Churches.[28] The ferment precipitated by the Council throughout Catholicism convinced numerous observant Protestants that the Roman Church was embarked earnestly upon a quest for renewal, that their own churches needed to do likewise, and that Protestants could learn from the example of their Catholic brothers.[29] But Vatican II also revealed that among Catholics there was sharp and increasing disagreement about how the Christian faith should be understood and presented in a secular age. Catholic disagreements closely paralleled the disagreements spreading among Protestants. By 1965 it was evident that Protestants of varied theological and religious complexions—fundamentalists, conservatives, progressives, radicals, etc.—could find their counterparts within the Church of Rome. The weight of Vatican II had been added to the forces that were stimulating new patterns of unity across traditional dividing walls as well as new patterns of division within churches that had been relatively homogeneous. The movement for Christian unity was thereby faced with a fresh and difficult challenge.

Decree on Ecumenism

In the months preceding the Council three preconciliar bodies began preparation of preliminary drafts that systematically treated questions of Christian unity. During the first session, the Council fathers were presented two of the resulting documents: *De Unitate Ecclesiae*, prepared by the Commission for the Eastern Churches, and chapter 11, "De Oecumenismo," of the Theological Commission's *De Ecclesia*. The document prepared by the Secretariat for Promoting Christian Unity was not released. Conciliar discussion of *De Unitate Ecclesiae* (which dealt primarily with the Eastern Catholic Churches) revealed wide dissatisfaction with the juridical approach it had taken to ecumenical questions, and the Council fathers voted on 1 December 1962 that the three documents should be consolidated. Principal responsibility for preparation of the new statement was assigned to Cardinal Bea and his colleagues in the Secretariat.[30]

The new schema, given the title *De Oecumenismo*, was developed chiefly by Belgian, French, and Dutch members and consultants of the Secretariat.[31] At their hands the new document had abandoned the traditional "return to Rome" orientation of the two earlier drafts. When *De Oecumenismo* was first discussed by the Council fathers in November 1963, some bishops indicated dissatisfaction with the document's too progressive orientation. But most immediately welcomed it, and some prodded the cautious Secretariat to make *De Oecumenismo* even more venturesome in its establishment of a Catholic ecumenical stance. A second version of the schema was published in April 1964, and after a further round of evaluation and emendation the following autumn, its successive chapters were favorably voted by an overwhelming majority. The complete final text then was prepared for the Council's formal vote on 20 November 1964. On 18 November representatives of Pope Paul met with Cardinal Bea and Monsignor Willebrands to request their acceptance of approximately forty slight textual changes. The pope's belated intervention apparently had been prompted by his wish to mollify bishops unhappy at the schema's progressive direction. Bea and Willebrands, unable to consult the whole Secretariat in time to meet pressing publication deadlines, accepted nineteen of the proposals. The next day considerable furor was raised by announcement in St. Peter's of the papal-initiated changes, but in retrospect most commentators have agreed that although several of the changes did weaken the document's positive assessment of Protestantism, none altered its fundamental thrust and the text gained greater precision.[32] In the final vote upon the schema, 2137 fathers voted in favor and only 11 against. On 21 November 1964 Pope Paul solemnly promulgated the *Decree on Ecumenism* "to the glory of God."

The essential purpose of the *Decree* (also known by its Latin title, *Unitatis redintegratio*) is to provide both direction and impetus for the Roman Church's participation with other churches in the quest for Christian unity. Its three chapters deal successively with the theological principles that guide Catholic ecumenical endeavor, the ways by which those principles should be implemented, and the churches with which the Roman Church is engaged in the pursuit of Christian unity.[33] The document's content is an incisive distillation and systematization of experience and convictions that had emerged among ecumenical pioneers during the preceding three decades. Remarkably few of even the most advanced positions of the early 1960s were not incorporated into the *Decree* (e.g., proposals for the relaxation of canonical discipline regarding mixed marriages). Understandably, Fr. Congar referred to it as a "great and beautiful text."[34] Rarely has a theologian witnessed so complete a fruition of his labor.

Earlier drafts of the *Decree* had followed Congar's 1937 lead by calling its theological statement "principles of Catholic ecumenism." But the Council decided that that formula must be replaced by one that would not encourage a Catholic ecumenical enterprise separate from the wider ecumenical movement. This movement, the *Decree* states, is responsive to the "grace of the Holy Spirit" (art. 1), and Catholics should join their efforts for unity to those of fellow Christians. They are to be guided by "Catholic principles on ecumenism" that reflect what the Roman Church—at this juncture of history—understands about the restoration of unity.[35]

The Council judged that indispensable to the responsible pursuit of unity is a theological understanding of its source. The *Decree*'s compact statement of God's redemptive deeds for mankind underscores his unitive intention. Jesus Christ has been sent so that "he might by his redemption of the entire human race give new life to it and unify it" (art. 2). The redeemed community is brought by the Holy Spirit into "a unity of faith, hope and charity" which is nourished by the teaching, ruling, and sanctifying ministry instituted by Christ and entrusted to the Apostles. The unity of the church is part of God's gift of redemption, and one's participation in that unity is an integral part of his experience of redemption.

The *Decree* conceives restored unity as "perfect ecclesiastical communion" (art. 4).[36] The task of ecumenism is to move toward this goal by fostering both a more complete realization of Christ's church in all segments of the Christian community and a transformation of the relationships existing among divided Christians and among their churches. Integral to this conception of the ecumenical task is a higher valuation of both Eastern and Protestant churches than Catholics had traditionally held. Present in them are "some, even very many of the most significant elements and endowments, which together go to build up and give life to the church itself; . . . the Spirit of Christ has not refrained from using them as means of salvation" (art. 3). Consequently, the baptized faithful of those bodies are "incorporated into Christ." The *Decree*

extols the abundant presence among Eastern churches of constitu-
tive realities of Christ's church and acknowledges that they are
churches. It notes that those realities are present in varying degrees
among Western bodies and refers to them collectively as "churches
and ecclesial communities," but without attempting to determine
which merit the one designation and which the other, as well as
without establishing the precise criterion by which to make that
determination.[37]

The ecclesiological perspective governing this evaluation of
other churches is an "ecclesiology of communion" that had been
first utilized for an ecumenical purpose in Congar's epochal
Chrétiens désunis.[38] Its more complete elaboration in the *Constitution on the Church* presents Christ's church as an organism in
which the corporate life of grace and the institutional means of
grace form "one interlocked reality" (art. 8). During consideration
of the constitution, a draft statement claiming that Christ's church
"is" the Roman Catholic Church was rejected in favor of a more
restrained statement asserting that Christ's church "subsists in"
the Roman Church. This formulation made possible the *Decree*'s
subsequent teaching that Christ's church extends beyond the
Roman Church to other "churches and ecclesial communities."
His church is present wherever, and to the extent that, church-
building elements and endowments exist among communities of
Christians.

In preconciliar theological discussion some Catholic ecumenists had moved beyond Congar's earlier limiting of "elements of
the church" only to visible instruments of grace. The *Decree*, too,
acknowledges a wide range of elements and endowments outside
the Roman Church: "the written Word of God; the life of grace;
faith, hope and charity, with the other interior gifts of the Holy
Spirit, as well as visible elements" (art. 3). No limit is placed upon
the extent to which the "interior gifts of the Holy Spirit" may exist
among non-Catholic churches. Nor is a claim made about the extent of their presence within the Roman Church. The *Decree* does,
however, assert that no other church has the same fullness of
means of grace possessed by the Roman Church. She alone has
been given the "fullness of the means of salvation;" she is "the all-
embracing means of salvation" (art. 3). That self-evaluation is a

consequence of her unique fidelity to the apostolic constitution of the church: "It was to the apostolic college alone, of which Peter is the head, that we believe that our Lord entrusted all the blessings of the New Covenant, in order to establish on earth the one Body of Christ into which all those should be fully incorporated who belong in any way to the people of God" (art. 3).

The *Decree*'s conception of "perfect ecclesiastical communion" affirms a pluralistic pattern of Christian unity like that envisaged by some Catholic ecumenical pioneers. The document finds a partial model of the desired communion in an earlier period of Christian history: "For many centuries the Churches of the East and West went their own ways, though a brotherly communion of faith and sacramental life bound them together. If disagreements in faith and discipline arose among them, the Roman See acted by common consent as moderator" (art. 14). Restored communion between the Roman and Eastern churches will not require conformity of the latter to Roman ways, for the Roman Church recognizes the richness of Eastern theological, liturgical, canonical, and spiritual traditions, and she regards their co-existence with her own traditions as a proper expression of the freedom and diversity that befits the unity of Christ's church. But today the communion between the Roman and the Eastern churches is incomplete. A principal task of ecumenism is to transform their incomplete communion into perfect communion. That transformation will occur as the visible and invisible elements of Christ's church are more completely realized on each side of the Catholic-Eastern split. Then the institutional and personal bonds that develop between them will reflect the communion that is Christ's will, and their communion finally will be expressed in the full sharing of eucharistic worship.[39]

By its formulation of the Catholic vision of restored unity principally in reference to the Eastern churches, the *Decree* continued a pattern begun in Leo XIII's pontificate. Its consideration of Protestantism moves within the framework of the goal of "perfect ecclesiastical communion." Western "churches and ecclesial communities . . . are bound to the Catholic Church by a specially close relationship as a result of the long span of earlier centuries when the Christian people had lived in ecclesiastical communion" (art. 19). The presence of partial, imperfect communion must foster no illusions about the ease with which perfect communion can be restored, for between the Roman and the Western churches "there are very weighty differences not only of an historical, sociological, psychological and cultural character, but especially in the interpretation of revealed truth" (art. 19). The *Decree*'s appraisal of these bodies acknowledges both strengths and deficiencies in their confession of Christ, in their respect for Scripture, in their sacraments, and in their Christian way of life.

The *Decree*'s discussion of dialogue accepts the methodological program developed in preceding years by the Roman Church's ecumenical pioneers. Through their respectful, probing conversation, Catholics and non-Catholics can understand each other better and grow into "a deeper realization and a clearer expression of the unfathomable riches of Christ" (art. 11). The document's most provocative statement about dialogue is the recognition that "in Catholic doctrine there exists an order or 'hierarchy' of truths, since they vary in their relation to the foundation of the Christian faith" (art. 11). Typically, the statement is undeveloped, but possibly its authors intended it to be interpreted in the light of Archbishop Pangrazio's claim that Christians are united in the primary truths of Christianity and separated in those that are secondary.

The *Decree* also acknowledges that divided Christians must do more than talk with one another. Because they already share a measure of common Christian faith and life, together they must confess Christ among non-Christians and work for a more just social order. They also must pray with one another, and they may worship together insofar as their worship is judged by church authorities not to violate the two principles governing *communicatio in sacris*: "The expression of unity very generally forbids common worship. Grace to be obtained sometimes commends it" (art. 8).

The *Decree* confirms the conviction of such pioneers as Congar and Couturier that the essential contribution Catholics can make to the advancement of Christian unity is the renewal of their church and of their own lives. The Roman Church's unique endowment from Christ is no warrant for Catholics to overestimate either the perfection of their church or their own sanctity. They must ever move toward the goal which is ahead: "During its pilgrimage on earth, this people . . . is growing in Christ . . . until it shall happily arrive at the fullness of eternal glory in the heavenly Jerusalem" (art. 3). The more completely the Roman Church's discipline, moral conduct, and doctrinal formulations are submitted to that "continual reformation of which she always has need" (art. 6), the more vividly she will manifest and experience the presence of Christ's church. And the more thoroughly individual Catholics are converted to a deeper union with God, the more intense will become the love that binds them to other Christians. As the same renewal spreads contagiously among other churches and other Christians, the unity that God intends between the churches and between Christians will become more perfectly realized.

More clearly than any previous official statement, the *Decree* recognizes the complementarity of the preservationist and transformationist tasks in the pursuit of unity. Assertions of the Roman Church's uniqueness are found throughout the document, but the nature and consequences of that uniqueness are freshly viewed. Thus, the *Decree* affirms that the Roman Church alone has been given the fullness of the means of grace, but it also recognizes that she enjoys no monopoly over those means. Nor does she perfectly manifest them or derive all the benefits of grace that are offered through them. She rejoices in their presence elsewhere and seeks to learn from other churches how her own manner of being Christ's church can be perfected. Indeed the fact of her unique endowment from Christ demands that she be engaged in constant self-transformation, so that the presence of Christ's church may become ever more manifest—both within her own life and, through the stimulus of her winsome example, in other churches. Faithfulness to her preservationist task, therefore requires dedication to the companion task of self-transformation. Significantly, the *Decree* concludes by calling for ecumenical activity that is both "loyal to the truth we have received from the Apostles and the Fathers, . . . and at the same time tending toward that fullness in which our Lord wants his Body to grow in the course of time" (art. 24).

* * *

Most Council fathers agreed that change must come to the Roman Church, but few of them realized how ardently hopeful

Catholics would press for far-reaching change once the conciliar venture in aggiornamento had ended. In the stormy years since 1965, Catholic innovators' collective impact upon the life and thought of their church has been pronounced. A measure of their impact is Lutheran scholar George Lindbeck's observation that "developments greater than those which have occurred slowly and amorphously in a period of generations within Protestantism have been compressed into months and years" within Catholicism.[40]

Resistance to those developments has been most conspicuous among members of the Roman hierarchy, but a growing number of laity and clergy have protested what they regard as some innovators' too rapid and indiscriminate jettisoning of traditional ways. Like the proposals for change, the proposals for conservation reflect a considerable variety of views regarding the Catholic future. Conflict between the competing camps has brought the Roman Church into a condition of disarray perhaps not matched since the Reformation. But it must also be noted that some influential Catholics are attempting to move constructively through this period of ferment, determined to shape a Catholicism in which values from both traditionalist and renewalist sources are fruitfully joined.

As was remarked in the first page of this study, the Roman Church's ecumenical involvements have been enormously creative in the volatile years since Vatican II. Whether future decades will prove as ecumenically productive is problematic. It is conceivable that conservative resistance to innovation will lead the Roman Church to reaffirm and update familiar separatist patterns. That possibility is encouraged by several elements in the current cultural climate. For instance, in many quarters one finds a reaction against the homogenizing, standardizing pressures of modern mass society in favor of traditional ethnic and religious identities which have been determinative in establishing self-identity. There is also widely present a disenchantment with all institutions, a fissiparous retreat by the individual from corporate engagement to privatization and intensely subjective life styles. The prospect of continued Protestant-Catholic convergence toward more inclusive forms of Christian community is further dimmed by a pervasive pessimistic mood: so many ideals have been compromised and hopes quashed that people do not readily commit themselves to the ideal of Christian unity. That commitment is made the more difficult when it is recognized that Catholic-Protestant unity requires far-reaching change and long-range strategies rather than the instant remedies in vogue today.[41]

A further sobering note issues from the Christian theological tradition: the doctrine of sin suggests that human beings will use even religion to indulge their desire to assert superiority and dominance over other persons. The spoken or unspoken claim that "my church is better than your church" remains an appealing way for Christians to yield to that temptation and betray the gospel of reconciliation.

If such factors preclude a glibly optimistic view of the Catholic ecumenical future, one must also recognize other factors that indicate the likelihood of continued movement toward Catholic-Protestant unity.

It is evident that the Second Vatican Council will influence Catholic thinking and behavior for many years. Even though the Council did not unambiguously promote ecumenism, one can expect that as new leaders emerge in the Roman Church, their minds will have been colored more decisively by the ecumenically favorable teachings and orientations of the Council than by those which reflect an earlier era. Especially important in the Council's legacy to the future is the three-fold insistence that unity is central to God's redemptive intent for humankind; that the unity he intends for the church requires discovery of pluralistic patterns of ecclesial life which allow all Christians to experience their reconciliation in "one Lord, one faith, one baptism;" and that Christians' corporate life should illumine the human family's groping for unity-in-diversity. No church has made a more thorough formal acknowledgment that faithfulness to the gospel requires commitment to ecumenism.

The Council's affirmations about unity reflect fundamental Christian convictions about the activity of man and God. Those convictions suggest that although many people today shun involvement in the demanding quest for new community, they nevertheless yearn for human solidarity. That longing is a consequence of the fact that human beings are created by God for community, not separation. Their lives are fulfilled through participation in patterns of community that nurture both their distinct identities and their interdependence. However difficult the task, Christ's church is intended to demonstrate the deepest meanings and the highest potentialities of human community. Her mission in the world requires that she be freed from whatever denies the richness of the human family's diversity and perpetuates its estrangements. God himself is committed to that transformation and by his Spirit empowers those persons who attempt to be his instruments of liberation and reconciliation. The Christian theological tradition affirms that those persons who strive for unity-in-diversity move concurrently with human aspiration and divine providence.

Continued Catholic-Protestant rapprochement also is encouraged by developments that have occurred quietly since the Council's adjournment. In numerous communities around the world Catholics and Protestants have entered into respectful, caring relationships which constitute a connective tissue between their churches. As many as fifteen different realms of current ecumenical collaboration were identified in 1975 by the Vatican Secretariat for Promoting Christian Unity. So remarkable is the breadth of collaboration that all fifteen realms deserve mention: (1) sharing in prayer and worship; (2) common Bible work; (3) joint pastoral care; (4) shared buildings; (5) collaboration in education; (6) joint use of communications media; (7) cooperation in the health field; (8) national and international emergencies; (9) relief of human need; (10) social problems; (11) Sodepax groups (promoted by the international agency which was created by the Roman Church and the World Council of Churches to deal with peace and development issues); (12) bilateral dialogues; (13) meetings of heads of communions; (14) joint working groups; and (15) councils of churches and Christian councils.[42]

For most of these realms no figures are available indicating the full scope of Catholic involvement, but in some cases they are available. For instance, Catholics officially collaborate in 133 Bible translation projects, and the Roman Church is a member body in nineteen national councils of churches (in Denmark, Sweden, Finland, the Netherlands, Swaziland, Belize, Samoa, Fiji, New Hebrides, Solomon Islands, Papua-New Guinea, Tonga,

West Germany, Botswana, St. Vincent, Sudan, Uganda, Guyana, Trinidad and Tobago).[43]

The approaches that Catholics and Protestants take to most issues rising in these fifteen realms have been increasingly shaped by identical perceptions and objectives. Their convergence mirrors that which has been noted at higher levels by Cardinal Jan Willebrands, President of the Secretariat for Promoting Christian Unity: "The great problems and tasks that now concern the churches are seen by the World Council of Churches and by the Catholic Church in the same way, indeed they are also formulated almost in the same way."[44]

Another volume would need to be written to report and analyze all that has been accomplished in the many realms of post-conciliar collaboration. We must content ourselves with only a sampling of the progress made in several of the more critical realms.

The Secretariat's explanation of "joint pastoral care" notes both the special need for such effort among the partners in mixed marriages and the significant encouragement given to this ecumenical ministry by a 1970 papal letter, *Matrimonia Mixta*. But the ecumenical import of interchurch marriages has moved beyond their providing an occasion for collaborative pastoral care. *Matrimonia Mixta* took certain other cautious forward steps (including a cessation of the requirement that the non-Catholic partner promise to rear the couple's children as Catholics) that have helped to make such families an important frontier for the advancement of Catholic-Protestant unity. This fact has been noted with increasing frequency, as in the Belgian Catholic bishops' statement that the partners in such a marriage "are not only called to assume personally the suffering of the division between the churches; in the little church of their family they can also be a prefiguration of the Christian unity which is yet to come."[45] The possible long-range ecumenical consequences of such marriages was evident in a German scholar's observation that "a significant number of interchurch couples are finding that it is possible to bring up their children to feel at home in both their traditions, and thus to experience unity before they become aware of divisions. Such couples have no interest in any reductionist form of Christianity; it is the fullness of their two traditions that they seek to share with each other; it is this fullness that they strive to give to their children. They beg the churches to consider this aim and achievement seriously, with all its implications, including those for the administration of the sacraments."[46]

The Secretariat's brief commentary upon collaboration in education calls attention to the increasing number of institutions engaged in ecumenical patterns of theological education. Catholic seminaries have joined with Protestant counterparts to share facilities, to offer common courses, and to encourage crossing by faculty and students of traditional Catholic-Protestant dividing lines. Here, too, a future impact of far-reaching consequence is being prepared.

Catholic and Protestant scholars engaged in official bilateral conversations have reached significant agreements on most of the doctrinal issues traditionally controverted between their churches. A discerning 1972 Catholic critique of eight bilaterals then underway in the United States made this appraisal of the theologians' efforts: "The bilateral conversations have already been of great service in the revitalization of all the communions involved. They have helped to overcome prejudices, to establish friendship and trust, to suggest realistic ecumenical goals, and to prompt a healthy reexamination of the doctrinal positions that have become habitual in the various confessional traditions."[47]

Theological progress has been especially notable in the conversations between Catholic and Lutheran scholars in the United States. By 1970 these men had reached sufficient agreement regarding the ordained ministry and the eucharist to recommend that their respective churches move toward recognition of each other's ministries and eucharists.[48] In March 1974 the group affirmed— and urged their churches seriously to consider—the possibility of a renewed papacy exercising its unitive ministry in a communion of "sister churches" that includes both the Roman Catholic and Lutheran Churches.[49] Although their recommendations had not yet been rejected or endorsed by the churches they represented, the scholars turned next to a consideration of the difficult issue of papal infallibility. Their preliminary sketch of a future communion of sister churches appeared compatible with the *Decree on Ecu-*

menism's vision of "perfect ecclesiastical communion" as well as with central features of the goal of a "conciliar fellowship of local churches" affirmed by the World Council of Churches Nairobi Assembly in December 1975.[50]

By the end of the first decade following Vatican II, signs of ecumenical advance coexisted with signs of ecumenical retreat. Often it appeared that the ecumenically significant experience of ordinary Christians and the ecumenically significant conclusions of scholars outpaced the ecumenically significant decisions of ecclesiastical hierarchies. Among many the great hope for unity awakened by the Council had waned. But we have seen that ecumenical pilgrims have repeatedly encountered impasses, delays, and detours; their presence today should occasion no surprise. Neither should there be surprise when again people and events conspire to lift the churches over obstacles to greater unity. The record of twentieth-century ecumenical progress makes it plausible to anticipate that Catholic and Protestant sister churches will continue to move toward discovery of a mutually acceptable form of "perfect ecclesiastical communion."

NOTES

1. Signs of the conservatives' power in Rome at the beginning of the Council are discussed in Henri Fesquet, *The Drama of Vatican II*, trans. Bernard Murchland (New York: Random House, 1967), pp. 6-9, 66; Michael Novak, *The Open Church: Vatican II, Act II* (New York: Macmillan, 1964), pp. 3-8; and Xavier Rynne, *Vatican Council II* (New York: Farrar, Straus and Giroux, 1968), pp. 30-36.

2. George A. Lindbeck, "Reform and the Council," *Lutheran World* 9 (1962): 315.

3. Marc Boegner, *The Long Road to Unity* (London: Collins, 1970), p. 288. Cf. Lindbeck, "Reform," p. 308; Vischer, "The Ecumenical Movement," in Fey, ed., *Ecumenical Advance*, p. 330.

4. Walter Abbot, ed., *The Documents of Vatican II* (New York: Guild Press, America Press, and Association Press, 1966), p. 715.

5. Hans Küng, Yves Congar, Daniel O'Hanlon, eds., *Council Speeches of Vatican II* (Glen Rock, New Jersey: Paulist Press Deus Books, 1964), pp. 145, 146, 148. Paul's expression of respect for other Christians went a step further the following spring in his Easter greeting to the non-Catholic churches of the world. Here the pope used the word "church" in speaking of Protestant bodies: "Peace and salvation to the

whole of the Anglican Church, while with a sincere love and the same hope we wish one day to see her once again as an honored member of the one universal fold of Christ. . . . Salvation and peace to all the other Churches which originated from the Reformation in the sixteenth century, and who separated themselves from us at that time." Bea, *Ecumenism*, p. 87.

6. Fesquet, *Drama*, p. 175; Bea, *Ecumenism*, p. 74.

7. Fesquet, *Drama*, pp. 178, 378; Bea, *Ecumenism*, pp. 203-4; Brown, *Ecumenical Revolution*, p. 169; Douglas Horton, *Vatican Diary 1965* (Philadelphia: United Church Press, 1966), pp. 173-4.

8. Cf. Albert Outler, *Methodist Observer at Vatican II* (Westminster: Newman Press, 1967), p. 15; Oscar Cullmann, *Vatican Council II, The New Direction* (New York: Harper and Row, 1968), p. 61.

9. Some curial officials resented this newcomer in their midst. The Holy Office's displeasure that responsibility for ecumenical matters no longer resided exclusively in its hands had been evident when Catholic observers were appointed to the 1961 World Council of Churches Assembly. The Holy Office had claimed the right to respond to the World Council invitation and had decided that no Catholic observers would be sent. The Secretariat appealed to Pope John and succeeded in having the Holy Office's decision overruled. But rather than being allowed to send observers from its own ranks, the Secretariat was required to appoint persons not among its consultants or members. See Vischer, "The Ecumenical Movement," p. 328; cf. Fesquet, *Drama*, pp. 774-5. The Secretariat's difficulties within the Curia did not end when the Council adjourned; see Grootaers, "Willebrands," *One In Christ* 6 (1970): 26-42.

10. Bea, *Ecumenism*, pp. 48, 187. One finds discrepancies among authors regarding the number of observers and guests actually present at the Council. Congar, for instance, reported that at the first session 39 observers and guests were present, the former representing 18 ecclesiastical bodies. Congar, *Report From Rome* (London: Geoffrey Chapman, 1963), pp. 139-42. The figures cited in the text are from Cardinal Bea's account of the Council. It should be noted that although there was a technical distinction between "observers" (originally called "observer delegates") and "guests of the Secretariat," the two groups were treated essentially alike and frequently all were called "observers."

11. Bea, *Ecumenism*, p. 50; Horton, *Vatican Dairy 1962* (Philadelphia: United Church Press, 1964), p. 21.

12. Bea, *Ecumenism*, pp. 51, 136-7, 165, 189; Fesquet, *Drama*, p. 371; Edmund Schlink, *After the Council*, trans. Herbert J. A. Bouman (Philadelphia: Fortress Press, 1968), p. 29. Visser 't Hooft has reported the remark of an unnamed Catholic theologian that "if an edition of the Council documents could be issued in which all passages that had been changed in the light of the remarks of the observers were printed in red the result would be a most colorful production." *Memoirs*, p. 330.

13. Horton, *Vatican Diary 1965*, p. 193. Similar sentiments have

been expressed in other accounts of the Council written by observers; e.g., Outler, *Methodist Observer;* Cullmann, *Vatican Council II;* Robert McAfee Brown, *Observer in Rome: A Protestant Report on the Vatican Council* (New York: Doubleday, 1964).

14. These statements are reproduced (along with comparable ones) in Küng, Congar, O'Hanlon, eds., *Council Speeches*, pp. 190-92, 216-18, 150-51.

15. A sampling of the myriad of such events is reported in *EPS*, passim, and Ward, *Documents of Dialogue*, passim.

16. Vischer, "The Ecumenical Movement," pp. 339-40, 342, 349-52. See also Bea and Visser 't Hooft, *Peace Among Christians*, trans. Judith Moses (New York: Association Press, Herder and Herder, 1967), pp. 7-27. A more recent stage of Roman Church-World Council rapprochement is reported in "Patterns of Relationship between the Roman Catholic Church and the World Council of Churches," *Ecumenical Review* 24 (1972): 247-88.

17. Bea, *Ecumenism*, pp. 158, 238-40; *EPS*, 17 June 1965; *EPS*, 9 September 1965. In July 1965 a bilateral conversation also had been inaugurated among scholars appointed by Lutheran and Catholic authorities in the United States. A study of those and other "bilaterals" has been made by Nils Ehrenström and Günther Gassmann, *Confessions in Dialogue* (Geneva: World Council of Churches, 1972).

18. *EPS*, 1 July 1965; *EPS*, 15 July 1965; Bea, *Ecumenism*, pp. 250-53; *EPS*, 6 January 1966. The idea for the Jerusalem center (established after the Council) emerged from exchanges between Pope Paul and Professor Skydsgaard at meetings of the pope with the observers and guests.

19. See especially *Dogmatic Constitution on the Church*, art. 13; *Pastoral Constitution on the Church in the Modern World*, art. 2; *Declaration on the Relationship of the Church to non-Christian Religions*, art. 1; and *Decree on the Missionary Activity of the Church*, art. 7. A useful study of the Council's reflection on these and related points has been made by Bea, *The Church and Mankind*, trans. James Brand (London: Geoffrey Chapman, 1967).

20. *Non-Christian Religions*, art. 2. Cf. *Church*, art. 16; *Modern World*, art. 22; *Missionary Activity*, art. 9.

21. The desire to fathom the meaning of modern history grew during the Council, and its effect can be seen especially among the final documents promulgated. As various scholars have indicated, this aspect of the Council's intellectual development represents a historicized version of the Thomistic view that grace does not destroy but perfects nature. The principal texts interpreting the significance of modern history for the church's unitive mission are in *Modern World*, especially arts. 24, 26, 39, 40, 42, and 92. Cf. *Church*, arts. 1, 13, 48; *Missionary Activity*, arts. 8, 11. See also Bea, *Church and Mankind*, pp. 249-53.

22. Prof. Lindbeck has pointed to the presence of both an "incarnationist" and an "eschatologist" tendency in the Council's pronouncements

about the church's relation to the world. The former emphasizes that movement toward mankind's transformation and unification will proceed through the progressive Christianization of the world and growth of the church. The latter looks toward a consummation more dependent upon God's intervention than upon the ambiguous progress of the church and the world. *Future*, pp. 41-50. It should be noted, too, that the question of the mutual relation of modern history and Christian unity, so provocatively raised by *Modern World*, emerged relatively late in the conciliar process and unfortunately had not been thoroughly pursued in the circles chiefly responsible for the *Decree on Ecumenism*. On this important issue the problematics of the two documents thus were not instructively joined at Vatican II. Significantly, the question of the relationship of Christian unity and mankind's growing unity became prominent in World Council of Churches circles in the early 1970s.

23. *Modern World*, art. 92; cf. Lindbeck, *Future*, pp. 77-80. Conciliar documents indicated at least five arenas for the exercise of Catholic ecumenical responsibility: (1) Joint Bible translations, *Divine Revelation*, art. 22; (2) common witness, *Missionary Activity*, arts. 15, 29, 36, 41; *Decree on the Apostolate of the Laity*, art. 27; *Modern World*, arts. 88, 92; (3) training of priests, *Decree on Priestly Formation*, art. 16; (4) bishops' leadership, *Decree on the Bishops' Pastoral Office in the Church*, art. 16; (5) theological dialogue, *Declaration on Christian Education*, art. 11.

24. Cullmann, *Vatican Council II*, pp. 79-80, 85. But not all Protestants were as pleased as Cullmann with the Bible's role; Edmund Schlink, for instance, stressed that "as a whole, the Bible was used for apologetics and for illustrations. It was not the norm for the decisions of the Council." "The Decree on Ecumenism," in Lindbeck, ed., *Dialogue on the Way*, p. 222.

25. Skydsgaard, "Scripture and Tradition," in Warren A. Quanbeck, ed., *Challenge and Response* (Minneapolis: Augsburg Publishing House, 1966), pp. 25-58; Schlink, *After the Council*, pp. 169-83; Paul S. Minear, "A Protestant Point of View," in John H. Miller, ed., *Vatican II: An Interfaith Appraisal* (Notre Dame: University of Notre Dame Press, 1966), pp. 68-88; George B. Caird, *Our Dialogue With Rome* (London: Oxford University Press, 1967), pp. 28-51.

26. Skydsgaard, "The Church as Mystery and as People of God," in Lindbeck, ed., *Dialogue on the Way*, pp. 145-174; Quanbeck, "Problems of Mariology," in Ibid., pp. 175-85; Schlink, *After the Council*, pp. 65-99.

27. Cf. Vilmos Vajta, "Renewal of Worship: De Sacra Liturgia," in *Dialogue on the Way*, pp. 101-28; Schlink, *After the Council*, pp. 50-64, 137-68; Joseph Sittler, "A Protestant Point of View," in Miller, ed., *Vatican II*, pp. 422-27; Lindbeck, "The Declaration on Religious Liberty," in Quanbeck, ed., *Challenge and Response*, pp. 145-60; Brown, *Ecumenical Revolution*, pp. 244-66; A. F. Carrillo de Albornoz, *Religious Liberty*, trans. John Drury (New York: Sheed and Ward, 1967).

28. This convergence was noted in Schlink, "The Theological Basis

of the Pastoral Constitution on the Church in the Modern World," in Quanbeck, *Challenge and Response*, pp. 173-184.

29. Among the many expressions of this theme were Karl Barth, *Ad Limina Apostolorum: An Appraisal of Vatican II*, trans. Keith R. Crim (Richmond: John Knox Press, 1967), especially pp. 63-79; Albert Outler, *Methodist Observer*, pp. 62-8, 172-89; and G. C. Berkouwer, *The Second Vatican Council*, pp. 249-58.

30. The most complete account of the debate and maneuvering that accompanied formulation of the *Decree on Ecumenism* is Werner Becker, "History of the Decree," in Herbert Vorgrimler, ed., *Commentary on the Documents of Vatican II*, 3 vols., trans. William Glen-Doepel et al., (New York: Herder and Herder, 1968), 2: 1-56.

31. Lorenz Jaeger, *A Stand on Ecumenism: The Council's Decree*, trans. Hilda Graef (New York: P. J. Kenedy & Sons, 1965), p. 14.

32. Becker, "History," pp. 52-5; Johannes Feiner, "Commentary on the Decree," in Vorgrimler, ed., *Commentary*, 2: 159-64; Thomas F. Stransky, "Commentary," *The Decree on Ecumenism of the Second Vatican Council* (Glen Rock: Paulist Press, 1965), pp. 10-12; Jaeger, *A Stand*, pp. 52-5. Cf. Wolfgang Dietzfelbinger, "The Council Continues: Third Session," in Lindbeck, ed., *Dialogue on the Way*, pp. 92-3.

33. An earlier version of the *Decree* included additional statements on religious freedom and the Jewish people, but in the end the Council accepted the Secretariat's original intention to have separate conciliar declarations on each of those subjects.

34. Cited in Becker, "History," p. 56.

35. The *Decree* does not attempt to answer every question it raises or to explain how all juxtaposed statements are to be related. Such a text requires and encourages interpretation in the light of understandings brought to it. Doors are left open for a variety of interpretations, as well as for shifting interpretations with the passing of time and the accumulation of experience. The following discussion of the *Decree* is admittedly an interpretation—one that has been informed especially by the commentary of Johannes Feiner.

36. Alternative formulations of the ecumenical goal used in the *Decree* are "full ecclesiastical communion" (art. 3) and "the reconciliation of all Christians in the unity of the one and only church of Christ" (art. 24).

37. It should be noted that the Secretariat justified application of the "churches and ecclesial communities" formula to Western ecclesiastical bodies by arguing that the Old Catholic Church (found predominantly in Europe) merits the title "church" because like the Eastern churches, it has a valid ministry and eucharist. See Hamer, "Die Ekklesiologische Terminologie des Vatikanum II und die Protestantischen Amter," *Catholica* 26 (1972): 146-53.

38. Gustave Thils, *Le décret sur l'oecuménisme* (Paris: Desclée de Brouwer, 1966), p. 38.

39. Although the *Decree* does not directly relate its discussion of re-

stored ecclesial communion to a consideration of the communion already present within the Roman Church, some commentators have provocatively done so. Feiner writes: "There is naturally no question that each of these communities may be another Church of Christ; the text of the decree excludes this itself in emphasizing the uniqueness of the Church of Christ. But are they not to be regarded as individual Churches, in which the one Church of Christ is visibly present? Just as in the primitive Church each individual Church (Ephesus, Thessalonica, Corinth, etc.) was regarded as the realization of the one Church of Christ at a particular place . . . , so that it was possible to speak of 'Churches' in the plural, so also the dioceses of the Catholic Church are not merely administrative districts of the one universal Church, but the concrete presence of the one Church in a particular place, so that one can speak of (particular or local) Churches in the plural (the Church of Paris, the Church of Cologne, the Catholic Eastern Churches). Should not the non-Catholic Christian communions be regarded in a similar way as different realizations and different kinds of presence of the one Church of Christ, and therefore be known as (particular) Churches?" "Commentary," p. 76. Cf. Stransky, "The Decree on Ecumenism," in Miller, ed., *Vatican II*, p. 382, and Gregory Baum, "The Ecclesial Reality of the Other Churches," in Küng, ed., *The Church and Ecumenism*, Concilium, Ecumenical Theology Vol. 4 (New York: Paulist Press, 1965), pp. 76-86.

　　40. Lindbeck, "The Crisis in American Catholicism," (Taylor Lecture delivered at Yale Divinity School Alumni Convocation, April 1973), p. 5.

　　41. This brief statement about the "current cultural climate" draws from numerous sources. Articles in the Golden Anniversary Issue of *Saturday Review/World* are especially insightful, e.g., in Part I, August 10, 1974: Norman Cousins, "Musings on a Golden Anniversary," pp. 4-7; Henry Steele Commager, "America in the Age of No Confidence," pp. 15-21. In Part 2, August 24, 1974: Norman Cousins, "Prophecy and Pessimism," pp. 6-7; Kurt Waldheim, "Toward Global Interdependence," pp. 63-4, 122.

　　42. "Ecumenical Collaboration at the Regional, National and Local Levels," *Ecumenical Trends* 4 (1975): 118-23.

　　43. Ibid., pp. 119, 126.

　　44. Willebrands, "Roman Catholic Ecumenism in 1973," *Ecumenical Trends* 2 (1974): 9.

　　45. "*Matrimonia Mixta*: Some Episcopal Directories," *One in Christ* 7 (1971): 223.

　　46. D. Joachim Lell, "Interchurch Marriages," *Ecumenical Review* 27 (1975): 379-80.

　　47. "The Bilateral Consultations Between the Roman Catholic Church in the United States and Other Christian Communions: A Theological Review and Critique by the Study Committee Commissioned by the Board of Directors of the Catholic Theological Society of America,"

Proceedings of the Twenty-Seventh Annual Convention of the CTSA 27 (1972): 228.

48. *Lutherans and Catholics in Dialogue IV: Eucharist and Ministry* (New York: USA National Committee of the Lutheran World Federation, and Washington: Bishops' Committee for Ecumenical and Interreligious Affairs, 1970).

49. Paul C. Empie and T. Austin Murphy, eds., *Lutherans and Catholics in Dialogue V: Papal Primacy and the Universal Church* (Minneapolis: Augsburg Publishing House, 1974).

50. A helpful background document prepared before the Nairobi Assembly is " 'The Unity of the Church—Next Steps,' Report of the Salamanca Consultation convened by the Faith and Order Commission, WCC, on 'Concepts of Unity and Models of Union,' " *Ecumenical Review* 26 (1974): 291-303.

Index

Abbott, Walter A., 134
Adam, Karl, 53, 87-9, 100, 102, 122 n. 6, 161, 231
Adrian VI, Pope, 13, 209
Alfrink, Archbishop Bernhard, 134
Amitié (Christian Association of Professors), 177
Anglican orders, 18, 35, 37, 55-6
Anglicans. *See* Church of England
Apostolate of Reunion, 65
Association for the Promotion of the Unity of Christendom, 23
Athenagoras, Ecumenical Patriarch, 227
Aubert, Roger, 165
Augsburg Confession, 14, 16
Augustine, Saint, 52

Baptism, 87, 100, 102, 200, 204, 210, 231
Bares, Bishop Nicolaus, 83
Barth, Karl, 80-81, 95 n. 25, 142, 181, 214-7
Baudrillart, Alfred, 43
Baum, Gregory, 185
Bea, Cardinal Augustine, 171, 185, 200, 210, 227-8, 236
Beauduin, Lambert, 50, 56, 60-66, 78, 83, 196 n. 82, 226
Beaupère, René, 177-8, 203
Benedict XV, Pope, 40, 54, 76-7
Benedictines, 60, 64, 66, 175, 178, 180-81, 194 n. 59
Berdyaev, Nicholas, 99
Bible. *See* Scripture
Blanshard, Paul, 190 n. 19
Boegner, Marc, 133, 171-2, 178
Bonhoeffer, Dietrich, 126
Bossuet, Bishop Jacques-Benigne, 16
Bouyer, Louis, 206-7, 209
Boyer, Charles, 169, 172-4, 182, 185

Brandenburg, Albert, 208
Brown, Robert McAfee, 184
Brunner, Emil, 80
Brunner, Peter, 199
Bultmann, Rudolf, 142
Butler, Charles, 22

Cahiers du témoignage chrétien, 128
Calvin, John, 205, 207
Carlhian, Victor, 108
Carnegie, Andrew, 84
Cassander, George, 14-5
Catholic Conference for Ecumenical Questions, 183
Catholica, 80, 144, 175
Charles, Pierre, 54, 69 n. 18, 82
Charles I, King, 15
Charrière, Bishop François, 179, 183, 185
Chrétiens désunis, 99-107, 119, 238
Christian Commission on Cooperation, 130
Christian Unity Association, 176
Church of England: Gallican overtures to, 17-9; and nineteenth-century ecumenism, 22-3; viewed by Manning, 27 n. 29; and Leo XIII, 34; and Portal, 37; in Octave petition, 40; and Monks of Union, 61; contrasting views of, 74; Beauduin's hope for, 83; and Sword of the Spirit, 128-9; participation in Belgian dialogues, 164; Vatican visit of Archbishop of Canterbury, 183; evaluation of, 202, 213, 248 n. 5. *See also* Anglican orders; Malines, Conversations of; Thirty-nine Articles
Church Peace Union, 84
Clement VII, Pope, 13
Cochlaeus, John, 205

Committee of Liaison Between the Communities, 130
Communism, 50, 137
Congar, Yves Marie-Joseph: influenced by Mercier, 56; on Protestant ecumenical advances, 79-80; edits journal series, 90-92; writes *Chrétiens désunis*, 98-108; affirmed by Lortz, 119; significance of, 120-21; varied names of, 122 n. 2; and Couturier, 123 n. 21; in prison camps, 127; urges Catholic reform, 136; advocates dialogue, 138; and Week of Prayer, 162; criticism against, 172; and ecumenical specialists, 182; Pope John agrees with, 185; in dialogues, 189 n. 13; view of baptism, 200; and Pope Paul, 226; influences Vatican II, 231, 236-8, 240
Constitution on the Sacred Liturgy, 234
Contarini, Cardinal Gasparo, 14
Copec Conference, 85
Cornoldi, Giovanni, 31
Couturier, Paul: view of Providence, 44; influenced by Mercier, 56; initiates Week of Prayer, 107-12; significance of, 120; and Congar, 123 n. 21; expands impact, 162-4; responds to *Instructio*, 169; criticism against, 172-4; successor of, 176; Pope John agrees with, 185; contribution of, 218; and Vatican II, 227, 240
Cullmann, Oscar, 134, 178, 217 228, 233
Curia, Roman, 13, 184, 224, 226

Dachau, 127
Davenport, Christopher. *See* Sancta Clara, Franciscus a
Davidson, Archbiship Randall, 55
Dawson, Christopher, 51, 150 n. 14
Declaration on Religious Freedom, 228, 234

Declaration on the Relation of the Church to non-Christian Religions, 228
Decree on Ecumenism, 24, 99, 210, 228-9, 235-41
de Lisle, Ambrose Phillipps, 23
Delp, Alfred, 126
Denifle, Heinrich, 42-4, 52
De Saussure, Jean, 111
Dez, Jean, 15-6
Dogmatic Constitution on Divine Revelation, 233
Dogmatic Constitution on the Church, 231, 234, 238
Doi, Archbishop, 130
Dombes, Group of the, 163, 192 n. 40
Dominicans, 65, 80, 90, 99, 177
Dondeyne, Albert, 138
Döpfner, Archbishop Julius, 175
Doyle, Bishop James, 22
Dulles, Avery, 72 n. 39, 204
Dumont, Christophe, J., 65, 177, 185, 203
Du Pin, Louis Ellies, 17-8, 26 n. 17

Eastern Churches Quarterly, 66, 73 n. 46, 144
Eastern Orthodoxy: viewed by Oxford Movement, 22-3; and Leo XIII, 34-5; and Fernand Portal, 37; in Octave prayer intentions, 40; and Malines Conversations, 56; stimulates Catholic ecumenism, 58-66; in early ecumenical organizations, 75; evaluated by Congar, 103; and scholarly cooperation, 134; participation in dialogues, 162-5; evaluation of, 199, 201-2; future unity with, 213; and Jerusalem study center, 230; viewed by Vatican II, 237-9
Ecumenical Review, 147
Edinburgh Conference (1910), 76
Elchinger, Coadjutor Archbishop Leon, 229
Equidem verba, 60, 175
Erasmus, Desiderius, 14, 19, 62, 117

Eucharist: interpreted by Du Pin, 17-8; and liturgical movement, 81, 142; Catholic concessions on, 83; in Protestantism, 204; Catholic reinterpretation of, 214; and Vatican II, 231, 251 n. 37
Eugene IV, Pope, 64
Evangelical-Catholic Ecumenical Work Circle, 161, 192 n. 40

Faith and Order. *See* World Council on Faith and Order; World Council of Churches
Febronius, Justinius, 19, 216
Fischer, Anton, 52
Florence, Council of, 48, 64, 72 n. 39

Gallicanism, 17
Gerlier, Cardinal, 110, 162, 176
German Christian Fellowship, 21
German High Church Union, 82
Girardin, Patrick Piers de, 17
Griffin, Archbiship Bernard W., 134
Grosche, Robert, 80, 175

Halifax, Second Viscount (Charles Lindley Wood), 36-7, 55
Hamer, Jérôme, 185, 189 n. 13
Hanahoe, Edward Francis, 173-4, 201, 204
Heenan, Archbishop John, 179
Heiler, Friedrich, 82
Heresy: sixteenth-century reaction against, 12; viewed by Bossuet, 16; combatted by Holy Office, 24; and Pius IX, 45 n. 4; Council of Florence's evaluation of, 48; and Protestants, 74; Congar's assessment of, 101-2; viewed by Journet, 104; of Luther, 118; re-evaluation of, 197-8, 219 n. 1
Herte, Adolf, 205
Hessen, Johannes, 119, 207-8
Heufelder, Emmanuel, 175
High Church Ecumenical Federation, 82

Hinsley, Archbishop Arthur, 128
Hitler, Adolf, 80, 218. *See also* Nazis
Holy Office: repudiates APUC, 23; combats heresy, 24; forbids Lausanne attendance, 76; and High Church Ecumenical Federation, 82; forbids Amsterdam attendance, 145; statements on ecumenism, 166-9; cancels Spanish conference, 181; contact with ecumenists, 183; on *extra ecclesiam nulla salus*, 199; and Secretariat, 248 n. 9
Humani generis, 169

Instructio, 167-9, 210, 224
Integralism, 51, 170, 173
International Fellowship of Reconciliation, 85, 113
Invisible Monastery, 163
Irenaeus Center, Saint, 177
Irénikon, 61-2, 64, 144, 164
Istina (journal), 144, 177
Istina (study center), 65, 177

Jaeger, Archbishop Lorenz, 160, 167, 175, 185
Jesuits, 64, 77-8, 88, 90, 130, 134
Jews: prayer for conversion of, 40; in Church Peace Union, 84; make statement with Christians, 85; in National Conference of Christians and Jews, 86; Nazi contempt for, 86; and Holocaust, 126; cooperate during World War II, 130; participate in biblical project, 135; make statement with Christians, 151 n. 17; cooperate in integration crisis, 180; prayer for sanctification of, 189 n. 10; spiritual state of, 199; and *Decree on Ecumenism*, 251 n. 33
John XXIII, Pope, 139, 148, 183-8, 195 n. 82, 209, 224
Joint Working Group, 230
Journet, Charles, 74-5, 104, 198
Justification, doctrine of, 11, 20, 104, 117, 206-7, 214-6

Karrer, Otto, 54, 217
Kennedy, John F., 139
Kiefl, Franz Xaver, 52
Kinder, Ernst, 146, 154 n. 35,
  160, 188 n. 4
Kreisau Circle, 126
Küng, Hans, 120, 135-6, 186-7,
  214-7

Lackmann, Max, 143
Lagrange, M. J., 32, 132
Laros, Matthias, 160, 167
League for Evangelical-Catholic
  Reunion, 143
le Courayer, Pierre Françgis, 18-9
Leenhardt, Franz, 148
Léger, Cardinal Paul-Emile, 210
LeGuillou, M. J., 145-6, 177
Leo XIII, Pope: career and teach-
  ing of, 30-37; Wattson agrees
  with, 41; concerned for all hu-
  manity, 45 n. 9, 148, 232; Pope
  John's continuity with, 184;
  and *Decree on Ecumenism*, 239
Léonard, Augustin, 138
le Quien, Michel, 18
Lialine, Clément, 65
Life and Work. *See* Universal
  Christian Council on Life and
  Work
Lilienfeld, André de, 77
Lindbeck, George, 216, 242, 249
  n. 22
Lord's Prayer, 113, 127, 129, 167-
  8, 227
Lortz, Josef, 52, 115-20, 124 n.
  37, 188 n. 4, 205-9
Louvain, Catholic University of,
  156 n. 54, 179
Luther, Martin, 13, 41-4, 52, 101,
  104, 114-9, 204-9
Lutheran World Federation, 147,
  196 n. 86, 230
Lutherans: viewed by Erasmus,
  14; Bossuet's plan for return of,
  16; unity of faith with, 19;
  prayer for return of, 40; overtures to Catholics, 82; viewed
  by Congar, 99, 101; Lortz's
  evaluation of, 118; die

Sammlung formed by, 143;
  evaluate preconciliar Catholicism, 146-7; in Germany, 162;
  in Swedish conference, 165; cooperate in Berlin, 175; evaluate
  Vatican II teaching; 234; in
  postconciliar bilateral dialogues, 246. *See also* Augsburg
  Confession; Luther, Martin;
  Lutheran World Federation

Malines, Conversations of, 38,
  55-8, 61, 65, 70 n. 22, 78
Manning, Henry, 23, 27 n. 29
Maritain, Jacques, 51, 138
Mary, Blessed Virgin, 29, 40-41,
  146, 170-72, 216, 231, 234
Mayr, Kaspar, 85
Meinhold, Peter, 209
Meissinger, Karl August, 161
Mercier, Cardinal Désiré, 32, 52,
  55-8, 61, 65, 70 n. 22, 70 n. 23
Mersch, Emile, 69 n. 18, 88-9,
  100, 102-3, 122 n. 6, 131, 185
Metzger, Max Josef, 112-5, 120,
  126, 160
Michalon, Pierre, 176-7, 211
Missionary movement: viewed by
  Leo XIII, 33-4; and Octave of
  Prayer, 39-40; in early twen-
  tieth century, 54-5; Monks of
  Union, 64; and International
  Missionary Council, 76; and
  salvation, 96 n. 42; postwar fer-
  ment in, 140; converging with
  ecumenism, 141, 155 n. 53; and
  Week of Prayer, 176; and Vati-
  can II, 232-3
Mixed marriage, 182, 236, 245-6
Modernism, 38, 42, 47 n. 29, 170
Moeller, Charles, 164, 214
Möhler, Johann Adam, 21-2, 53
Möhler Institute, Johann Adam,
  175
Molanus, Gerhard Walter, 16
Monitum, 166-7, 169
Monks of Union, 60-65, 77, 81,
  99, 108, 164, 179, 192 n. 40,
  214
Mortalium animos, 77-9, 82, 169

Morren, Lucien and Hélène, 164, 179
Munificentissimus Deus. See Mary, Blessed Virgin
Murray, John Courtney, 130-31
Mystical Body of Christ, 53, 61, 66, 100, 198
Mystici Corporis Christi, 198-9

National Catholic Welfare Conference, 85
National Conference of Christians and Jews, 86
Nazis, 50, 86, 112-6, 126-8, 137, 164. *See also* Hitler, Adolf
Newbigin, Lesslie, 202
Newman, John Henry, 22-3, 116
Nouvelle revue théologique, 88

Octave of Prayer for Church Unity, 39-41, 108-10, 165, 172, 179, 184, 193 n. 50
Observers (at Vatican Council II), 185, 196 n. 86, 226-9, 248 n. 10, 248 n. 12
Occam, William of, 117
Orthodox. *See* Eastern Orthodoxy
Osservatore Romano, 105
Oxford Movement, 22-3, 27 n. 28, 37-8

Pangrazio, Archbishop Andrea, 229, 240
Papacy: viewed by Du Pin, 18, by Febronius, 19; conflicting understandings of, 20; Vatican I definition of, 29; Wattson's approach to, 41; discussed at Malines, 55; Beauduin's interpretation of, 63; denounced at Stockholm, 71 n. 26; interpreted by Adam, 161, by Boegner, 172, by Küng, 186, by Lortz, 206, by Cullmann, 217; role in future union, 246
Pastoral Constitution on the Church in the Modern World, 234
Paul III, Pope, 13
Paul IV, Pope, 12
Paul VI, Pope, 216, 225-7, 236

Pius IX, Pope, 29-30, 42, 219 n. 3
Pius X, Pope, 42-3
Pius XI, Pope, 40, 50, 54-5, 58-60, 77-9, 201
Pius XII, Pope, 40, 114, 126, 128, 132-3, 146, 166-74
Pole, Cardinal Reginald, 14
Portal, Fernand-Etienne, 36-8, 44, 46 n. 15, 55-7, 123 n. 25, 226
Preservationist motif: in Leo XIII, 35; in Paul Wattson, 41; in Beauduin, 62; in papacy of Pius XII, 166; in Boyer and conservative ecumenists, 172, 174; in progressive theologians, 210; in Pope John, 225, in Pope Paul, 227; in teaching of Vatican II, 232, 241
Pribilla, Max, 82, 90
Protestant churches (Catholic evaluation of), 57, 102-3, 200-204, 213, 237-8

Quintero, Cardinal J. Humberto, 230

Rahner, Karl, 136, 171, 188 n. 4, 208
Rampolla, Cardinal, 46 n. 15
Reformation, The, dividing Christians, 20; viewed by Möhler, 21; reassessment of, 52; fresh study of, 90; values of, 91; Congar's view of, 101-2; and reunion, 104; viewed by Visser 't Hooft, 105; Lortz's interpretation of, 115-9; postwar analysis of, 206-9; churches dating from, 248 n. 5
Reformed churches, 78, 110, 162-4, 180, 190 n. 18
Religiöse Besinnung, 82-3
Revised Standard Version (Catholic Edition), 134
Revue des sciences philosophiques et théologiques, 80
Rousseau, Olivier, 80
Russian Orthodox Church, 58, 61, 65, 108, 131

Sacraments. *See* Eucharist; Baptism
Sailer, Johann Michael, 21
St. John, Henry, 56
Saint Sergius Theological Academy, 65
Sancta Clara, Franciscus a, 15
Sartory, Thomas, 175, 191 n. 30, 208-9, 220 n. 14
Satis cognitum, 35-6, 45 n. 10
Saulchoir, Le, 99, 105
Schillebeeckx, Edward, 136, 139, 204
Schlink, Edmund, 188 n. 4, 228, 250 n. 24
Scripture: and tradition, 11; in nineteenth-century scholarship, 32-3; and mystical body, 53; viewed by Congar, 99; honored by Protestants, 102; role of, in Protestantism, 106; and Luther, 118; use in Dachau, 127; fresh impact of, 132-5; as meeting-ground, 134-6; common obedience to, 163; study in Holland, 179; normative role of, 213, 215; at Vatican II, 233-4
Secretariat for Promoting Christian Unity, 183-85, 196 n. 85, 224-8, 230, 235-6, 244-5, 248 n. 9
"Separated brothers," 16, 26 n. 12, 34, 102, 127, 198, 219 n. 1
Shehan, Archbishop Lawrence, 180
Skydsgaard, Kristen E., 146-7, 228, 249 n. 18
Smith, Al, 85
Society for Ecumenical Work, 78, 82-3
Society of Christ the King, 112
Society of the Atonement, 39, 41, 172
Söderblom, Archbishop Nathan, 81
Soldiers and Sailors Prayer Book, 130
Stählin, Bishop Wilhelm, 161
Stakemeier, Eduard, 175
Stauffer, Richard, 205, 209

Stimmen der Zeit, 90
Suhard, Cardinal Emmanuel, 140
Suprema haec sacra, 199
Sword of the Spirit, 128-9, 150 n. 14

Taizé, Community of, 142-3
Tavard, George H., 173, 185
Teilhard de Chardin, Pierre, 139
Temple, Archbishop William, 107
Theological Studies, 130
Thieme, Karl, 83
Thijssen, Frans, 165, 182
Thils, Gustave, 185, 189 n. 13, 203-4
Third Hour, 165
Thirty-Nine Articles, 15, 17
Tillich, Paul, 142
Thomism, 31-2, 44, 52, 69 n. 15, 104, 106, 122 n. 13, 138, 170, 204, 215
Transformationist motif: limits to, 13; in Erasmus, 14; in Du Pin, 18; in Leo XIII, 34; required for unity, 36; in Portal, 41; in Beauduin, 62-3; in Couturier, 163; suspect in Rome, 166; gains cautious support, 169; prompts criticism, 173; advocated by Pope John, 225; in *Decree on Ecumenism*, 241
Trent, Council of, 14, 16, 64, 208, 213, 215-6

Una Sancta (earlier journal), 82
Una Sancta (later journal), 175, 208
Una Sancta Brotherhood, 113-4, 160-1, 166, 175, 177
Uniate churches, 56, 83-4
Unitas, 144, 172
Unitas Association, 165-6, 172
Universal Christian Council on Life and Work, 76, 79, 107, 128

Valensin, Albert, 108
Van der Pol, W. H., 164
Vatican Council I, 29, 63-4
Vatican Council II: nineteenth-

century contrast with, 24; Leo XIII's preparation for, 33; ecumenical outlook endorsed by, 120; and Bible translations, 135; Lutheran preparation for, 147; dialogue brought to, 148; and Pope John, 183-7; and episcopacy, 217; ecumenism accepted by, 218; proceedings and teachings of, 224-41; influence of, 243
Vers l'unité chrétienne, 144, 177
Vestigia ecclesia, 201, 220 n. 14
Vie Intellectuelle, La, 90, 96 n. 48
Villain, Maurice, 162, 164, 176, 189 n. 11
Visser 't Hooft, W. A., 105-6, 143, 174
Von Loewenich, Walther, 119, 209
Von Moltke, Helmuth, 126

Wake, Archbishop William, 17-9
Wattson, Paul, 38-41, 44, 174, 176. *See also* Octave of Prayer for Church Unity
Week of Prayer for Christian Unity: developed by Couturier, 109-12; observed in prison camps, 127; affirmed missionary task, 144; postwar observance of, 162-5; decline of, 171; criticized, 173; expansion of, 176-9; survey of, 193 n. 50
Weigel, Gustave, 155, 180, 185
Wesen des Katholizismus, Das 53-4, 87-8, 96 n. 41
Wesley, John, 12, 205

Willebrands, Jan G. M., 165, 179, 182, 185, 189 n. 13, 236, 245
Willibrord, Association of Saint, 165, 179
Winslow, Bede, 66, 165
Witte, J. L., 216
Wood, Charles Lindley. *See* Halifax, Second Viscount
World Conference on Faith and Order, 76, 107, 110, 113, 144-5
World Council of Churches: agencies merged into, 75; Provisional Committee of, 80; headed by Visser 't Hooft, 105; interest in reform, 136; 1961 membership of, 143; Catholic interest in, 144-5; Amsterdam Assembly, 145-6, 166, 189 n. 10; Evanston Assembly, 145, 183; New Delhi Assembly, 145, 221 n. 30, 248 n. 9; Lund Conference, 145; Oberlin Conference, 144-5; St. Andrews meetings, 145; reasons against Catholic membership in, 145-6; sponsors prayer for unity, 177; usage of vestigia ecclesia concept, 201; Joint Working Group, 230; convergence with Vatican II, 234; collaboration in Sodepax, 244; Nairobi Assembly, 247; interest in unity of mankind, 250 n. 22
World War II, 111, 119, 126-31, 159

Zwingli, Huldreich, 205